The
Iranian
Revival

The Making of the Past

The Iranian Revival

by Georgina Herrmann

Advisory Board for The Making of the Past

Series Editor   Graham Speake
Managing Editor   Giles Lewis
Picture Editors   Hilary Kay, Andrew Lawson
Design   Keith Russell
Production   Elizabeth Digby Firth
Index   Griselda Taylor

Frontispiece: a Parthian nobleman drawing his bow: a piece of shell inlay found with several others in a tomb at Shami. They probably once formed the decoration for a box. Ht. 4·5 cm. Tehran Archaeological Museum.

ISBN 0 7290 0045 1

Elsevier-Phaidon, an imprint of Phaidon Press Ltd,
Littlegate House, St Ebbe's Street, Oxford

Origination by Art Color Offset, Rome, Italy

Filmset by Keyspools Limited, Golborne, Lancs.

Printed and bound by Brepols, Turnhout, Belgium

Contents

Maps

Preface to the series

This book is a volume in the Making of the Past, a series describing
the early history of the world as revealed by archaeology and related
disciplines. The series is written by experts under the guidance of a
distinguished panel of advisers and is designed for the layman, for
young people, the student, the armchair traveler and the tourist. Its
subject is a new history – the making of a new past, uncovered and
reconstructed in recent years by skilled specialists. Since many of the
authors of these volumes are themselves practicing archaeologists,
leaders in a rapidly changing field, the series is completely
authoritative and up-to-date. Each volume covers a specific period
and region of the world and combines a detailed survey of the modern
archaeology and sites of the area with an account of the early
explorers, travelers, and archaeologists concerned with it. Later
chapters of each book are devoted to a reconstruction in text and
pictures of the newly revealed cultures and civilizations that make up
the new history of the area.

Titles already published

The Egyptian Kingdoms

Biblical Lands

The Aegean Civilizations

The New World

The Spread of Islam

Man before History

The Emergence of Greece

The Greek World

The Rise of Civilization

Barbarian Europe

The First Empires

The Roman World

Rome and Byzantium

Ancient Japan

Indian Asia

Future titles

Prehistoric Europe

Ancient China

Archaeology Today

The Kingdoms of Africa

Introduction

The 970-odd years between Alexander's comet-like conquest of the Orient and the irresistible tramp of the armies of Islam were years of flux and change. Foremost among these changes was the massive increase in the size of the civilized world. The focus of the ancient world had been the eastern Mediterranean and the great river valleys of Egypt and Mesopotamia, while the new world of the Iranian Parthians stretched from China to Britain, connected by the arteries of trade. The Parthians, enjoying the profits and privileges of middlemen, exchanged friendly embassies with Han China in the east and in the west met the expanding power of the Republic of Rome.

It was not only rare merchandise that traveled along the trade routes but also men and ideas. This was a time of ferment which saw the birth and spread of new religions. It began with a spirit of tolerance and syncretism, although it ended with oppression and bitter fighting. Out of India came Buddhism, fired with proselytizing zeal. Entrenched in Iran and to become the state church in the 3rd century AD was Zoroastrianism, with its strange western deviation, Mithraism. After the death of Jesus, Christianity spread both east to Iran and west, and by the 4th century had become the state religion of Byzantium. With the formal adoption of different faiths by the two great rivals, Byzantium and Sasanian Iran, the stage was set for centuries of religious war and persecution. From 240 AD the Prophet Mani preached a new universal faith, an amalgam of all of these, but, like Jesus, he died for his vision, as did Mazdak two centuries later for teaching a simple communism at a time of disastrous political and economic failure. It was the burning fervor of yet another new message, that of the Arab merchant Muhammad, which inspired the Arabs to sweep away the old order. By that time, interrupted only by the brief rule of the quarreling Hellenes, the Iranians had been masters of the Orient for over 1,000 years. It was time for a change, for a pause, before once again the Iranian genius and thirst for power flared up to form fresh empires under the banners of Islam.

But who were these restless Iranian warriors, who conquered and ruled Western Asia for so long? As far as we know today, they belonged to a large loose confederation of tribes, the earliest of which probably entered the land now known as Iran in the late second millennium BC and we first hear of two tribes, the Medes and the Persians, in the 9th century BC. This book is not concerned with the early history of these Iranian peoples and of their first world empire, that of the Achaemenian

Persians, but with their achievements after the cataclysm that was Alexander the Great. Alexander had dreamed of the fusion of east and west but he died too young. His ideas were partially realized by his successors, the dynasty founded by his general Seleucus, and, more surprisingly, also by the succeeding dynasty of Iranian rulers, the Parthians. These nomads had only recently arrived in northeast Iran but embraced Hellenism so enthusiastically that their kings called themselves Philhellenes. After 400 years of rule the Parthians were followed in the 3rd century AD by another Iranian dynasty, the Sasanians, who claimed to be the heirs of the Achaemenians.

Iran has long been called the crossroads of Asia, for it occupies a strategic position between east and west and forms a land bridge between the Persian Gulf and the Caspian Sea. It is a land of contrasts, between the dry, incredibly clear and invigorating air of the Iranian plateau lying over 1,500 meters above sea level and the humid heat of the sea coasts; between gray desert and barren mountain and immensely fertile plains and valleys; between the restless world of the Central Asian nomads and the rich farmers and merchants of Mesopotamia. During the period covered by this book the Mesopotamian alluvium was the grain bowl of the Iranian empires.

There were no obvious and easily held frontiers, either to the east or to the west, and their establishment and maintenance were a constant problem. The Iranians themselves had come from the east, but pressing behind them were more land-hungry hordes, who continually harassed the eastern borders. And the Iranian dream of recreating the Achaemenian empire also caused recurrent conflict in the west.

Until recently this millennium has been comparatively neglected, but this has now changed and major new discoveries are made each year. This book, written when I was a Calouste Gulbenkian Research Fellow at Lucy Cavendish College, Cambridge, attempts to give an outline of the history and archaeology of the Parthians and Sasanians. The subject is, however, a complex one covering many disciplines and I should like to apologize for any errors and to thank friends and colleagues who generously helped me, among them David Stronach, Richard Frye, Dietrich Huff, Ed Keall, John Hansman, John Curtis, and Michael Roaf, who kindly read my typescript. I am also indebted to Basil Gray, Graham Speake and Hilary Kay for their patience and help and, above all, to my husband, Luke. I dedicate this book to my cousin, Jocelyn Baber, who first taught me, in the depths of her Italian castle, to love unearthing the past.

Chronological Table

	The West		Iranian Empires		The East
	Seleucids				
BC 300	Seleucus I 312–281 Antiochus I 281–261 Antiochus II 261–246 Seleucus II 246–226		**Parthians** Arsaces	Revolt of Parthia and	**Greco-Bactrians** Diodotus I Diodotus II
BC 200	Antiochus III 223–187 Seleucus IV 187–175 Antiochus IV 175–164/3	Antiochus defeated by Rome 189	Artabanus c. 211–191 Phraates I c. 176–171	Bactria c. 240	Euthydemus c. 230–200 Demetrius II c. 190–167
			Mithradates I c. 171–138	Foundation of Parthian empire	Greek empire divides into two warring kingdoms
	Demetrius II 147–140/39	Demetrius captured by Mithradates	Phraates II c. 138–128	Saka hordes overwhelm Greeks and nearly defeat Parthians c. 130	Eucratides
BC 100	Antiochus VII 138–129 Seleucid kingdom reduced to small state in Syria, annexed by Pompey 64		Mithradates II 124/3–87	Chinese/Parthian empires in direct contact in Central Asia. First silk caravan c. 109	**Kushans** Yueh-chih occupy Bactria
	Rome	Sulla insults Parthian ambassador in 92			
	First Triumvirate, Caesar, Pompey and Crassus 60–53	Battle of Carrhae 53	Orodes II c. 57–38		Yueh-chih unified by Kushan chief
AD	Augustus 27 BC–14 AD	Pacorus conquers Syria *Pax Augusta*	Phraates IV 38/7–2 BC Phraates V 2 BC–4 AD	Kushan maritime trade with Rome	Kajula Kadphises founder of Kushan empire
			Artabanus III c. 12–38 AD Gotarzes II c. 38–51		
	Nero 54–68	Parthia invaded by Alani 72 World epidemic of plague	Vologases I c. 51–76/7 Constant struggles for throne	Kushan empire at height, frequent contacts with Rome and China	Kanishka I c. 110/20–c. 140/50
AD 100	Trajan 98–117 Hadrian 117–138 Lucius Verus 161–169	First Parthian War Alani invade c. 136 Second Parthian War	Vologases IV c. 148–192		Kushans continue in power for another century until forced to recognize Sasanian suzerainty
AD 200	Septimius Severus 193–211	Third Parthian War	Vologases V c. 190/1–206/7 Artabanus V c. 213–224		
			Sasanians Ardashir I 224–c. 243		
	Alexander Severus 222–235	at war with Ardashir	Shapur I c. 242/3–273	Prophet Mani	
	Gordian III 238–244 Philip the Arab 244–249 Valerian 253–260	Shapur's Roman triumphs Carus sacks Ctesiphon 283	Bahram I 273–276 Bahram II 276–293 Narseh 293–302 Hormuzd II 302–309	Revolt of Sakas and Kushans	
AD 300	Diocletian 284–305 Constantine 305–337	Constantine converted to Christianity	Shapur II 309–379 Ardashir II 379–383	re-establishes control over Kushans to Kabul	Arrival of Hephthalite Huns in Bactria
	Julian the Apostate 332–363	Huns raid Anatolia	Shapur II 383–388		
AD 400			Bahram IV 388–399 Yazdigird I 399–421 Bahram V 421–439	Sasanians control Gulf to Indus	Empire of Hephthalite Huns
			Yazdigird II 439–457 Peroz 458–484 Kavad 488–531	defeated and killed by Huns Mazdakite movement	
AD 500	Justinian 527–565	War resumed 540–561 Muhammad born c. 570	Khusrau I 531–579 Hormuzd IV 579–590	Bahram Chubin revolts	Hephthalite Huns crushed
AD 600	Maurice 582–602	Arabs defeat Persians at Dhu Qar 604 Persian armies overrun Near East	Khusrau II 591–628		Turks in Central Asia
	Heraclius 610–641	Heraclius sacks Shiz Arabs conquer Sasanian empire	Yazdigird III 632–642		

1. The European Discovery of the Orient

Sweet to ride forth at evening from the wells
When shadows pass gigantic on the sand,
And softly through the silence beat the bells
Along the Golden Road to Samarkand.

JAMES ELROY FLECKER

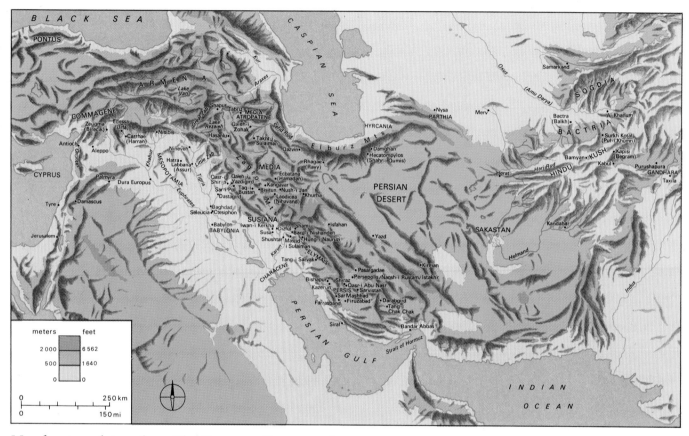

Merchants and travelers. The European discovery of Iran began as early as the 12th century AD with the journey of Benjamin of Tudela, a Jewish rabbi, who was one of the first Europeans to leave a record of his eastern travels. He was followed in the 13th century by members of the Polo family: they undertook their long and hazardous journeys to the court of the Great Khakhan in China to ensure the preeminence of Venetian trade, for commerce, together with religion, was one of the principal impulses which motivated people to travel so far at this time.

In his famous *Travels*, written in 1298 after his return to Italy, Marco Polo described for the European public both the landscape through which he had traveled and the customs of the people he had met. Of Iran he wrote that it was "a very great country" with a "great supply of fine horses." By that time Iranian horses had been famous for more than 2,000 years. Early in the first millennium BC the Assyrians of northern Iraq, then masters of a considerable empire, exacted a tribute of horses from the Iranian Medes, then living in the western Zagros. A few centuries

Above: Western Asia in the time of the Iranian revival.

Previous page: Mount Demavand (5604 meters high) in the Elburz Mountains in north Iran.

later Darius, king of the Achaemenian Persians, described his country as "possessed of good horses, possessed of good men." Persian horses were also considered to be exceptional by the Greeks, and the most efficient fighting unit of both the Parthian and the Sasanian armies was the cavalry, both light and heavy-armed. It is perhaps of interest that the Turkoman horse, still highly prized in Iran today, is one of the ancestors of the English thoroughbred.

Marco Polo commented on the dangers of travel at that time: "In this country there are many cruel and murderous people, so that no day passes but there is some homicide among them. Were it not for the Government ... they would do great mischief to merchants; and indeed, maugre the Government, they often succeed in doing such mischief."

He also praised Iranian craftsmanship: "In the cities there are traders and artizans who live by their labour and crafts, weaving cloths of gold and silk stuffs of sundry kinds ... The people are very skilful in making harness of war, their saddles, bridles, spurs, swords, bows, quivers and arms of every kind are very well made ... The ladies of the country and their daughters also produce exquisite needlework in the embroidery of silk stuffs in different colours with figures of beasts and birds, trees and flowers and a variety of other patterns. They work hangings for the use of the noblemen so deftly that they are marvels to see."

The first European to report on the ancient monuments of Iran was the Italian friar Odoricus of Pordenone, traveling a few decades after Marco Polo in the early 14th century. He visited the ruins of the Achaemenian capital at Persepolis where he would have been able to see both the massive platform, much as it is today, as well as considerable remains of a number of the palaces. These he described as "palaces yet standing entire, but without inhabitants."

Towards the end of the 15th century Venice achieved commercial supremacy in the Mediterranean and sent a number of merchant-ambassadors to Iran to negotiate favorable trading terms. One of these was Josefa Barbaro, who traveled in 1471 to 1475 and who concluded an alliance in Tabriz with Uzun Hasan, the leader of the White Sheep dynasty, against their common enemy the Ottomans in Turkey. In his diaries Barbaro commented on the monuments of Persepolis and Naqsh-i Rustam, though there was little realization of their correct identification. For instance, he identified the great king on his charger in the largest Sasanian relief at Naqsh-i Rustam as "seemyng to be the ymage of a boysterouse man, who they saie was Samson" rather than as even a Persian king.

The old pattern of trade, whereby the spices and silks of the Orient were brought by caravan to the shores of the Mediterranean for further carriage by small coast-hugging ships, was radically changed with the introduction of large ocean-going vessels and, as a result, Venice lost her advantageous trading position. When he sailed around the Cape of Good Hope in 1497 Vasco da Gama discovered a new and faster route to the riches of India, of which the Portuguese were quick to take advantage. Portugal rapidly acquired complete control of maritime trade with India and by 1514 Portuguese ships had sailed to China for the first time. Three years later a Portuguese took up residence in Canton. In the same year that they first sailed to China the Portuguese attacked and conquered the strategically sited island of Hormuz at the head of the Persian Gulf. Hormuz was the center of a vast trade with every part of the east, receiving rich cargoes of spices, precious stones, pearls, ivory, silks and cloth of gold. The island itself was just a barren rock, but it had been converted into a rich and thriving city described by the Abbé Raynal as "a more splendid and agreeable scene

A fragment of green and yellow silk decorated with the Sasanian motif of a fabulous winged creature or *senmurv*, enclosed in a roundel. It was once used to wrap the relics of St Lupus of Troyes. Diameter of the outside circle 37 cm. Musée des Arts Decoratifs, Paris.

than any city in the east." The Portuguese were not thrown out of Hormuz until 1622, when they were defeated by a joint force of Iranians and soldiers of the British East India Company. But to trace British involvement in the area it is necessary to go back a century in time.

Trade with the east. One of the first British ventures to attempt to gain a share in the lucrative eastern trade was initiated as a result of a journey made in 1553 through the White Sea to Archangel. Having reached Archangel, Richard Chancellor traveled inland to the court of the Grand Duke of Muscovy, Ivan the Terrible, by whom he was favorably received. Chancellor's reports resulted in the formation of the "Russian or Muscovy Company," which proposed to conduct an overland trade through Russia with the lands lying to the east and south of the Caspian. The first expedition, led by Master Anthony Jenkinson, set out in 1557 to explore and open the projected trade routes with Central Asia. They reached the Caspian Sea and flew the Red Cross of St George upon it, and they were the first Englishmen to visit Bokhara. An unexpected result of Jenkinson's journey was that it roused Russian interest in Central Asia and during the next decades Russian ambassadors traveled to Bokhara where they negotiated to secure the freedom of Russian slaves.

Between 1561 and 1581 the Muscovy Company launched six more trading expeditions under very adverse conditions before finally abandoning the enterprise. A more successful attempt to tap some of the wealth of Oriental trade was made by the Turkey and Levant Company, formed in 1581, which proposed to use the old trade route overland to Aleppo and then across the Mediterranean in small ships. Following this route in 1583, four British merchants set off to India via Aleppo, Basra and Hormuz. When in Hormuz, they were seized by the Portuguese, imprisoned and thence transferred to Goa. They managed to escape two years later and it was the report of one of them, Ralph Fitch, that encouraged the promoters of the East India Company. By this time Elizabeth I had been on the throne of England nearly 30 years, during which time commerce had been given every form of royal encouragement. The English historian G. M. Trevelyan summed up the spirit of the time in the following words: "Commerce was the motive of exploration as well as of warfare, and all three were combined in some of the greatest deeds of that generation." With the defeat of the Spanish Armada in 1588 British merchants were able to contemplate challenging the Portuguese monopoly. In 1600 the East India Company obtained a charter and began to trade with India, sailing around the Cape of Good Hope in well-armed merchantmen, prepared to do battle when necessary with the "Portugalls."

In Iran itself conditions were favorable for an increase in trade. A new power was emerging with the rise of the Safavid dynasty in 1502, the greatest monarch of which was Shah Abbas (1586–1628). Not only did he re-establish the internal security of the country and reclaim former Iranian territory, he also built a beautiful new capital city at Isfahan. Isfahan is sited in a fertile plain, which had long contained an important city but never a capital. It was a sensible choice for it was sited in the center of Abbas' new empire. To this city with its beautiful palaces and gardens, its colorful mosques and teeming bazaar, its wide tree-lined avenues and many-arched bridges, flocked "the embassies of mighty sovereigns . . . from the uttermost parts of Europe and [they] were received with all the splendour of a court immensely rich and versed in a fanciful and fastidious etiquette. The factors of great trading corporations occupied a position little short of the accredited representatives of royalty; and a life of gorgeous ceremonial, mingled with holiday festivity, rendered Isfahan the most famous and romantic of the cities of the East." (Curzon.)

Adventurers in the Orient. A new class of traveler now arrived in the Orient, neither merchants nor pilgrims nor missionaries but adventurers who offered to the Oriental courts the benefit of their knowledge, primarily in the military field. Two Italians were among the first of this group: in 1502 Ludovico Varthema of Bologna left Venice, traveling first to Egypt and Syria. There he dressed himself in local clothes, joined a caravan of pilgrims and visited Mecca, one of the first Europeans to do so. He later traveled to Iran, India and Malacca before attempting to cross Central Asia. He reached Herat, but political conditions forced him to return to India. Local princes employed him to cast cannons but, when he

realized that these were to be used against fellow Christians, he ran away and the Portuguese, forewarned, were able to defeat the attack.

The second Italian adventurer was the Roman, Pietro della Valle, who sailed from Venice in 1614 via Constantinople and Egypt to Syria. Having visited Jerusalem, he returned to Syria and rode on to Mesopotamia, where he paused long enough to marry a Nestorian lady before continuing his journey to Iran. She unfortunately died there, but she continued to accompany him even after death, for he had her body embalmed and carried her coffin with him through all his travels right back to Rome. Della Valle gained considerable influence at the Persian court and wrote many letters, as well as a book on the history of the period. His descriptions were novel in that they were not confined merely to the appearance of the countries but also discussed the political events and personalities of his time. Furthermore his report provided European scholars with the first concise account of the ruins of Babylon and a detailed report on Persepolis, including an early copy of Old Persian cuneiform writing.

A pair of contemporary English adventurers at the court of Abbas were the Shirley brothers, Robert and Anthony. They, like della Valle, advised the shah in military tactics and were employed by Abbas as ambassadors to the European courts with the aim of forming alliances against the Turks. Anthony, sent first, never returned to report on his mission, which was a failure. Robert, however, traveled to Europe twice on the shah's business, first from 1608 to 1615 and then, setting out from Isfahan again almost immediately, from 1615 to 1627. His attempts to establish trading relations between England and Iran were frustrated by the Levant Company. By the time he returned in 1627 with the embassy sent by Charles I and led by Sir Dodmore

Cotton, Shirley's position at court had been eroded and he died penniless in Qazvin in 1628.

Accompanying Sir Dodmore and Robert Shirley was Sir Thomas Herbert who described their landing at Hormuz as follows: "Wrapped in smoak and flame, we landed safely, though Neptune made us first to dance upon his liquid billows, and with his salt breath seasoned the epicinia. The Cannons also from the Castle and Cittadel vomited out their choler, ten times roaring out their wrathful clamours, to our delight but terrour of the Pagans, who, of all noise, most hate artificial thunder."

Attracted to the Safavid court of luxury were two French jewelers, Tavernier and Chardin, both of whom wrote about their travels. Jean Baptiste Tavernier, who worked for the Great Sophy (as the shah was then known) and for the Great Mogul, did not succumb to the romance of the Orient. Writing of the Chehel Situn in Isfahan, he said "I cannot make any handsome description of it in regard there is nothing of beauty either in the Building or in the Gardens."

John Chardin, however, was overwhelmed. When writing of the Palace of Hasht Behesht or Eight Paradises, his enthusiasm was carried to exceptional heights: "When one walks in this place expressly made for the delights of love, and when one passes through all these cabinets and niches, one's heart is melted to such an extent that, to speak candidly, one always leaves with a very ill grace. The climate without doubt contributes much towards exciting this amorous disposition; but assuredly these places, although in some respects little more than cardboard

The great cliff of Naqsh-i Rustam near Persepolis in the 17th century. An engraving from Chardin's book after a drawing by G. J. Grelot, a French artist who accompanied the jeweler on one of his journeys. In the engraving the whole scene is reversed.

castles, are nevertheless more smiling and agreeable than our most sumptuous palaces."

Chardin first visited Iran during the reign of Shah Abbas II (1641–68), who "had a peculiar love for the Europeans, and a mighty inclination to enter into the strictest leagues and bonds of friendship with our princes." As Chardin records, however, Abbas' predecessor, Shah Sefi (1628–41), had sent 60 men to the Persepolis area with orders to deface the sculptures so as to discourage the visits of Europeans, and some Sasanian reliefs there show traces of such a deliberate destruction. Chardin visited Persepolis in 1674 and drew many views as well as publishing a complete cuneiform inscription. The Dutch painter Angel also spent eight days drawing the ruins for Abbas II.

India and the Parsees. By the middle of the 17th century the British East India Company was firmly established. The first English colony had settled at Surat in 1611; its factors had taken up residence in Isfahan from 1617; in 1622 the Company soldiers had helped the shah to throw the Portuguese out of Hormuz; in 1662 Charles II married the Portuguese princess, Catherine of Braganza, and was ceded Bombay as part of her dowry; in 1757 Robert Clive decisively defeated the French at Plassey; and in 1765 the East India Company signed a treaty with the Great Mogul, which made them the paramount power in India. From 1784 administration was in the hands of governors-general, responsible only to the British Crown, and the many journeys undertaken by their ambassadors to Iran, Afghanistan, Central Asia and elsewhere, together with the foundation of the Asiatic Society of Bengal, came to have a fundamental influence on Oriental studies.

Though little recognized at the time, the visit to Surat of Anquetil-Duperron, a young French Orientalist and scholar then serving in the French army, was of considerable importance. There he met a community known as the Parsees, descendants of Persians who had fled from Iran to India after the Muslim conquest of their land. They were Zoroastrians, worshipers of the Good Lord Ahuramazda. Zoroastrianism had been the official state religion of the Sasanian empire, as also of the earlier Achaemenian empire, although the Muslim conquest ended its official role. The Parsees, however, succeeded in preserving their ancient literature and rituals in their new home and Anquetil was able to secure a copy of the *Avesta*, the sacred book of the Zoroastrians, which he brought back to Europe in 1761. Ten years later he published the first translation of it and thus started serious Zoroastrian studies in Europe.

Russian interest in trading with India began in the mid-17th century, when they dispatched a number of missions, not one of which actually got there. The first embassy to reach India traveled in the reign of Peter the Great (1689–1725) but it too was unsuccessful for only one servant survived the return journey. Peter's reign, however, completely changed the face of Russia and advances were made on many fronts, including the foundation of an Academy of Sciences and the publication of the first serious scientific works. The colonization of Siberia had already focused Russian interest on the east and had brought awareness of the need for accurate maps of their new territories. The map published in 1698 was a major Russian contribution to knowledge at this time, for it showed that the Aral Sea was not part of the Caspian Sea. Peter was also exceptionally enlightened in his realization of the importance of antiquities and it is thanks to this awareness that the magnificent Scythian gold, found in barrows in Siberia and the Black Sea region, is preserved in its entirety in the Hermitage Museum, Leningrad (St Petersburg) today. Among other incomparable treasures in that museum is a superb series of silver dishes of the Sasanian period, the collection of which was also inaugurated by Peter the Great.

The 18th and 19th centuries. The 18th century was one of considerable internal weakness in Iran. The last Safavid king had been deposed by the future Nadir Shah, a brilliant general but poor administrator, and after his murder in 1747 three factions fought for power: the descendants of Nadir Shah, the Zands in the Shiraz area, and the Qajars, who finally succeeded in suppressing all opposition in 1794. These unsettled conditions did not encourage foreign visitors and as a result there were many fewer. One of the more important for the study of antiquities was Carsten Niebuhr, a member of a Danish expedition, who took advantage of the comparatively settled conditions in the Shiraz area in the 1760s during the time of Karim Khan Zand. He took astronomical bearings, which aided the preparation of better maps, and also published copies of several cuneiform inscriptions from Persepolis. Niebuhr was the first to recognize that these were composed in three systems of writing, which ran from left to right. The German scholar, G. F. Grotefend, used his copies when working on the decipherment of cuneiform in 1802. It was Grotefend who finally realized that the inscriptions were those of the Achaemenian kings and that they consisted in the main of the names and titles of those kings.

In establishing this, Grotefend was greatly helped by the decipherment in the last years of the 18th century of some epigraphic Pahlavi or Middle Persian texts of the Sasanian kings by the French Orientalist, Silvestre de Sacy. These included the standard formula of "great king, king of kings, king of Iran and non-Iran, son of . . ., great king, . . ." The most important advance, however, in the decipherment of cuneiform came when Henry Rawlinson, who was in the military service of the East India Company, was posted to Kermanshah in 1836. While there he noticed the sculpture and trilingual inscription of Darius the Great (522–486 BC), which was carved on the cliff of Bisitun. Rawlinson traveled widely and also visited Parthian Qaleh-i Zohak and Sasanian Takht-i Sulaiman.

A silver dish, partially gilded, decorated with a vivid scene showing Shapur II (309–79) hunting lions. Diameter 23 cm. Hermitage Museum, Leningrad.

The return of politically settled conditions in Iran in the 19th century led to a considerable increase in the number of foreign visitors and to a marked improvement in the recording of ancient monuments. The latter was particularly helped by photography which was introduced in Iran towards the end of the century. This century also saw the beginning of the archaeological excavation of sites, begun by the French and the British in northern Iraq.

George Curzon, later Viceroy of India, writing at the end of the century, listed no fewer than 197 visitors to Iran, each of whom wrote some record of his or her journey in a European language. One of the first of these was the British ambassador, Sir John Malcolm, who visited Iran twice in 1800 and 1810 and later wrote his pioneering *History of Persia*. James Morier accompanied two British missions, those of Sir Harford Jones in 1808–09 and of Sir Gore Ouseley in 1811–12. Although today principally remembered for his delightful romance, *Hajji Baba of Isfahan*, he was surprisingly the first European to visit the Sasanian site of Bishapur, which had been recorded by the Persian geographer Istakhri as early as the 10th century,

and which is located beside one of the principal routes from the Persian Gulf to Shiraz. Istakhri described it in the following terms:

"Bishawar was built by King Shapur. It has four gates, and in the midst of it is a singular hill or eminence like a tower or dome. ... In the territory of Shapour is a mountain, and in that mountain are the statues of all the kings and generals, and high priests, and illustrious men who have existed in Pars; and in that place are some persons who have representations of them and the stories of them written."

While Morier recorded the ruins of the great city of Shapur, the fortress overlooking it, and the six Sasanian sculptures carved in the nearby gorge, he failed to find the famous statue of Shapur carved out of a stalactite in a cave, which was described by Hamd 'Allah Mustawfi of Qazvin as "a black statue of a man, larger than life, standing in a temple; some say it is a talisman, others that it is merely a real man whom God had turned to stone." The 10th-century geographer Mukaddasi had previously referred to the cave lying one league distant from the city and to the colossal figure of King Shapur which stood at the mouth of the cave, in which water fell continually. The great statue was discovered a few weeks after Morier left Bishapur in 1811 by a Major Stone and was published by

Sir William Ouseley. Sir William, a great Oriental scholar, was the first to visit the Sasanian sculpture at Darabgird, of which he wrote "One glance enabled me to recognise in the supposed figure of Rustam, another monument . . . of the glory or the vanity of Shapur."

The new spirit of scientific inquiry which pervaded the 19th century is well illustrated in the instructions given to the British artist and traveler Sir Robert Ker Porter by A. Olinen, President of the Russian Academy of Fine Arts. Ker Porter was urged to "draw only what you see! Correct nothing; and preserve in your copies, the true characters of the originals. Do not give to Persian figures a French tournure, like Chardin, nor a Dutch, like Van Bruyn, nor a German, or rather Danish, like Niebuhr, nor an English grace, like some of your countrymen, in your portraits of the fragments at Nakshi-Roustam."

Ker Porter was a professional artist, who had studied under Benjamin West at the Royal Academy from 1790, when he was only 13. He had an adventurous and romantic career, ending up as British consul in Venezuela. But first he was appointed "historical painter" to the czar of Russia and while at St Petersburg he fell deeply in love with a Russian princess. He had to flee the country before he could marry her because of the Franco-Prussian alliance and retreated to Sweden, where he was knighted by

Gustav IV. He then went to Spain with the British Army but returned to Russia in 1811, married his princess and stayed to describe the campaign of 1812 against Napoleon. He was knighted by the prince regent in 1813. Meanwhile his energy had been noticed by his wife's cousin, Olinen, and it was Olinen who encouraged him to travel to the Orient with the object of accurately recording ancient monuments. His drawings were a considerable improvement on earlier ones and he was the first European to record the magnificent late Sasanian grotto at Taq-i Bustan near Kermanshah, which he visited in 1818.

Layard and the later 19th century. While Ker Porter was traveling in Iran, Austen Henry Layard was born in Paris of English parents. Much of his childhood was spent traveling, particularly in Italy, where he passed his time visiting the museums of Florence and collecting flowers and butterflies on the hills of Fiesole. He was already fascinated by the Orient, after reading *The Arabian Nights*, which made him long to visit Aleppo, Damascus,

Opposite: a watercolor of the Sasanian grottoes at Taq-i Bustan by Sir Robert Ker Porter. The drawing is of particular interest for it shows the site's magnificent setting in the early 19th century before its recent enclosure. British Library.

Below: Ker Porter's drawing of the royal boar hunt of Khusrau II, one of two delightful scenes carved on the walls of the Great Grotto at Taq-i Bustan. The hunt takes place within a huge enclosure or paradise, and, in typical Sasanian manner, all stages of the hunt are illustrated. British Library.

Baghdad and Isfahan. As he grew older he read every volume of eastern travel that he could obtain, including those of Morier and Malcolm. He prepared himself for his travels by learning some Arabic and Persian, how to read a sextant and some elementary medicine, all of which were to prove of considerable value. Layard was an exceptionally gifted traveler, not only because of his powers of observation and superb gifts for writing and drawing but also because of his incredible endurance and human compassion for the troubles of others. Much of his time in Iran was spent as a guest of the Bakhtiari tribe and he became personally involved in their problems. Dressed in Bakhtiari clothes, he rode alone or with Persian companions through the mountains, subject to attack by robbers, wild animals or sudden illness. One bad night was spent in a guest tent in the mountains:

"The winter had now set in and . . . there were constant heavy rains, with thunder, lightning, and high winds. The . . . guest-tent offered but little protection when these storms broke over us, and I was frequently drenched to the skin during the night. On one such occasion a pack of wolves made a descent in the darkness upon the sheep, and breaking through the tents, carried off nine of them. The screams of the women, the cries of the men, and the barking of the dogs – the thunder rolling in awful peals and the lightning flashing with the most dazzling brightness – added to the terrors of the night. Tents were blown down. Torrents from the hills swept into the plains carrying everything before them. We had to seek for refuge behind rocks and wherever we could obtain shelter.

The horses, terrified, broke loose from their tethers and fled. Such a night I had never before, and have never since, witnessed."

One of Layard's aims was not to leave "untrod one spot hallowed by tradition or unvisited one ruin consecrated by history" and among those he visited in Iran was the "vast mound which marks the site of the ancient city of Susa." However, it was not Susa but the cities of Assyria in northern Iraq which were to start his remarkable archaeological career. Layard was among the early visitors to the magnificent stone city of Hatra, located in the old Assyrian heartland just a day's journey away from the capital Assur.

Traveling in Iran at the same time as Layard, 1839 to 1841, were the Frenchmen Charles Texier, Eugène Flandin and P. Coste. Texier was the first to sketch the Sasanian relief at Salmas near Lake Rezaieh, while Flandin and Coste prepared plans and drawings of buildings and rock reliefs. They were the first to publish the Sasanian palaces at Firuzabad and Sarvistan, which are still standing to a considerable height today. They were followed some 40 years later by Marcel and Jane Dieulafoy. He was a competent architect and antiquarian scholar whose accurate plans and drawings were supplemented by photographs taken by his wife. The results of their first visit were published in 1883 in the beautifully illustrated *L'Art antique de la Perse*. That year saw them beginning excavations on the acropolis mound at Susa, where work had been started in 1851 by W. K. Loftus. Having established that the ruins were those of the Biblical Shushan or Classical Susa, Loftus turned his attention to other sites and it was left to the French to undertake large-scale excavation at Susa. This work has continued from 1884 to the present day, apart from interruptions caused by two world wars. In 1890 the French were granted a monopoly in Iran which excluded archaeologists of other nations for a considerable period.

Other important travelers at the end of the 19th century included Messrs Stolze and Andreas (1874–81). Stolze was the first to prepare a photographic record of the monuments he visited and from this time photography largely replaced drawing as a method of recording sculptures. The British scholar E. G. Browne visited Iran in 1888 and began a life-long attachment to the country, its people and its literature. His *Year among the Persians* (1893) and *Literary History of Persia* remain standard works, as does Curzon's *Persia and the Persian Question* (1892). Lord Curzon spent six months in Iran working as a correspondent for *The Times* and traveling widely. His book combined careful observation of the conditions of the day and of the monuments he saw, together with a scholarly appreciation of what had been written earlier.

Considerable progress in Oriental studies was also made in Russia in the 19th century. The Academy of Sciences, a large part of which was devoted to human studies, was given its first statutes in 1804, which were renewed in 1830.

A faculty of Oriental languages was created in St Petersburg in 1854. After the conquest of Turkestan, completed in 1881, exploration in the field was speeded up and many expeditions set out to record the geography, natural history, ethnography and archaeology of the area. Museums and libraries were founded in Bokhara and Tashkent and early texts and manuscripts were collected, including some from the famous library at Ardebil, which were sent to St Petersburg.

20th-century discoveries. Thus, as the 20th century began, the conditions were ripe for the spate of discoveries that have widened our understanding of Iran's past during

Above: a 19th-century traveler at bay. Madame Jane Dieulafoy, suddenly confronted by eight nomads, announces in her loudest voice "J'ai quatorze balles à votre disposition."

Below: still partially covered with silken clothes of Sasanian inspiration, a life-size clay statue found at Tun-Huang, E Turkestan.

the last 75 years. At the beginning of the century important finds for the understanding of the ancient religions of Iran were made in distant eastern Turkestan, which was located on the Great Silk Road and was a natural refuge area for those fleeing from religious persecution. Foremost among the many expeditions visiting eastern Turkestan at this time were those of the explorer Mark Aurel Stein, a Hungarian by birth, though for many years he worked as a servant of the government of India and adopted British nationality. At the great Buddhist site of Tun-Huang, which ranges in date from the 5th to the 12th centuries AD, Stein found thousands of manuscript scrolls, as well as fine wall paintings and early silks decorated with designs of Sasanian inspiration, all preserved in excellent condition by the dry air.

As well as his life-long interest in discovering traces of Alexander, Stein's later years were much occupied in the archaeological reconnaissance of northwest India and southeast and northwest Iran. He was the first to discover the ruins of Kuh-i Kwaja in Seistan, which he published in the *Geographical Journal* in 1916 and later in *Innermost Asia* (1928). The ruins were visited in the winter of 1924–25 by the German Orientalist Ernst Herzfeld, who "did some excavating during the spring of 1929." The site is built on an impressive table-hill in a lake and Herzfeld found important buildings there, including a palace and a fire temple, which probably date to the Parthian and Sasanian periods. Some of the walls had been lavishly decorated with colorful frescoes and an ornate stucco design.

Above: one of the Parthian frescoes from the palace at Kuh-i Kwaja: a man's head in profile.

Below: the ruined palace and fire temple of Kuh-i Kwaja, built in the Partho-Sasanian period on an island in Seistan.

Herzfeld was one of the most important pioneers of Iranian archaeology and had an overall knowledge of other relevant fields including literature and numismatics. He summed up his approach to archaeology in the Preface to his *Archaeological History of Iran* (1935): "It may well sound desultory if I jump from architecture to legends, from sculpture to coins, from paintings to inscriptions, but it is not losing the thread. For the quality common to all such material is that it has something to tell about cultural developments of high antiquity, which means it is material eminently archaeological in the real sense of that word."

It was his close attention to coins that enabled Herzfeld to make a major advance in the attribution of Sasanian rock reliefs, for he realized that the kings could be recognized by the distinctive shape of their crowns, and that the different crowns were identified on the coins. With Friedrich Sarre, who visited the sites in 1897–1900, he published the first serious study of Iranian rock reliefs, which were illustrated by Sarre's excellent photographs. Also with Sarre he traveled extensively in Mesopotamia and, among other monuments, published in 1920 the great Sasanian palace at Ctesiphon, near Baghdad. A year later came his description of the ruins of the stone tower of Narseh at Paikuli in Iraqi Kurdistan. A long inscription had been carved on some of the blocks, but these had fallen and were scattered at the bottom of the hill. With painstaking care he recorded them and gradually, over the years, pieced them together to form a coherent whole.

A number of excavations undertaken in Mesopotamia in the first half of this century finally put the Parthians on the archaeological map. Until then they had only been known from references in Classical literature and from their coins. Foremost among those working there was the brilliant German archaeologist Walter Andrae. At Assur-on-Tigris overlying the Assyrian capital Andrae uncovered a complete Parthian city with its palaces, temples, private houses and burial vaults. He excavated with such meticulous attention to detail that he did not merely record the plans of the buildings and their associated finds but also noted exactly how the walls and vaults were constructed, recording the brick lays. He was thus able to suggest convincing reconstructions and his work still provides the most vivid illustration of a Parthian city in its entirety. Andrae also rode to the contemporary site of Hatra and his work there has recently been amplified by the Iraq Antiquities Department who are carrying out an ambitious project of excavation and restoration.

Working as an architect with Andrae was Oscar Reuther who later carried on the excavations begun by Herzfeld at Ctesiphon, a site also currently being worked on by the Iraq Antiquities Department. Reuther wrote two articles on Parthian and Sasanian architecture which were published in the *Survey of Persian Art* (edited by Arthur Upham Pope) and which remain essential reading for anyone interested in ancient architecture.

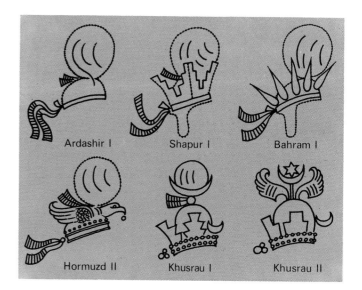

Above: crowns of the Sasanian kings. Each king wore a different crown, which can be identified from the coinage and which included divine attributes, such as the rays of Mithra, the wings of Verethragna, or the crenellations of Ahuramazda.

Below: silver drachm of Shapur I wearing his personal crown. Above the crown can be seen the balloon-like *korymbos*, presumed to be hair held in a silken covering. British Museum.

In 1926 the founder of the present dynasty, Reza Shah Pahlavi, ascended the throne of Iran. Among many reforms which Reza Shah initiated he invited the French architect, André Godard, to create an archaeological service and to draw up a methodical inventory of historical remains. Godard arrived in Iran in 1928 and stayed there for over 30 years, during which he designed and established the Tehran Archaeological Museum. In the 1930s Reza Shah passed an antiquities law, which opened the country to intensive archaeological research. This opportunity was taken advantage of both by the French, who had been working in Iran since 1884, and by the British and Americans. American interest in archaeological exploration was considerable at this time and many missions were dispatched to Mesopotamia and Iran. In Mesopotamia the Americans turned their attention to the exploration of the previously ignored Seleucid period and they undertook excavations at two important foundations, Seleucia-on-Tigris, capital of the Seleucid east, and Dura Europus on the Euphrates, founded halfway between Seleucia-on-Tigris and the western capital of Antioch-on-the-Orontes. Material found at these sites at last illustrated the Hellenistic impact on Mesopotamia under the Seleucids and documented its continuation and gradual absorption during the succeeding Parthian period.

In Iran the Oriental Institute of Chicago sponsored work at Persepolis: the expedition was initially directed by Ernst Herzfeld, who was replaced by Erich Schmidt in 1934. Schmidt's first excavations in Iran, on behalf of the University Museum, Philadelphia, had been at Tepe

Above: the facade of the palace of Khusrau I at Ctesiphon, seen in an old photograph before the right side collapsed.

Below: a decorative plaster roundel of the early Parthian period, found during the 1930s at Seleucia-on-Tigris.

Hissar, near Damghan, a site strategically located at the foot of the Elburz Mountains, close to the famous "Caspian Gates," one of the easiest routes through the mountains to the lush Caspian littoral. At Tepe Hissar the expedition had concentrated on the prehistoric levels but also excavated a Sasanian palace lying 200 meters away. Schmidt found many Sasanian stucco panels in the Sasanian palace which could be closely paralleled by stuccoes found by the Germans at Ctesiphon and by another American team working at Kish, where two Sasanian villas were recorded. From 1934 Schmidt was not only in charge of the excavations at Persepolis and the associated work of the expedition at the nearby sites of Naqsh-i Rustam and Sasanian Istakhr, but also of the Oriental Institute's work at Rumishgan in Luristan and at Rayy near Tehran.

Aerial photography. Despite this burden of work Schmidt pioneered a breakthrough in archaeological method. It was mainly thanks to the initiative and energy of his wife, Mary Helen Warden Schmidt, that they were able to buy a small aeroplane, the necessary cameras and to persuade the Iranian authorities to allow them to make aerial photographs of archaeological sites. Schmidt used these extensively in planning the excavations, as at Naqsh-i Rustam: "The impressive photograph . . . was taken as the 'Friend of Iran', about 90 meters above the ground, with wide open throttle, raced past the rock of Naqsh-i Rustam . . . The test excavation at Naqsh-i Rustam was entirely planned by means of aerial photographs.

Of the value of aerial photographs, the editor of Schmidt's magnificent and invaluable volume, *Flights over Ancient Cities of Iran* (1940), commented: "For meeting both the general and the specific problems the vision of the earth-bound traveler is limited. To see things as they are – ancient cities and towns in their complete geographic environment, streets and buildings revealing the ancient plans – the camera-equipped airplane has proved its outstanding usefulness."

Fortunately Schmidt did not confine his aerial photography to the sites on which he was working but also made extensive flights over other ancient sites. Flying over Firuzabad, Ardashir's city of Gur, Schmidt wrote: "One of our most striking photographs records the circular city of Gur or Jur . . . The present view, taken roughly toward the northeast, . . . suggests a double peripheral city enclosure, the two walls being separated by a deep moat . . . Only seventeen hundred years have passed since the city of Ardashir I – thousands of homes, shops, barracks, and governmental buildings – throve in the apparent safety of its girdles of defence. The onslaught of the Arabs and Islam crushed in the 7th century the dynasty and the empire of the Sasanians. Their magnificent palaces turned into desolate ruins and their cities into mounds and fields leveled by the elements and by the peasants of later generations."

Schmidt also took aerial photographs of the Sasanian cities of Qasr-i Abu Nasr near Shiraz, where an American expedition sponsored by the Metropolitan Museum of New York was working, and of Bishapur near Kazerun. At Bishapur Roman Ghirshman's main effort, during a series of campaigns which lasted from 1935 to 1941, was concentrated on clearing the temple and the nearby palace, in which he found fragments of some outstanding mosaics, strongly Roman in style. Ghirshman then transferred for a time to Afghanistan, where the French had been active from the 1920s under the leadership of A. Foucher and J. Hackin. They had made major discoveries at a series of important sites which included the dramatic Buddhist monastery built in the cliff of the Bamiyan valley with its two enormous figures of Buddha, as well as the Buddhist site of Hadda with strong Indian connections, and the site of Begram, a former capital of the Kushan kings.

Aurel Stein continued his reconnaissance in Iran during the 1930s. While exploring the Malamir region he heard of the discovery of a magnificent bronze sculpture, now in the Tehran Museum. Hurrying to the spot, he excavated the important Parthian shrine of Shami and found fragments of many other bronzes. For these travels in the mountains he was given an escort of "a dozen hardy Gendarmes, equal to trying marches and content with a minimum of kit." Transport suitable "for the rough journey" was secured in Shiraz with the help of the governor-general of Fars province "in the shape of a dozen and a half of sturdy Shirazi mules. In 1915, when travelling during the war from Meshed to Sistan along the Perso-Afghan border, I had learned to appreciate the excellent qualities of these animals bred in the valleys about Kazerun and Shiraz. Trying experiences with camels and donkeys in the wastes of Baluchistan and the Gulf coast had made me eagerly look forward to mules as the ideal means of transport amidst old-world traffic conditions. My expectations proved fully justified. During a journey which, in the course of five months, covered aggregate marching distances of close on 1,300 miles, no trouble was ever experienced on account of our brave mules, however bad the stony tracks or however difficult to secure fodder and grazing. It is pleasant, too, to remember the hardy men who knew so well how to look after their animals and to save them from galls and sores." Stein died in Kabul in 1943 at the age of 81, still exploring.

Both before and after World War II the Russians have been excavating at sites in south Russia and Central Asia, many of which have illumined previously unknown aspects of archaeology. Working at Nysa, the first capital of the Parthians in their homeland near the Caspian Sea, they found monumental buildings, including a palace and a temple, and discovered a hoard of superb ivory rhyta. These discoveries have cast an entirely new light on the cultural background of the Arsacid kings. In addition to excavation, Russian scholars have prepared numerous studies of coins, seals and other antiquities, and in

Above: a mosaic panel from Bishapur showing a lady playing a harp, cut by Roman prisoners-of-war captured by Shapur I. Musée du Louvre, Paris.

Right: the fertile Bamiyan valley, once the site of a thriving Buddhist monastery, dominated by the gigantic figures of Buddha carved out of the rock.

particular the work of Vladimir Lukonin of the Hermitage Museum has been of outstanding originality and usefulness.

After the war Roman Ghirshman was made director of the French Delegation in Iran, in which position he continued until 1967. In addition to conducting the annual French dig at Susa, he also worked at many other sites, which he has continued to do since his "retirement." His excavations at Iwan-i Kerkha, Masjid-i Sulaiman and Bard-i Nishandeh have provided much new material belonging to the Seleucid, Parthian and Sasanian periods. In Afghanistan too, where the French Delegation was headed until recently by Daniel Schlumberger, our knowledge of the archaeology of the Greco-Bactrians and the Kushans was radically changed by the excavation of the Kushan dynastic shrine of Surkh Kotal, near Pul-i Khumri, and the Greco-Bactrian city of Ai Khanum on the banks of the Oxus.

The spread of knowledge and modern technology.
A flood of new journals has echoed this increase of archaeological activity. In 1961, together with the Belgian Louis Vanden Berghe, professor at Ghent University, Ghirshman initiated a journal dedicated to the study of the

past of Iran, called *Iranica Antiqua*. This publication has been followed by many others, *Iran* of the British Institute of Persian Studies (1963), the resumed *Archaeologische Mitteilungen aus Iran* of the German Archaeological Institute (1968), which had been founded by Ernst Herzfeld, the Dutch *Persica*, and the *Cahiers de la Délégation Archéologique Française en Iran*, a supplementary journal to their long-standing series, *Mémoires de la Délégation en Perse*. Prior to the appearance of *Iranica Antiqua*, Louis Vanden Berghe had already published a book which remains the "Bible" of Iranian archaeologists, *Archéologie de l'Iran ancien* (1959). This described all the known archaeological sites, listed both by area and by period, together with a full bibliography; a supplement to bring this invaluable work up to date is currently in the press. Vanden Berghe has, in addition, conducted regular field trips to little-known areas of Iran and among his prodigious output has published numerous previously unknown Sasanian buildings.

The end of the 1950s witnessed the beginning of a long-term project by the German Archaeological Institute at Takht-i Sulaiman in northwest Iran. Takht-i Sulaiman was a major Sasanian shrine built around a mountain top which

The terraced shrine of Bard-i Nishandeh in the ancient province of Elymais, southwest Iran. Seleucid to Parthian periods.

had itself been formed by the mineral deposits of the everlasting lake near its center. With this remarkable natural feature it is hardly surprising that the city was an important religious center and a monumental religious complex has been unearthed there by Professor Rudolph Naumann. In addition to its work at the Takht, the German Archaeological Institute, with a Tehran branch set up in 1961, has undertaken a wide range of fieldwork in Iran, including a survey of Sasanian Firuzabad by Dietrich Huff. The British Institute of Persian Studies was set up in the same year with the aim of encouraging all aspects of Iranian studies, though their main emphasis is archaeological. One of their digs was at the Persian Gulf port of Siraf, a site first surveyed by Aurel Stein. According to Arab geographers, Siraf had been extremely prosperous in the early Islamic period, when it was a focus of trade with China. As well as the expected Islamic levels, excavations also revealed that the port had been founded by the Sasanians and it may have been they who initiated direct maritime trade with China.

The last 15 years have been a period of intense archaeological activity in Iran, undertaken both by foreign missions and by the Iranians themselves. This work has been encouraged by the personal interest which T. I. M. Mohammad Reza Pahlavi and the Shah-banou, the Empress Farah, take in the discovery of their country's past. Sites from caves of the Palaeolithic period through to medieval Islamic cities have all been investigated and it is only possible in this brief survey to mention some of the Parthian and Sasanian sites worked on in the recent past. These include the temple of Anahita at Kangavar, excavated by Kambaksh Fard, and the new excavations at Bishapur under the direction of Ali Sarfaraz, both of which are sponsored by the Iranian Archaeological Center; the Parthian city at Shahr-i Qumis and a Parthian village at Tepe Nush-i Jan, excavated by the British; the Parthian and Sasanian cemetery at Dailaman dug by the Japanese; and the mountain-top Parthian site of Qaleh-i Yazdigird, which is being excavated by the Royal Ontario Museum.

The increase in archaeological work in the last half-century has been matched by a corresponding increase in technology, both in the field and in the laboratory. Excavation techniques are constantly being improved and excavation nowadays is usually linked to wide-scale field survey. The scientific techniques used include methods of dating – by measuring the radiocarbon in organic samples (C-14), and by thermoluminescence, determining the age of fired pottery – as well as increasingly sophisticated studies of the floral and faunal remains with the aim of reconstructing the ecology of the period being studied. Vastly superior methods of conservation, both of objects and of buildings, are now employed. All these methods greatly increase the amount of information which can be retrieved from an excavation: they still depend, however, on the validity of the original fieldwork.

2. The Hellenistic Heritage and the Rise of Parthia

> And in the heat of the combat that followed, the clash of shields, the shouts of the men, and the doleful sound of the whirring arrows continued without intermission.
>
> AMMIANUS MARCELLINUS

"There was weeping and mourning in the land." So wrote a Babylonian scribe living at the time when Alexander's generals battled to win control of his vast conquests, for Alexander the Great had died without an heir. From the time of his death in Babylon in 323 Alexander's generals had fought each other for 12 weary years until the eastern part of his empire was won by Seleucus, formerly chief of the Macedonian cavalry, while Ptolemy ruled in Egypt and Antigonus in Asia Minor. But still the battles continued, Greek fighting Greek, and Greek against non-Greek or "barbarian."

The Seleucids. Seleucus' early years after his accession in 311 were occupied in reconquering the territories won by Alexander in the east. He only secured the allegiance of Bactria in northern Afghanistan in 306, after fighting both the Greeks settled there by Alexander and barbarians. A year later he crossed the Indus river, where conditions had changed considerably since Alexander's triumphs. Instead of meeting a number of independent local princes, Seleucus was opposed by a united northern India ruled by Chandragupta (Greek Sandrocottos), founder of the Mauryan empire. Conquest was clearly impossible and Seleucus wisely made a treaty with Chandragupta, which included an exchange of ambassadors and probably a marriage alliance. Among the gifts exchanged by the two kings were some fighting elephants and these were to be a deciding factor in the Battle of Ipsus in which Seleucus defeated and killed one of his major rivals in the west, Antigonus. The devastating effect of elephants in battle has been described by a Roman soldier fighting in the 4th century AD called Ammianus Marcellinus: "The gleaming elephants with their awful figures and savage gaping mouths could scarcely be endured by the faint-hearted; and their trumpeting, their odour, and their strange aspect alarmed the horses still more."

After the death of Antigonus at Ipsus in 301 Seleucus had won for himself the greater part of Alexander's empire. He ruled an area which stretched from Syria and Anatolia in the west to Afghanistan and south Russia in the east. To impose foreign rule on this vast territory he continued Alexander's policy of founding cities organized on Greek lines and run by Greek settlers – islands of Hellenism in a barbarian sea. The constant exposure of the locals to Hellenism began to make one of Alexander's dreams come true, for he had wanted to promote a fusion of east and west. One of his most spectacular gestures to try to achieve this had been the mass marriage of his Macedonian soldiers to Oriental women, an event which took place at Susa shortly before he died. He himself had already married the beautiful Roxana, daughter of the Iranian king Oxyartes, and some of his generals including Seleucus had also married Iranian noblewomen. Seleucus' son and heir, Antiochus, was therefore half-Greek and half-Iranian and uniquely suited to rule an Oriental empire on Greek lines.

In his later years Seleucus entrusted Antiochus with the rule of his eastern provinces, both to prepare him for kingship and because his own interests were primarily western: he had built himself a new capital city at Antioch-on-the-Orontes in Syria, which became his favorite residence. Like Alexander and his father, Antiochus had to campaign vigorously in the east to restore and maintain order. By this time some of

Previous page: the magnificent bronze statue of a Parthian prince from Shami, nearly 2 meters high. The loose cross-over tunic and baggy over-trousers are typical of both the Parthian and the early Sasanian periods. The date is uncertain: 1st century BC to 1st century AD. Tehran Archaeological Museum.

Below: reverse of a silver tetradrachm of Seleucus I showing an elephant, probably one given him by Chandragupta Maurya. Bibliothèque Nationale, Paris.

Alexander's Alexandrias had fallen into disrepair and these he rebuilt, as well as initiating new works, one of the most ambitious of which was to enclose the entire oasis of Merv in Central Asia within a massive wall to defend it against nomad attacks. It was, once again, a period of considerable nomad pressure and it was probably at about this time that the Iranian Parni, a tribe of the Dahae, moved into the old Achaemenian satrapy of Parthava, from which they were to take their name – the Parthians.

By his vigorous measures Antiochus I (281–261 BC) securely re-established Hellenistic rule in Central Asia and there was no serious challenge to Seleucid authority in the east until after the middle of the 3rd century BC, when Seleucus II Callinicus (246–226) was preoccupied fighting Ptolemy of Egypt. Taking advantage of Seleucus' engagement in the west, both the provinces of Parthia and Bactria defected. As Justin wrote in his *History of the World*, "One Arsaces [the Parthian king], a man of uncertain origin, but of undisputed bravery, happened to arise at this time and ... overthrew Andragorus [the Seleucid satrap or governor] ... and took upon himself the government of the country." Seleucus II tried to regain his rebellious eastern provinces in 228, by which time the Parthian king had raised a large army and had formed an alliance with Diodotus II of Bactria, son of the rebel satrap. Again in the words of Justin, Arsaces

View of the site of the ancient city of Merv in Central Asia.

"engaging with King Seleucus, who came to take vengeance on the revolters, obtained a victory."

This Parthian victory securely established the new power which expanded south of the Elburz Mountains and occupied the Seleucid city of Hecatompylos. Hecatompylos has only recently been identified with the site of Shahr-i Qumis near the modern city of Damghan. By 211 when Artabanus succeeded to the throne, the Parthians may have held territory which stretched as far west as Ecbatana (modern Hamadan) in Media. Meanwhile, further east, the Greeks in Bactria also took advantage of Seleucid weakness and established themselves as a major force. At this time the Greco-Bactrian kingdom probably consisted only of the old Achaemenian satrapies of Bactria and Sogdia. Expansion south of the Hindu Kush was not possible for the Kandahar region was in the hands of the greatest of the Mauryan emperors, Asoka (274–232), who controlled much of the Indian subcontinent. Political decline, however, set in soon after his death, and the Mauryan empire rapidly broke up, leaving the way open for Greco-Bactrian expansion southwards.

The last successful Seleucid attempt to re-establish their slackening control over the eastern territories was made during the reign of Antiochus III (223–187 BC). Having first defeated a rebellious general Molon in Babylonia and Media, he replenished his treasury by looting the Temple of Anahita at Ecbatana before marching east. He succeeded in reconquering much Parthian territory,

Silver tetradrachm of the Greco-Bactrian king, Euthydemus. British Museum.

although he failed to defeat the Parthian king, Artabanus, with whom he eventually made peace and signed an alliance. He then marched on into Afghanistan to challenge the Greco-Bactrians and had to besiege the great city of Bactra for more than two years before the Greco-Bactrian king Euthydemus finally acknowledged his supremacy. Antiochus III was able to return to Mesopotamia triumphant, having restored Seleucid authority over both Parthia and Bactria – but for the last time.

After this success Antiochus III had to face a formidable new enemy on his western frontier – that of the expanding Republic of Rome – and he was defeated at the Battle of Magnesia in 189 BC. Two years later he was killed, while once again trying to refill his depleted treasury by looting a temple, this time the Temple of Bel in Elymais.

The formation of the Parthian empire. The kingdom of Parthia had survived two determined Seleucid attempts to crush it – those of Seleucus II Callinicus and of Antiochus III. The death of the latter and the inactivity of his successor Seleucus IV Philopator (187–175) not only made further Parthian expansion possible but also provoked widespread revolts in many other parts of the Seleucid empire including the kingdoms of Armenia and Media Atropatene. Phraates I of Parthia (c. 176–171) conquered much of the Elburz mountain area and retook Hyrcania, thus providing a successful base for the conquests of his successor and brother, Mithradates.

Mithradates I (c. 171–138) was a man of exceptional military ability who during his lifetime transformed Parthia from a small kingdom in northern Iran to an empire stretching from Babylonia to Bactria. He first took advantage of a time of Bactrian weakness, caused by internal struggles for the throne, to wrest territory from them. He then prudently waited for the death of Antiochus IV Epiphanes (175–164/3) before expanding westwards. Antiochus IV had attempted to regain Seleucid territory and had campaigned in Armenia and in the Zagros, with some success. By about 148, however,

Silver tetradrachm of Mithradates I the Great, the founder of the Parthian empire. Bibliothèque Nationale, Paris.

Mithradates had probably occupied Media, after which he returned to the east, conquering land perhaps up to the borders of India. By this time the old Greco-Bactrian empire had split into two warring kingdoms, the Greco-Bactrians north of the Hindu Kush and the Indo-Greeks in southern Afghanistan and northwest India. Marching swiftly westwards, Mithradates took advantage of internal problems over the succession of the youthful Demetrius II Nicator to the Seleucid throne, and by July 141 he had entered Seleucia-on-Tigris. He soon had to withdraw to quell a Bactrian attack but he was back in time not only to defeat but also to capture Demetrius II. Using Demetrius' own die-cutters in the Seleucid capital and mint-town of Seleucia, he issued a fine and dated coinage to commemorate his victories.

After these early successes the Parthians suffered a number of serious reverses shortly after the death of Mithradates I, for the newly created empire was attacked both in the southwest and in the north and east. In about 130 the Seleucids, led by Antiochus VII Sidetes (138–129), counterattacked and recaptured Babylonia and Media. Meanwhile, in the north and east, another Iranian group, the Saka, had brought the two east Greek kingdoms to a sudden end, before challenging the Parthians in their Parthian homeland, which they overran. Phraates II (c. 138–128) succeeded in beating off the Seleucid challenge, but both he and his successor died fighting the Saka, and it was only the succession of another great Parthian king, Mithradates II (124/3–87), that enabled the Parthians to survive at all.

Mithradates II faced a desperate situation, his homeland overrun and Babylonia again in revolt, this time led by

Opposite: view of the walls of the Seleucid city of Dura Europus on the Euphrates.

an Arab prince of a kingdom near the Persian Gulf, Hyspaosines of Charax. Mithradates was, however, an exceptional man "to whom his achievements procured the surname of Great; for being fired with a desire to emulate the merit of his ancestors, he was enabled by the vast powers of his mind to surpass their renown. He carried on many wars, with great bravery, against his neighbours, and added many provinces to the Parthian kingdom" (Justin). Mithradates II first reconquered Babylonia, overstriking the coins of Hyspaosines, and then reclaimed the Parthian homeland. He either conquered the newly formed Saka kingdom in Seistan (Sakastan) or forced it to accept vassal status. By 113 he had extended Parthian control westwards making the Euphrates the new frontier and capturing the Seleucid caravan city of Dura Europus. In ten years he had completely transformed the situation which had confronted him on his succession and had securely refounded the Parthian empire, which was to last for more than 300 years.

Foreign affairs. Mithradates was not only a military genius but also a brilliant ruler in times of peace and his reign was marked by expanding diplomatic and commercial contacts throughout the then known world. In the Seleucid period regular embassies had traveled between Asoka's India and the Hellenistic kingdoms, but under the Parthians contacts were made and maintained between Parthia and Rome on the one hand and Parthia and China on the other. These contacts were stimulated by the insatiable desire of the wealthy Romans for an ever-increasing quantity of Oriental luxuries, silks, precious stones, scents and spices, which Rome paid for with gold specie and Roman glass and bronzes. Meanwhile Parthia flourished and grew rich, benefiting from its lucrative position as middleman.

The Parthians came in direct contact with the Chinese, then ruled by the great Han dynasty, in Central Asia towards the end of the 2nd century BC. Chinese interest in the west had been shown as early as c. 138 BC when the Han emperor Wu-ti (141–87) had sent an ambassador, Chang Chien, to Central Asia. Chang Chien had brought back reports of fine horses, of wine and of many useful plants. The Ferghana horse was a great improvement on those indigenous to China, and to obtain them Wu-ti campaigned as far west as Sogdia. Known as "celestial" or "blood-sweating" in China, this horse was said to be both stronger and faster than those previously used, and was almost certainly the one employed by the Parthians. The importance of the horse to the Parthians, whose cavalry tactics were based on their use of an agile charger, was described by Justin: "they ride on horseback on all occasions; on horses they go to war, and to feasts; on horses they discharge public and private duties; on horses they go abroad, meet together, traffic and converse."

Mithradates II and Wu-ti exchanged ambassadors and presents, the Parthian sending such novelties as ostrich

A Parthian charger standing at an altar: the incised design on the base of a silver vase of the 1st century AD found at Bori in Georgia.

eggs and conjurors to the Han court, and this friendship led to the organization of trade between the two empires. The principal Chinese export was silk, in exchange for which they received all kinds of luxury goods, including carpets, precious stones and medicines. The first caravan probably traveled west in c. 106 BC, and the Chinese were successful in maintaining their monopoly in the production of silk until the middle of the first millennium AD.

The peaceful and profitable relations which the Parthians had established with Han China were not mirrored in the west – but this was no fault of the Parthians. Mithradates II was prepared to welcome contacts with Rome and he sent an ambassador, Orobazus, to greet the Roman general Sulla in 92 BC on the Euphrates. Rome, preoccupied with the threat posed by an alliance between Tigranes the Great of Armenia and Mithradates of Pontus, knew little about this new eastern power: When Orobazus offered Sulla friendship and an offensive and defensive alliance, he was treated with contempt. Sulla arrogantly assumed that he was applying for vassal status and this affront led to centuries of confrontation between Rome and Parthia. In response to this rebuff Mithradates II formed a powerful anti-Roman group, strengthening his links with Tigranes of Armenia, a man whom he had himself installed on the Armenian throne, and forming an alliance with Mithradates of Pontus.

The end of his long and brilliant reign was marred by internal revolt. A man named Gotarzes set himself up as an independent king in Babylon, as the occurrence of his name on tablets dated 91 BC proves. Mithradates II continued to rule in northern Mesopotamia and Iran, for

we hear of him in 87 when he captured the Seleucid king Demetrius III. We do not know why he tolerated the independence of Gotarzes, presumably the same man as the one described as "satrap of satraps" on Mithradates' damaged victory relief at Bisitun. This tendency for powerful nobles or sub-kings to assert their independence recurred throughout the Parthian period and illustrated an essential weakness in the feudal organization of the state. The state was governed by the king together with a council of nobles, which was composed of three groups – members of the royal family, the nobles and the priests or Magi. The army was raised and paid for by the nobles: as Justin wrote, "as anyone is eminent in wealth, so he furnished the king with a proportionate number of horsemen for war." This obviously resulted in the formation of private armies loyal to their master rather than to the king, whose authority was consequently weakened. Just how powerful members of the principal families could be is shown by the entourage of the brilliant general Suren, a member of one of the most important families, who went to war with a personal bodyguard of 1,000 armored horsemen.

Religion. When Alexander conquered the Orient, the worship of the Olympians and of the deified Alexander was added to the many faiths already followed within the empire. The Seleucids also encouraged worship of themselves and their families, as is shown by an inscription of Antiochus III found at Nihavand (ancient Laodicea). This promotes the worship of his wife, Queen Laodice, "considering this very necessary, not only because she shows her affection and her tender care in her life with us, but also because she is pious towards the divinity . . . we decree that . . . there be established . . . high priestesses of Laodicea who shall wear gold crowns with her portrait and whose names shall be inscribed in the deeds after those of the high priests of our ancestors and ourselves."

The worship of the Olympians was easily accepted throughout the Seleucid empire for there was at that time a spirit of syncretism which enabled people to amalgamate them with more specifically local deities. Thus in Iran Greek Zeus and Iranian Ahuramazda, Greek Apollo and Iranian Mithra, Greek Heracles and Iranian Verethragna, and Greek Artemis and Iranian Anahita were thought of as the same.

Although the Parthian kings called themselves Philhellenes, there is little doubt that the Parthians continued to worship the Iranian pantheon. This is shown by their names such as Mithra-dates and Arta-banus (Arta = truth), by their use of the Magi, the Iranian tribe of priests, and by their adoption of the Zoroastrian calendar on the records of a wine store found at Nysa. The prophet Zoroaster, who probably lived in about the 7th century BC, had initiated a basically monotheistic religion, promoting the worship of the Good Lord Ahuramazda above all other old Iranian deities. His vision was essentially one of opposed forces. It enjoined the worship of Ahuramazda together with abhorrence of Ahriman, Spirit of Evil, and it stressed the free choice of man between good and evil, light and darkness, truth and deceit.

However, even in the Achaemenian period the sole worship of Ahuramazda, if it had ever been strictly followed, had been supplemented by that of other Iranian deities such as Mithra, Lord of the Contract, and Anahita, Goddess of Water and of Fertility, and by the Parthian period Verethragna was one of the most popular deities, frequently depicted in clay and stone. An example of this is the statue of Heracles/Verethragna carved beside the main east-west highway, the Great Silk Road or the Great Khurasan Road, at Bisitun near Kermanshah. The god is shown reclining on his side, one bare leg indolently crossed over the other and holding a goblet in his left hand. His club is by his feet and a lion skin is outlined on the rock below. The sculpture is dated by an inscription to year 163 of the Seleucid era (148 BC), about the time of the first Parthian annexation of Media.

Although the Parthians were Zoroastrians, there is no evidence that they attempted to impose their faith on their new subjects. Indeed all the evidence points to a refreshing tolerance, greatly at variance with the heavy hand of their Sasanian successors. Excavated sites have produced a bewildering variety of temple plans, and statues of many different deities, both male and female, have been found.

The archaeological evidence. As outlined above, the Parthians had moved into an area ruled by the Seleucids and, even after they had secured their independence in c. 240 BC, the principal powers around them continued to be Hellenistic – in the west the Seleucids and in the east the Greco-Bactrians. It is, therefore, hardly surprising that the culture these nomads adopted to express their new-found power shows strong Hellenistic influence.

Because of the Hellenistic content of early Parthian art any attempt to separate Seleucid from Parthian excavation levels is difficult and at times impossible. The futility of such an attempt can best be understood when the composition of the population is considered. The indigenous population throughout the empire was itself composed of many different peoples and varied from region to region. Despite changes of dynasty it remained essentially the same. To this had been added Greek colonists, who continued to enjoy a superior social status under the Parthians. These three divisions of society, the Parthian masters, the Greek colonists, and the indigenous peoples, have to be remembered when discussing the art and architecture of the time. For instance, Seleucid cities, such as Seleucia-on-Tigris, continued to prosper and remained predominantly Greek in both population and urban organization for much of the Parthian period. Indeed, so as not to offend the citizens of Seleucia, the Parthians set up their camp, which later grew into the city

of Ctesiphon, on the other side of the Tigris. Seleucia's autonomy is illustrated by the fact that when it revolted against the Parthians in the 1st century AD it was able to hold out for seven years before being forced to capitulate. After this revolt the buildings were influenced by new, decisively Parthian elements, but previously had been essentially Greek.

The sites discussed below are selected to illustrate the Seleucid and early Parthian periods as we know them today. The evidence is sparse and uneven in distribution and more excavation is required before we can hope to establish a coherent picture. The Hellenistic period is known from excavations at Seleucia-on-Tigris, Dura Europus and Babylon in Mesopotamia, while eastern Hellenism is currently being revealed by the excavation of the site of Ai Khanum on the banks of the Oxus in ancient Bactria, only discovered in the 1960s, and by Russian excavations. Prior to this the Greco-Bactrians were principally known by their superb coins, struck both in gold and silver. Our knowledge of the early Parthians has also been transformed by Russian excavations at one of the first Parthian capitals at Nysa. For many years Seleucid and Parthian Iran has been relatively an archaeological blank, but here too the situation is changing rapidly, particularly with the discovery of another early Parthian royal city, Hecatompylos, at which excavations are still continuing. Excavations at Masjid-i Sulaiman and Bard-i Nishandeh in southwest Iran have also contributed much new material. Though serious archaeological study of the Hellenistic and Parthian periods is only just beginning, already enough new evidence has been recovered to enable us to understand something of the impact of Greek art on the Orient after Alexander's conquest.

Guarding the Great Silk Road at Bisitun. A life-size sculpture of a reclining Heracles, dated by a Greek inscription to c. 148 BC. His club is by his feet and the skin of the Nemean lion is indicated on the rock beneath him.

The Greeks in the east. Hellenistic culture was remarkably uniform whether in Central Asia or in Mesopotamia. It was essentially urban and Greek cities had regular plans which are easy to recognize, especially from the air. For instance, Seleucid Merv in Central Asia, built by Antiochus I, was rectangular in plan with straight streets intersecting at right angles. Seleucia-on-Tigris, probably built on top of the earlier city of Opis, was also laid out on a grid. Seleucia became the largest and wealthiest city in Mesopotamia with a population of some 60,000 inhabitants. Like other Seleucid cities, it was the home of an alien population, and had therefore to be strongly defended against attack by massive fortification walls, reinforced by rectangular towers, the ruins of which still form huge mounds today.

Oriental Greeks preserved their Greek culture even though they were living in a foreign country, and each city was arranged on Greek lines with an agora or market

Plan of the Greek theater and gymnasium at Babylon, an indispensable social center for the local Greek population.

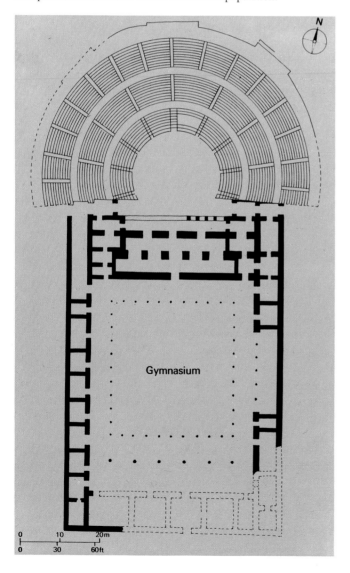

Gymnasium

place, a gymnasium and a theater. A combined theater/gymnasium was discovered in the early years of this century at Babylon. Although built in brick, for there is no stone on the alluvial Mesopotamian plains, the plan is uncompromisingly Greek. The rows of seats of the theater were built in the usual semicircle facing the stage, the front of which was decorated with reliefs in gypsum plaster. A row of statues set on brick pedestals was placed at the edge of the orchestra. Behind the stage the gymnasium or palaestra was sited in a peristyle courtyard. This structure must have been an indispensable social center for the Greek population of Babylon.

An agora, "the focal point of Greek city life and the basic feature of the planned Greek city," was found at Dura Europus, another Seleucid royal colony, sited halfway between the twin capitals of Antioch-on-the-Orontes and Seleucia-on-Tigris. Like the theater at Babylon, and for the same reason, lack of stone, it was built of mud brick on stone foundations and had a tiled roof. The American excavators also discovered two palaces and two temples, dedicated to Greek gods, one to Artemis and Apollo, the other to Zeus. Like other Seleucid cities, Dura was strongly fortified and laid out on a regular grid plan.

Greco-Bactrian cities have been located in the Soviet Union as well as the one already mentioned on the Afghan banks of the Oxus, Ai Khanum. Work began there in 1964 and is still continuing under the direction of Paul Bernard. The site was first visited by the late Professor Daniel Schlumberger in the early 1960s when he was convinced that at Ai Khanum there lay the remains of a complete Hellenistic city, grand enough in scale and conception to be a foundation of Alexander himself. Proof of this has not yet been found, though Bernard considers it possible that the site should be identified as Alexandria Oxiana.

The city of Ai Khanum was well sited in an easily defensible position: roughly triangular in shape, it is bounded on two sides by the River Oxus and its tributary, the Kokcha, while the third long side was defended by a massive fortification wall. In typical Greek fashion the city consisted of a citadel or acropolis on a rocky plateau, and a lower town divided from the acropolis by a long straight street running north-south. Excavations so far have concentrated on major public buildings in the lower town. Among these a gymnasium, a temple, a shrine or mausoleum, perhaps belonging to the first governor of the city, and a large complex of buildings known as the administrative quarter have been uncovered.

The administrative quarter consisted of an enormous courtyard leading into a great hall and a square building. The courtyard, which measured 136·8 × 108·1 meters, was entered through a propylon from the north. It was lined with columns on all four sides, though those on the south were the tallest and were placed in front of an open three-sided hall. The columns were comparatively long and slender and had ornate painted Corinthian capitals. The

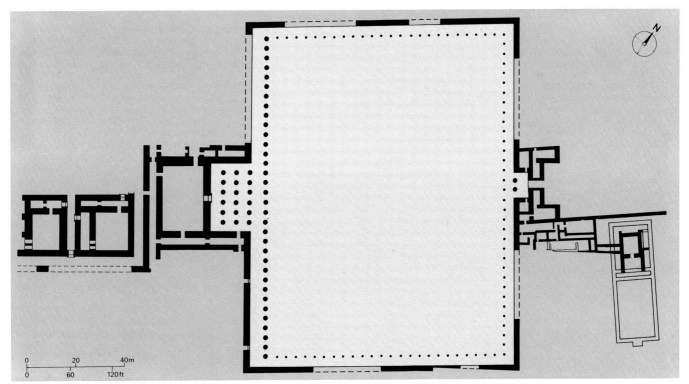

The Greco-Bactrian city of Ai Khanum on the Oxus: plan of the administrative quarter.

open hall led into the great hall which measured 17 × 26·5 meters. Unlike the open hall with its three rows of six columns, none were found in this room and the charred roofing timbers found on the floor were relatively thin – not more than 20 centimeters in thickness. Since there was no trace of vaulting, the roofing of this space remains problematic.

The walls of the great hall were decorated with engaged fluted columns and the plastered surfaces were gaily painted with geometric designs in black, white, red and yellow. In a suite of rooms to the west there were well-equipped bathing facilities.

The square building, perhaps built later, was separated from the great hall by an alley. Each side was 52·65 meters long and it was divided into four rooms surrounded by a corridor. The most interesting finds in this area included fragments of relief sculpture made of clay and stucco. One of these probably represented a mounted king, over-life-size and depicted in the Greek style. This tradition of monumental clay sculpture continued to flourish in Central Asia and northwest India.

The administrative quarter shows a mixture of Greek and eastern influences: the plan of the peristyle court, the Corinthian capitals and the stone-working techniques of the columns are clearly Greek, while there are also architectural links with Achaemenian palaces such as the massive brick walls which are up to 3·20 meters thick, the slender proportions of the columns and the adornment of the walls with sculpture. The roofs too

exhibit this fusion of east and west for these were probably mostly flat, although the discovery of tiles and antefixes suggests that they may have been given a decorative edging of tiles. The excavator is not yet sure what purpose this monumental complex served, though he suggests that it was used as a royal or perhaps vice-regal residence. Thanks to the thorough plundering, smashing and burning to which the site was subjected there are few small finds.

If Ai Khanum was indeed founded by Alexander, then the earliest settlement there can be dated to 329–327 BC, when Alexander was in Central Asia. The first major building program was probably undertaken during the reign of Seleucus I, particularly during the latter half of his reign when his son Antiochus was in charge of the eastern provinces. A second major building period is dated to the first half of the 2nd century BC, during the reigns of the Greco-Bactrian kings Demetrius and Eucratides. The city and the Greco-Bactrian kingdom were brought to an end c. 130, probably by the invasions of the Saka, whose attacks nearly caused the collapse of the newly formed Parthian empire.

Only two inscriptions have been found at Ai Khanum but both are of considerable interest. One in a courtyard building near the river dedicated it to Hermes and Heracles, an appropriate dedication for a gymnasium. The other was inscribed on slabs in a small temple-like building located near the center of the lower city. It was built over the grave of a hero, presumably the first governor of the settlement, who is named as one Kinneas. The shrine consisted of a rectangular *cella* or shrine, approached through a *pronaos* or porch, and the building was carefully

Above: view of the quadrilobate columns of the Parthian palace at Nysa revealed by Russian excavations.

Below: reconstruction of the Parthian palace built in the citadel at Nysa. Huge clay statues were placed in the niches.

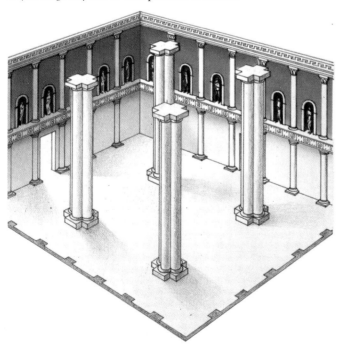

maintained throughout the life of the city. The inscription, which was written by a man called Klearchos after a visit to Delphi, was carved in the fine lettering of the 3rd century BC on a panel set in the *pronaos*. On it he recorded precepts that had been dedicated at the Delphic shrine and, as the excavator Bernard observed, "their presence on the banks of the Oxus more than 5,000 km as the crow flies from Delphi is an astonishing testimony to the fidelity of the Greek settlers of remote Bactria to the most authentic and general traditions of Hellenism."

Early Parthian sites: Nysa. The earliest Parthian settlement yet discovered is at Nysa or Parthanissa, not far from the modern town of Ashkabad. Russian excavations there have revealed many monumental structures, each built to a different plan and each lavishly decorated. The sculpture and small finds are similarly vigorous, owing much to Hellenism, yet with a distinct flavor of their own.

Nysa consisted of a walled lower town and a citadel built outside the town walls on a nearby hillock. This citadel, called Mithradatkert according to a tablet found there, was built by Mithradates I. The massive fortification walls were some 20 to 25 meters high and 5 meters thick and were built of packed earth or pisé faced with mud bricks. Access was by means of a ramp which followed the line of the walls around the citadel. Any invading army, attempting to storm it, would have had to climb up around the ramp, and would have been brought under constant fire.

Within the citadel walls the Russians discovered numerous public buildings, including a palace, the so-called "Square House," and some temples. The principal room of the palace was a pillared hall, some 20 meters square. It was roofed with great beams, supported on four large quatrefoil columns, which effectively divided the room into three aisles: this feature recurred frequently in later Parthian architecture. The walls were painted red and white and were divided horizontally by a frieze of terracotta plaques, and vertically by rows of engaged columns, six on each wall. In the lower register the column capitals were of the Doric order while in the upper they were of the Corinthian. Huge clay statues, today very fragmentary but probably representing deified ancestors, were placed in niches between the upper rows of columns.

The principal *cella* of one of the temples consisted of a huge circular room which measured some 17 meters in diameter. Like the great hall at Ai Khanum it had no columns and the method used to roof the span is not known. Like the Nysa palace, the interior was painted and decorated: the white walls were embellished with a figured terracotta frieze and in the upper register with engaged columns and niches. This circular room formed the core of a square complex, which was surrounded by corridors. Adjacent to this temple was another square central unit or tower with ambulatory. A similar plan occurs in the administrative quarter at Ai Khanum and such a unit continued to be built throughout the Parthian and Sasanian periods.

The architects of Nysa were clearly experimenting with many different forms of buildings. In the Square House they returned to the typical colonnaded courtyard building with long columned rooms on all four sides. Entrances too were equally experimental and ranged from simple doorways to entrance vestibules and to the familiar columned portico. There is no sign yet of what became the most characteristic Parthian architectural innovation and legacy, the *iwan* or open hall roofed with a high barrel vault and placed as the dominant feature in a courtyard. As we shall see in the next chapter, the earliest unequivocal example does not occur until the 1st century AD in Mesopotamia. It was possible at that time to erect such high barrel vaults because the builders were using gypsum mortar. This mortar sets very quickly; indeed it holds bricks almost as soon as they are placed in position. This advantage made it possible to build larger vaults than before and ones which did not require expensive wooden scaffolding; it was in other words a technological breakthrough.

It may be that there were two stages in the evolution of the typical Parthian *iwan*. Stage 1 involved only the use of an open three-sided hall, which at that time was roofed with beams, either supported on columns as necessary to bridge the span, or simply resting on the side walls. Stage 2 followed when it was possible to roof such halls with barrel vaults. Examples of Stage 1 can be found in early Parthian Central Asia. At Nysa itself it is possible, though the plan is somewhat conjectural at this point, that the vestibule to the tower temple complex was such an open three-sided hall, probably roofed by beams resting on the side walls. Another more convincing example of Stage 1 is to be seen in a palace discovered by Russian archaeologists at Saksanakhyr, some 40 kilometers north of Ai Khanum. This palace, a typical courtyard building, has been dated to the 2nd century BC. The dominant feature of the courtyard was an open three-sided hall, the 12-meter span of which was roofed with the help of only one or perhaps two columns; the building was poorly preserved, standing only a few centimeters above ground level, and only one column base has survived. This may well be an early example of an open hall which only took on its distinctive vaulted form some two centuries later in Mesopotamia.

According to Isidore of Charax who prepared an itinerary called *Parthian Stations*, Nysa was the necropolis of the Parthian kings. Unfortunately the royal tombs with their rich funerary offerings have not yet been discovered, although a great treasure was found sealed in some rooms of the Square House. Among the many beautiful objects found there were 40 ivory rhyta or drinking horns, so large and heavy that they must have been reserved for ceremonial use (pp. 41–46). They are decorated with figures at the bottom and friezes around the top in a mixture of Classical and Oriental motifs, and they illustrate the

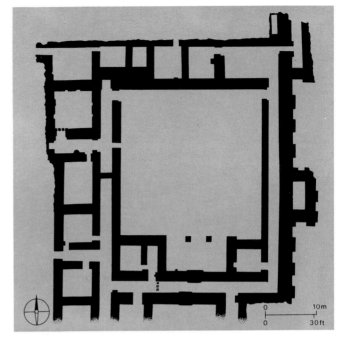

Above: plan of the 2nd- to 1st-century BC palace at Saksanakhyr.

Below: plan of part of Mithradatkert, the citadel built by Mithradates I outside the town walls at Nysa.

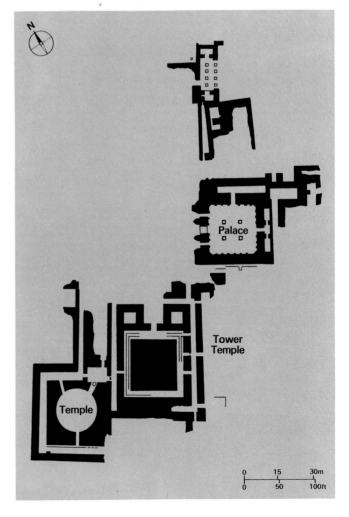

Parthian fusion of ideas from east and west. The seals on the doors date from no earlier than the 1st century AD, so the treasure can be dated to the earlier rather than the later Parthian period. The seal impressions themselves also provide valuable information on Parthian glyptic art.

Although the royal tombs have not yet been found, a building in the lower town may have served as a mausoleum for the nobility. It was a simple rectangular building constructed against the town wall, with columns running around the other three sides. The capitals were debased Ionic in style, a type of capital that was also popular in Iran. Inside the mausoleum there were several long chambers with loculi or recesses for coffins or pots containing the bones. These loculi are similar to those of the much later mausolea at Hatra, Dura Europus and Palmyra. The Nysa chambers were some 2 meters wide and were roofed with simple vaults.

Hecatompylos. Remains of buildings of the Parthian period, also possibly serving as mausolea, have recently been found at the site of Shahr-i Qumis near Damghan. This has been identified by John Hansman as the lost Seleucid/Parthian city of Hecatompylos, which the Parthians made one of their capital cities in the last quarter of the 3rd century B C. Situated in the plain on the southern side of the Elburz Mountains, it would have made a pleasant winter capital but in summer the court probably moved to cooler cities in the Parthian homeland.

The Parthian buildings at Shahr-i Qumis date to the early Parthian period, for the site ceased to be used as a capital in the 1st century B C, probably being replaced by a more western capital such as Ctesiphon. The site is a large one, though unfortunately one which has suffered considerably both from strong wind and water erosion. As the excavators John Hansman and David Stronach, Director of the British Institute of Persian Studies, write, "Such are the effects of these natural assaults that only the most substantial monuments appear to have survived in

Above: two architectural members from Nysa: at the top, an Ionic-style column capital; below it, a capital decorated with a bow-case.

Below: general view of Shahr-i Qumis, ancient Hecatompylos, from the north, showing the Parthian structures at Sites VI and VII.

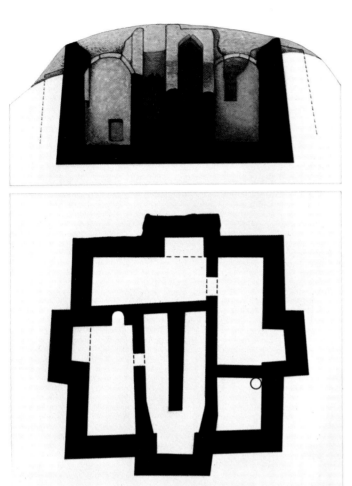

anything approaching an undisturbed condition. Elsewhere each natural fissure or artificial cut reveals more or less clean, tenacious clay, devoid almost of any trace of the original stratification." However "substantial monuments" have survived.

Only four seasons of excavation have taken place so far and work has been concentrated on clearing and recording the main monuments, already partially uncovered by local farmers collecting soil. Of the buildings recorded so far, three major structures belong to the Parthian period and still stand to a considerable height. The plans are all somewhat similar, basically square with a rectangular extension in the center of each side. Two of the structures contain L-shaped rooms while the third has rectangular or square rooms. None of the rooms was very wide and the problem of roofing was not therefore difficult.

Thanks to the remarkable preservation of these structures – Sites VII and XIII still stand some 6–7 meters above the plain, and fragments of a third story can be seen – the various forms of vaulting employed survive in many cases in a perfect state of preservation. Three systems of vaulting were used at Qumis: a simple barrel vault, a more wedge-shaped or triangular headed vault, and an

Left: plan and elevation of Site VII at Shahr-i Qumis.

Below: Shahr-i Qumis, details of stepped vaults with rounded and pointed arches from Sites IV (*left*) and VI (*right*). The ranging rod in the foreground of the right-hand picture is 2 meters high.

interesting variation on the latter type where the wedge-shaped vaults are only some three struts wide and ascend or descend in "steps" – a "step-vault," used under or over a stairway or ramp. All these vaults are built out of a special type of mud brick, a molded and curved strut. These measure c. $88 \times 9 \times 18$ cm, as opposed to the standard brick of c. 38–40 cm square by 10 cm thick. This use of a special member for vaulting was not new, for it had also been used in the Achaemenian period at Persepolis and at the Median site of Tepe Nush-i Jan near Hamadan (c. 700 BC).

Other tombs and shrines. While the Qumis buildings may or may not have been mausolea (their purpose is not yet certain), a different type of tomb has been found in the Zagros Mountains. These tombs consist of chambers cut into the cliffs, an idea obviously derived from the great rock-cut tombs of the Achaemenian kings at Naqsh-i Rustam. Some of these tombs consist only of a single chamber, while others have a number of "rooms" as well as an exterior adorned with sculptured reliefs. One of the most ornate occurs at Qizqapan in Iraqi Kurdistan. Internally there are three interconnecting chambers hollowed out of the rock, with recesses cut into the floor to receive the bodies. The Qizqapan facade is framed by a pair of engaged columns with capitals of debased Ionic style, decorated with a rosette motif between the volutes, and they are partially similar to capitals found at Nysa. The principal scene was placed above the entrance to the tomb and showed two men in Iranian dress saluting a large fire altar of Achaemenian type. The men, carrying bows, are wearing "Median" dress, a tunic and trousers with a

All that remains of the palace or temple at Khurha near Isfahan: slender stone columns with Ionic-style capitals (reerected) and the stone platform. Note the strapwork motif on the scolls (*above*). Seleucid-Parthian period.

The rock-cut tomb at Qizqapan in Iraqi Kurdistan: drawing of the sculpture which decorated the facade. Post-Achaemenian period.

coat slung over the shoulders. Above them are three religious symbols. For a long time scholars believed that these tombs belonged to the Median period but in recent years it has been realized that they date to the post-Achaemenian period, that is to the Seleucid or Parthian era. This new dating has been suggested by a number of factors including the use of Hellenistic architectural elements which were popular over a wide area at that time and by the results of technical studies of ancient stone working.

Hellenistic-style capitals have also been found at Khurha near Isfahan, where a palace or temple was built in a pleasant valley surrounded by mountains. The plan of the structure has not yet been recovered, although remains can be seen of a stone platform and a number of columns. The columns are an interesting combination of Iranian and Greek styles, for the drums are both thinner and higher than they would be in Greece, while the capitals are based on the Ionic order with the addition of a strapwork motif between the volutes.

A number of other structures also dating to the post-Achaemenian period and built on stone platforms have been found in the ancient province of Elymais. Two of these, at Masjid-i Sulaiman and Bard-i Nishandeh, have been excavated recently by Professor Roman Ghirshman, while another at Shami was the subject of a rescue sondage by Sir Aurel Stein in the 1930s. The Masjid-i Sulaiman terrace is next to Iran's oldest oilfield where a natural gas fire had long made it a sacred place for the fire-worshiping Persians. Occupation on the stone terrace is attested from Achaemenian to late Parthian times and the plans of no fewer than four different sanctuaries have been recovered. Professor Ghirshman suggests that there was a Macedonian military garrison located at Masjid-i Sulaiman guarding the route between the Susiana plain and the Persian Gulf in one direction and between Masjid-i Sulaiman and the Iranian plateau in the other, for he has found many clay figurines of Macedonian cavalrymen. One of the shrines they established, consisting of a *cella* and *pronaos*, was dedicated to Heracles, of whom Ghirshman found a stone statue showing the hero grasping the Nemean lion. Clay figurines of this popular subject have also been found at Susa, and representations of it occur on the ivory rhyta from Nysa.

The sculptures of Shami. At Shami, a remote valley in the Zagros Mountains, Stein found the remains of a rectangular building on a terrace. It measured some 24 × 12 meters and may have been partially open to the skies, for evidence of roofing was only found near the walls. The shrine had been completely wrecked and burned before abandonment and Stein found, among the debris, a number of stone bases with sockets sunk into them, which were obviously designed to receive the feet of statues displayed within the shrine. In the sack many of these statues had been smashed, including a sensitive

Above: a fragment of a bronze head, found by Aurel Stein in the ruins of the temple of Shami. Strongly Hellenistic in style, it is considered to represent one of the Seleucid kings, perhaps Antiochus III or IV. Ht. 26·5 cm. Tehran Archaeological Museum.

Below: bronze statuette of a worshiper found at Shami. Ht. 27 cm. Tehran Archaeological Museum.

bronze face in Hellenistic style which perhaps represented Antiochus III or IV. Other sculptures found at Shami include a small bronze statue of a man in Parthian dress, only some 27 centimeters high, of which unfortunately the head is missing, and a fine marble head similar in style to the head of the magnificent over-life-size bronze of a

Marble head of a Parthian prince from Shami, similar in style to that of the bronze prince. Ht. 11 cm. Tehran Archaeological Museum.

Parthian, for which the site is principally famous. This statue was found by villagers when digging foundations for new houses and the capable military administrator of the area immediately took charge both of the statue and of the find-spot. Stein, then traveling in the Bakhtiari hills and hearing of this exciting find, came and worked at the site for about a week to see what additional information he could recover.

The Shami bronze, one of the most remarkable works of art of the Parthian period, is nearly 2 meters high and measures some 66 centimeters across its massive shoulders. The head, somewhat small in proportion to the body, was cast separately and fits closely at the neck. The face has widely spaced eyes with heavy brows, a narrow straight nose and a long moustache; the carefully shaped beard is marked by fine chiseling around the jawline. The long hair is bound around the brows by a diadem and rolled back, away from the face. Around the neck hangs a simple torque, carefully represented to show the fine herringbone design of the heavy metal chain and the wide flat stone in the center. Since no rich hoard of Parthian jewelry has yet been found, information about the jewelry of the period comes in the main from sculptures, such as this one, and from coins.

The Shami prince's cross-over tunic with its wide lapels leaves much of his hairy chest bare. His belt was decorated with an incised oblong design probably representing metal plaques. He wore baggy pants and long loose over-trousers, inside the top of which the blades of his two daggers were hidden. The finish at the back of the sculpture was somewhat rough, and it is probable that the bronze was made to be placed against a wall.

Below the shrine, dug into the hillside, were many Parthian graves, and in one of them Stein found some pieces of shell inlay, presumably once adorning the sides of a box. One of these shows a Parthian archer with taut bowstring. The date of this terraced shrine, and therefore of the statues within it, is still disputed. It clearly began in the Seleucid period and continued in use in the Parthian period, but how long it lasted within the four centuries of Parthian rule is far from certain. It probably belonged to the earlier rather than to the later part and the late Daniel Schlumberger suggested that the great bronze belonged to the turn of our era.

The archaeological evidence for the last three centuries before the birth of Christ is fragmentary and does not yet form a coherent picture, nor does it link with evidence gleaned from coins and historical references. Much more work is needed before we can hope to gain a clearer picture of the gradual fusion of Hellenistic and Oriental cultures and of that evolved by the dynamic Parthians. Early Parthian art may not necessarily have been homogeneous, particularly in the early years, for they conquered a vast territory and the degree of control must have varied from province to province as it also did under the Seleucids. In some remote areas local traditions probably lasted longer and new ideas were only gradually absorbed. However, even though the material is still sparse, sufficient exists of high artistic quality to suggest that early Parthian art and architecture were a vigorous expression of the power of this new empire. Like that of the Achaemenians it undoubtedly drew on many sources of inspiration, Greek, eastern and indigenous, to evolve its own artistic style, which continued to develop during the later Parthian period.

The Shami bronze of a Parthian prince (see p. 25 for complete view): a detail of the back showing the baggy over-trousers and the hilt of a dagger. Tehran Archaeological Museum.

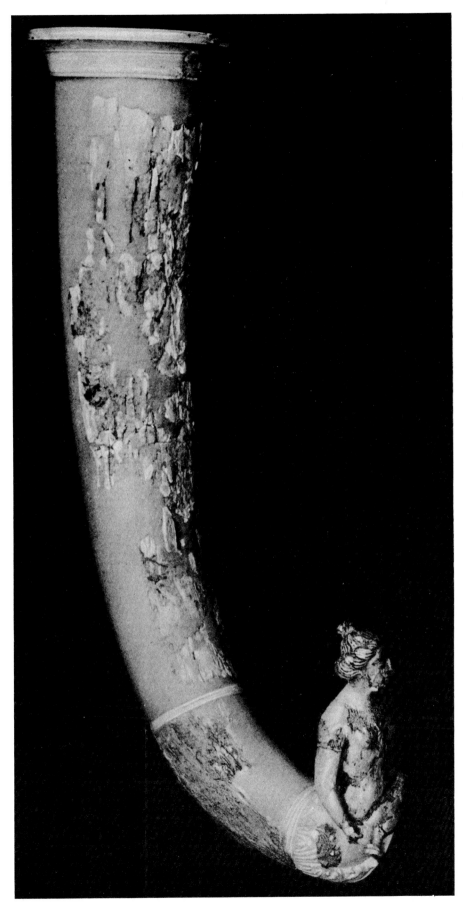

Ivory Drinking Horns from Nysa

A hoard of treasure including 40 huge drinking horns or rhyta was found in a sealed room in the Square House at Nysa. These horns were made from several sections of an elephant's tusk and were probably only used on ritual or ceremonial occasions, as they were so heavy. Seal impressions fixed to the blocked-up entrance of the treasure chamber probably date from the 1st century AD and thus prove that the rhyta are early Parthian rather than late.

This superb collection vividly illustrates the eclectic nature of early Parthian art. Some rhyta appear to be almost entirely Classical in inspiration, with an Aphrodite-type figure rising from the end and a frieze around the top illustrating a Greek legend, or showing the Olympians. Others are more Oriental, with a winged griffin completely Achaemenian in style at the base.

Left: a rhyton made in three sections. The body of a naked female, perhaps representing Aphrodite, rises from the base. Her upswept hair is typically Parthian. The join of the torso to the vessel is concealed by a foliate pattern. The frieze once decorating the top is too damaged for identification.

Left and below : decorative friezes were frequently placed around the tops of the rhyta. The two on this page probably represent scenes of Dionysiac sacrifice : the musicians are wearing animal skins, and rams are being led along. These friezes are carved in low relief in a strongly Classical style, but there are sufficient variations from the Classical canon to suggest that the rhyta were carved in Parthia itself rather than imported from the west. While the Dionysiac scenes were carved in low relief, the heads above (*left*) are cut fully in the round, and each differs from the other. This unusual use of heads later becomes a decorative feature on Parthian and Sasanian buildings. The rim of the rhyton *below* is decorated with an incised design representing bunches of grapes and vine leaves:

Above: detail of a frieze of heads placed immediately below the rim of a rhyton. Staring straight out, though set at different angles, each depicts a different face and is carved fully in the round. These could be placed so close to the rim because the wine was drunk or poured from a spout at the base and a smooth lip was not necessary.

Right: the figure from the base of a rhyton: a man, whose loins are covered with a skin, carrying a boy(?) on his shoulders. This most probably portrayed some Classical hero, but in its present fragmentary state it is impossible to be certain who is represented. It may be Heracles or, if the fragmentary remains of horse's legs can be seen, then it probably represents the centaur Nessus carrying off Deianira, the wife of Heracles.

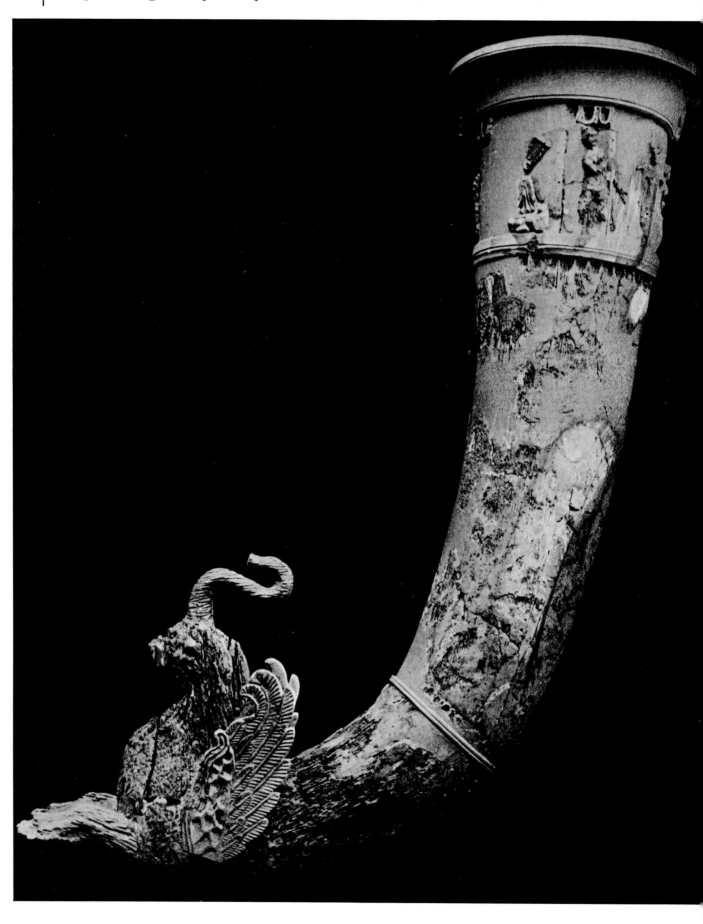

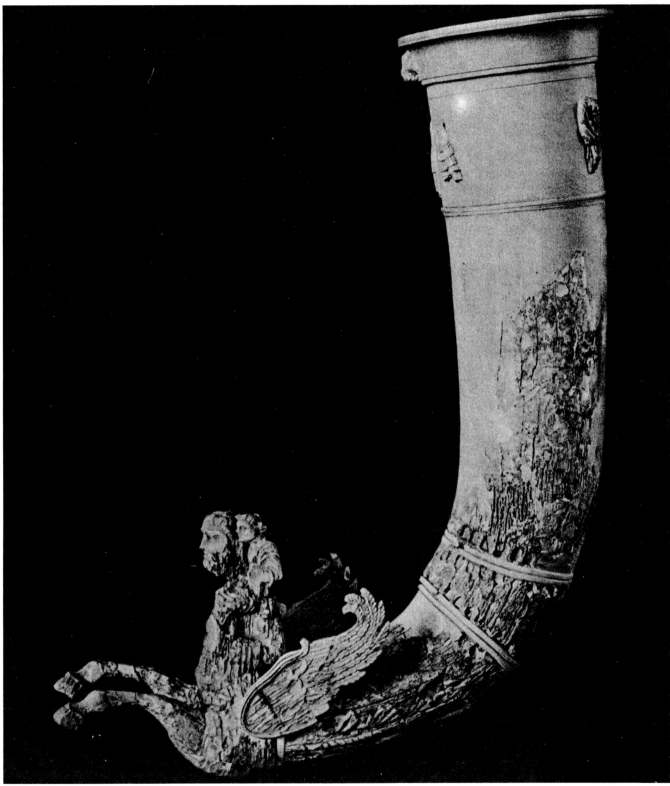

These two rhyta illustrate the eclectic and exploratory nature of early Parthian art. The rhyton *above* ends in a familiar Classical creature, the man/horse or centaur. On his shoulder can be seen the small figure of a woman, whom he is carrying off, so this figure may again represent Nessus abducting Deianira.

The rhyton on the *left*, however, terminates in a figure entirely Achaemenian in inspiration, a winged griffin. Such a motif had a long history in the ancient Near East. Typically Achaemenian are his unswept wings and curving horn. Yet, while the griffin is Oriental in origin, the frieze around the top (much damaged) again depicts some Classical scene.

Left: detail from a frieze, showing a woman holding a tablet, another with an alabastron and one with a box, perhaps containing jewels. The figures on this frieze may represent the nine Muses.

Below: an unusual ivory carving in the form of an elephant. Trumpeting loudly, the elephant seems to be charging forward. The remains of the mahout can be seen between his ears.

Right: the elegant back of an Aphrodite figure, similar to that shown on page 41.

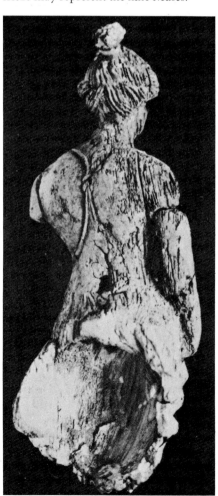

3. Conflict in the West

Being assailed by the Romans, also, in three wars, under
the conduct of the greatest generals, and at the most
flourishing period of the Republic, they alone, of all nations,
were not only a match for them, but came off victorious.

JUSTIN

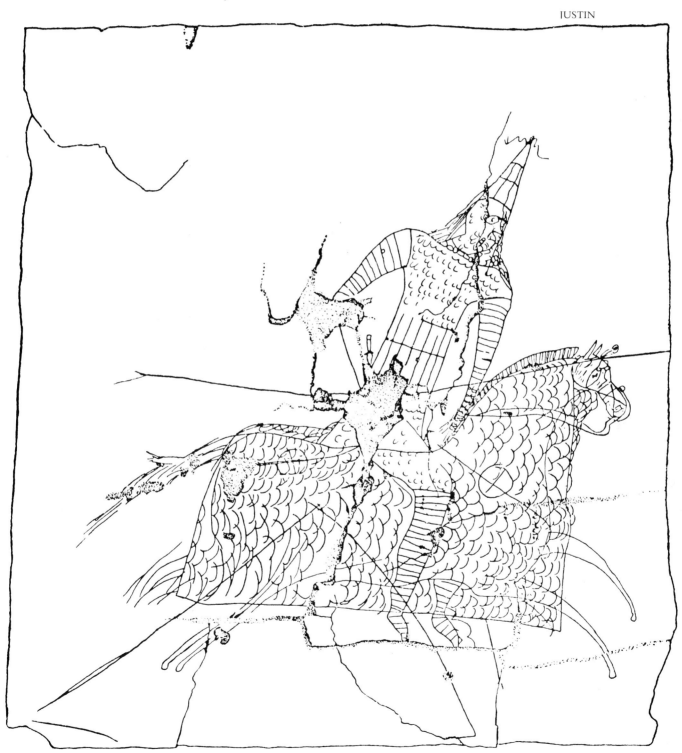

The long centuries of conflict between the Iranian and the Roman empires began in 92 BC. One cause of friction was the location of the frontier, the banks of the Euphrates. This frontier gave the Parthians a distinct military advantage, for the river takes a great westward curve deep into Syria, making a Parthian strike at the rich and important city of Antioch-on-the-Orontes, capital of the Roman east, all too easy. The Euphrates remained the frontier during the first three centuries of Parthian rule, in which time they inflicted a number of major defeats on the Romans and generally maintained an offensive role, sometimes raiding deep into Syria. By the 2nd century AD, however, this advantage was lost, for Parthia had been considerably weakened by internal dynastic and economic crises and Rome was able to extend her power east of the Euphrates. Three times in the 2nd century Rome succeeded in sacking the Parthian winter capital of Ctesiphon, a disastrous series of blows from which Parthia never recovered.

While the position of the actual frontier was one cause of friction between Parthia and Rome, another was control of the kingdom of Armenia. Each power wanted its own client king on the throne. Indeed when Sulla met the Parthian ambassador in 92, he was principally concerned about an alliance formed between Tigranes the Great of Armenia and the king of Pontus, also called Mithradates. He had no concept of the power and extent of the new Parthian empire, which was to be Rome's major rival in the east for the next three centuries.

Problems over the succession after the death of Mithradates II left Parthia divided and weak for a number

Above: the "Parthian shot," minutely inlaid in gold and silver on a Western Han dynasty bronze tube: a detail drawn from a chariot ornament found at Ting-hsien in Hopei, China, greatly enlarged.

Previous page: graffito on the wall of a house at Dura Europus: a Parthian cavalryman charging. He is armed with lance and dagger, and both man and horse are protected by armor. 2nd–3rd century AD.

of years, unable to respond either to an Armenian recovery of the "70 valleys" ceded to Mithradates II or to subsequent appeals for help against the Romans from Tigranes and Mithradates of Pontus. In 58 or 57 BC Parthia was plunged into civil war as the brothers Mithradates and Orodes, who had previously murdered their father, struggled for the throne. Mithradates finally surrendered to his brother in 55 BC hoping for clemency, but was promptly killed. The uniting of Parthia under the rule of Orodes was only just in time, for the following year Parthia was invaded by Rome.

Crassus in Parthia. Effective leadership in Rome at this time was divided between Julius Caesar, Pompey and Crassus. The elderly Crassus, then some 60 years of age, was appointed governor of Syria and left Rome in November 55, determined to undertake a Parthian war, extending "his hopes as far as to the Bactrians, and the Indians and the external sea" (Plutarch). This war had no possible justification, for Parthia was at peace with Rome and had indeed signed a treaty with her. Furthermore such a war was unpopular with the Roman citizens. Despite a rough sea passage from Brundisium, Crassus arrived in Syria safely and "matters at first turned out fully equal to his expectation; for he easily threw a bridge over the Euphrates, and got his army across safely, and he also obtained possession of many cities in Mesopotamia which surrendered." He garrisoned his newly captured territory and then returned to Syria for the rest of the winter. This was his first major blunder for not only did it give the Parthian king much-needed time to prepare for war, but it also committed the Romans to invading Parthia via Mesopotamia rather than through the foothills of Armenia. This cost Crassus the support of the Armenian king, Artavasdes, who had offered him considerable help, provided that he attacked through the hilly country of Armenia, where the superb Parthian cavalry would be hampered by the terrain. Crassus, however, had to collect his garrisons left in Mesopotamia.

Orodes prepared for war and committed the main Parthian force, which he himself commanded, to Armenia, where he met the unfortunate Artavasdes. The Armenian wisely came to terms with Orodes and the alliance was cemented by a marriage. Mesopotamia, however, was defended by a force of only 10,000 cavalry, led by the young Parthian noble, Suren. Suren, "in wealth, birth and consideration . . . was next to the king; but, in courage and ability, the first of the Parthians of his time; and, besides all this, in stature and beauty of person he had no equal. He used always to travel, when he was on his own business, with 1,000 camels to carry his baggage, and he had following him 200 carriages for concubines; and 1,000 mailed horsemen, with a larger number of light cavalry, escorted him; and he had in all, horsemen, clients, and slaves, no less than 10,000." (Plutarch.)

Suren's force consisted of both light- and heavy-armed horsemen. Justin described Parthian armor as "formed of plates, lapping over one another like the feathers of a bird," entirely covering both man and horse. The heavy-armed cavalryman carried a long two-handed lance, while the archers carried "bows which were strong and large and, owing to their great degree of bending, discharged the missiles with violence" (Plutarch). Parthian tactics were well described by Justin: "Of engaging with the enemy in close fight, and of taking cities by siege, they know nothing. They fight on horseback either galloping forward or turning their backs. Often too they counterfeit flight, that they may throw their pursuers off their guard against being wounded by their arrows. The signal for battle among them is given, not by trumpet but by drum . . . In general they retire before the enemy in the very heat of the engagement, and, soon after their retreat, return to the battle afresh; so that, when you feel most certain that you have conquered them, you have still to meet the greatest danger from them." Both the feigned retreat and the Parthian shot (firing backwards when retreating) became famous in Roman literature and live on in our own terminology.

Crassus' army consisted of about seven legions, in all some 40,000 men, mostly infantry. He had dangerously little cavalry, for which he had been relying on Roman client kings and particularly on Artavasdes, whose support he had forfeited. The Parthians attacked the Romans unexpectedly in open country, constantly wheeling about to confuse their enemies, and pouring a merciless hail of arrows into the barely complete Roman square. This, as Plutarch tells us, "the Romans endured so long as they had hopes that the Parthians would withdraw from the contest when they had discharged their arrows, or would come to close quarters; but when they perceived that there were many camels standing there, loaded with arrows, and that the Parthians who had first shot all their arrows, turned round to the camels for a fresh supply, Crassus . . . began to lose heart" and ordered his son to mount a desperate diversionary attack. This was decoyed away from the main force by the "retreating" Parthians, who then surrounded and slaughtered all the Romans. What was left of the main Roman force escaped and spent the night within the walls of Carrhae, from which they fled the following night only to be led astray by their guides and were once again surrounded by the Parthians. Suren offered a truce but while the terms were being negotiated Crassus was killed, perhaps accidentally, and his head sent to Orodes in Armenia where the king was celebrating his new alliance with Artavasdes. Of Crassus' force Plutarch reported that a total of 20,000 were killed, while 10,000 were taken prisoner and, according to Pliny, settled in Antiochia in Margiana – the Merv oasis. Only 10,000 succeeded in escaping to Syria. The brilliant Suren too died soon afterwards, murdered by order of Orodes who distrusted so able a subject.

Parthian supremacy. The result of this resounding Parthian victory was that Parthia's prestige was enormously enhanced and the Euphrates was securely established as the western frontier until 63 AD. Taking advantage of their success, the Parthians, led by Orodes' son Pacorus, campaigned in Syria in 51 BC. They were helped by a native population tired of Roman rule and their success seriously worried the Roman commanders. The Parthians failed, however, to follow up their advantage and withdrew the following year across the Euphrates, perhaps to attend to problems on their northern or eastern borders or perhaps because Orodes suspected his son of treachery. According to the later reports of Ammianus Marcellinus, a Syrian fighting in the Roman army in the 4th century AD, it was Pacorus who transformed the army encampment at Ctesiphon, which the Parthians had established near Seleucia, into "the crowning ornament of Persia," strengthening it with additional inhabitants and walls.

The Romans were unable to make a serious response to Parthian supremacy at this time because they themselves were plagued by the civil war between Caesar and Pompey, with the Parthians supporting the latter. Caesar began to plan a major campaign to solve the Parthian problem in 45 BC and made available 16 legions and 10,000 cavalry as well as sufficient gold and an enormous supply of arms. The lesson of Crassus' defeat had been well learned: the invasion was to be via the hills of Lesser Armenia and the legionaries were to be defended by an adequate cavalry force. But Caesar was murdered in Rome and the struggle for power continued – between Mark Antony and Caesar's nephew, Octavian. Antony planned a Parthian campaign in 41 BC but instead continued through Syria to Egypt where he spent the winter with Cleopatra.

In 40 BC a new offensive was launched by the Parthians against Syria under the joint command of Pacorus and a former Roman ambassador, Quintus Labienus. The Parthian force was overwhelmingly successful and took Antioch before splitting into two: Labienus' force campaigned victoriously in Asia Minor, perhaps even reaching Lydia and Ionia, while Pacorus captured all Syria, with the exception of Tyre which was impregnable from land, and continued into Palestine, taking Jerusalem and placing a Jewish king on the throne of the Holy City – the Jews had long supported Parthia against their hated Roman masters. Nearly all Rome's Asiatic provinces were in Parthian hands and the Parthians had nearly re-established the former Achaemenian empire. Antony sailed back to Rome from Egypt without attempting to intervene for he had to fight in Italy, though he did dispatch a force into Asia under the command of Publius Ventidius Bassus. This succeeded in inflicting a major defeat on the Parthian force commanded by Labienus, who was later taken prisoner and put to death. The Parthians were defeated a second time before withdrawing for the winter of 39 from Syria, which was reoccupied by the Romans.

Pacorus again invaded Syria in the spring ot 38 BC and since his administration had been popular there was a real danger of a popular uprising in support of the Parthians. But in a fierce battle near Gindaris a little west of the Afrin river, the brilliant Pacorus was killed along with many of his followers. Justin wrote of this defeat "nor did the Parthians, in any war, ever suffer a greater slaughter."

When the news of the Parthian defeat and the death of his son reached the elderly king, who had just been "boasting of his son Pacorus as the conqueror of the Romans," Orodes was overwhelmed by despair. "After long indulgence in grief another cause of concern troubled the unhappy old man, as he had to determine which of his 30 sons he should choose for his successor in the place of Pacorus" (Justin) and in 37 BC he abdicated in favor of his eldest son Phraates IV.

Phraates IV and Mark Antony. Phraates was an unfortunate choice for he "immediately proceeded to kill his father, as if he would not die, and put to death, also, all his 30 brothers. But his murders did not end with his father's sons: for finding that the nobility began to detest him for his constant barbarities, he caused his own son, who was grown up, to be killed that there might be no one to be nominated king" (Justin). Many nobles fled to escape the murderous impulses of their king, among them one who persuaded Antony that Parthia would be an easy conquest since the people would be ready to rebel against Phraates.

Antony prepared for a Parthian war and crossed the Euphrates at Zeugma in the spring of 36 BC with an army of some 100,000 men. Hearing that the Median army was away helping the Parthian king, he left behind the siege engines and baggage train guarded by two legions, while he "hurried on, confident that he would capture all the enemies' strongholds without a blow. He assailed Praaspa, the royal residence, and proceeded to heap up mounds and to make assaults. When the Parthian and the Mede ascertained this, they left him to continue his idle toil, for the walls were strong and were well manned by defenders" (Dio Cassius) and attacked and captured the baggage train, killing more than 10,000 soldiers. In a country without much timber the loss of the siege engines and of the great 24-meter ram was a disastrous blow.

Phraates then took advantage of the weak position of the Roman force encamped before the walls of Praaspa. The Parthians "showed themselves to the besiegers in gallant array" (Plutarch) and threatened them. Antony led out most of his force both to counterattack and to forage but only succeeded in taking 30 captives and killing 80 of the enemy despite following them for a long way. In the meantime the besieging force had been left in too weak a state to contain a sally by the citizens and the inadequate Roman response so enraged Antony on his return to camp that he "put in practice what is called decimation against the cowards; for he divided the whole number into tens, and put to death one out of each ten who was chosen by lot."

Antony was in an impossible position: he could only obtain food for his army by sending out foraging parties.

If these were small they were destroyed by the hovering Parthians; if they were large enough to defend themselves, the besieging force was so weakened that the citizens were able to break out and damage the improvised siege works. Antony was forced to withdraw with the city walls unbreached before the hard mountain winter set in and made life intolerable. He sent ambassadors to Phraates who received them "seated upon a golden chair and twanging his bowstring" (Dio Cassius). Having concluded an agreement that he could retreat in peace Antony broke camp and set off but was soon attacked by the Parthians, who continued to harry the Romans until they reached the frontier. However, grimly clinging to the hills, Antony avoided the fate of Crassus and was finally left by the Parthians. He reached Syria early in the winter, by which time he had lost more than 40,000 men although he had saved his army from annihilation. Phraates celebrated his triumph by overstriking tetradrachms of Antony and Cleopatra.

These two overwhelming Parthian victories – over Crassus and Mark Antony – should have secured Parthian supremacy for a considerable time but the murderous Phraates was an impossible king for his own people to accept, even though he had triumphed over the Romans. Antony twice more campaigned in the Zagros, though he achieved little by doing so, and by 31 BC a Parthian pretender, Tiridates by name, rebelled against his king. Phraates IV struggled for six years to suppress this rebellion, during which time each side appealed to Octavian for help against the other. Octavian, however, was at first too occupied in fighting Antony (finally defeated at the battle of Actium in 31) and later was himself planning a Parthian war!

Tetradrachm, struck at Seleucia, showing on the obverse (below) the bust of Phraates V and on the reverse (opposite) Musa, the Italian slave girl presented by the Emperor Augustus to Phraates IV. She became his queen, poisoned her husband, placed her own son Phraates V on the throne, and then married him. British Museum.

The Pax Augusta. The result of this sudden period of Parthian weakness – so dramatic a *volte face* after their years of victory – was that the Romans were able to negotiate the return of the standards and the prisoners lost at Carrhae and Praaspa. Phraates was, in fact, so alarmed that the Romans might be planning an invasion of Parthia, Justin writes, that "whatever prisoners, accordingly, remained of the army of Crassus or Antony throughout Parthia, were collected together, and sent, with the military standards that had been taken, to Augustus. In addition to this, the sons and grandsons of Phraates were delivered to Augustus as hostages; and thus Caesar effected more by the power of his name, than any other general could have done by his arms." This return of the standards was regarded as a great triumph by the Romans and was celebrated both by special issues of the imperial coinage and by the construction of a triumphal arch in Rome. Romano-Parthian relations were much improved and Parthia profited from a long period of peace.

Shortly after the return of the standards in 20 BC, Augustus sent Phraates IV a present – an Italian slave girl called Musa, who was to lead an astonishing life, described by the Jewish historian Josephus. "After he [Phraates IV] had begotten on her his son Phraataces he was so much besotted with her beauty, that he took her to his wife and held her in high estimation." The elderly king was so much in her power that she was able to persuade him to send his four older sons and their families to Rome so that "only Phraataces was brought up in the affairs of state." She then poisoned her husband in 2 BC and placed Phraataces or Phraates V on the throne. Four years later Musa married her son, an act that shocked the Hellenistic and Jewish world, though this practice had been followed by the Achaemenian Persians, who themselves had probably adopted an Elamite tradition. The heads of mother and son appeared together on their coins, but it was only another two years before Phraataces was deposed or killed and we hear no more of Musa.

"Who fears the Parthian . . . while Augustus lives," sang the poet Horace with truth, for Parthia was in no way able to resist the Romans ruled by the wise Augustus. Strong central government had collapsed under Phraates IV and the early death of Phraataces added to Parthian weakness, for no suitable candidate could be found for the throne who was acceptable to all the different powerful factions in the council of nobles. One of the kings whom they installed was Vonones, a son of Phraates IV, who had been sent by his father to live in Rome. However Vonones' Roman manners and dislike of the hunt displeased the nobles, and they approached another Arsacid, Artabanus, then king of Media Atropatene. After a struggle between the two, Artabanus III finally entered Ctesiphon in 12 AD and reigned for 26 years, during which time he succeeded in considerably strengthening central authority. The widespread distribution of his coins bears witness to the prosperity of his reign.

The general prosperity of the country under Parthian rule is attested by a considerable increase in the number and size of Parthian settlements, some of which have been discovered in recent surface surveys in the Diyala region and in parts of western Iran. It is important to realize that, although there were frequent periods of internal conflict during the years of Parthian control from 141 BC to 224 AD – either over succession to the throne or because of rebellion by a vassal – the majority of these struggles were confined to the ruling elite, which had an interest in preserving the wealth of the country and the expensive irrigation networks. And even in the 2nd century AD, when there were three major Roman invasions of Mesopotamian Parthia, destruction was limited to the relatively narrow path of the actual invasion and was quickly repaired. Thus the Parthian pattern of frequent political turmoil, interspersed with periods of strong central government, interfered little with the life and wellbeing of the people. The wealth of the country was based on two factors – successful agriculture and profits from trade. A greater area than ever before was brought into cultivation by widespread and large-scale irrigation works, requiring regular maintenance and dredging, all of which was almost certainly sponsored by the state. This increase in agriculture was needed to support the populations of the many new towns or cities founded by the Seleucids and the Parthians. Both dynasties are remembered in Classical sources as city-builders, a tradition borne out by the archaeological remains.

The Great Silk Road: some of the many routes along which the silks and spices of the east were carried to Rome. The improvement of communications was a major feature of Seleucid and Parthian government.

Trade and Communication. Another feature of Seleucid and Parthian government was the improvement of communications necessary to facilitate administration and long-distance trade. The most important trade route at this time was the Great Silk Road which brought the soft silks of China to the wealthy citizens of Rome. One of the routes was recorded in *Parthian Stations*, the itinerary prepared by Isidore of Charax. Caravans started in Antioch and, crossing the Euphrates at Zeugma, traveled to Seleucia before traversing the Zagros Mountains to Ecbatana (Hamadan) and then on to Rhagae (Rayy near Tehran), Nysa and Merv. There were of course numerous alternatives: for instance from Hamadan the route west might continue directly through passes into ancient Assyria where the former Assyrian capitals of Assur and Nineveh flourished again in the Parthian period. Another variation was for the goods to reach Babylonia by sea, having sailed up the Persian Gulf from northwest India.

Thus this luxury trade in silks and muslins, precious stones and pearls, bronzes and glassware, oils, perfumes and spices flowed along various roads and the spectacular buildings and rich statuary occurring in cities located beside them testify to the rich profits to be made. Perhaps the most spectacular and romantic of these caravan cities was Palmyra, located in an oasis in the Syrian desert and reached in a single long stage from Dura Europus on the Euphrates. This trans-desert route significantly shortened the journey and was indeed the shortest route between India and the Syrian ports. Although showing Parthian influence in a number of ways, Palmyra was essentially a city of the Roman east and therefore falls outside the scope of this book, though the inscriptions found there provide valuable evidence for the routes and organization of the trade. Palmyrene colonies were established in a number of

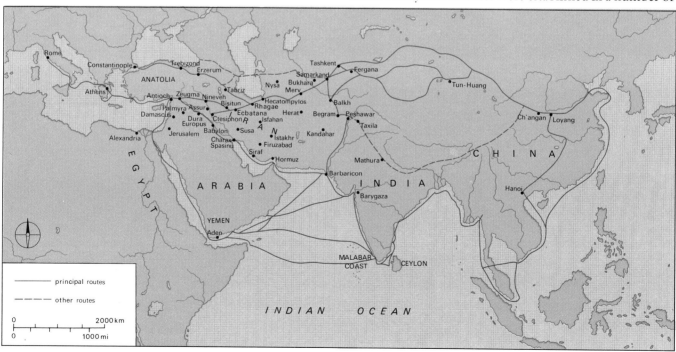

Parthian cities and merchants traveled freely between them. One Palmyrene inscription tells of a Palmyrene merchant who was honored by the erection of no fewer than four statues in Palmyra and three outside the town, one in Spasinu Charax at the head of the Persian Gulf, one in Vologesia, near Babylon, and one in the caravan station of Gennais. Palmyrene sculpture has even been found in distant Merv. There must have been a constant exchange of both men and ideas along the many roads leading east and west.

Parthia in the 1st century A D. We know comparatively little of events in Parthia during the 1st century A D, for this was the time of the *Pax Romana*, so western sources have little to say of Parthian matters. The Euphrates was still accepted as the frontier between the two empires but Rome had consolidated her hold on buffer states near the Euphrates, such as Palmyra, as a result of the prolonged period of Parthian weakness. This period of peace was a fortunate one for the Parthians for, had Rome invaded, their attack might well have been successful. In the latter part of Artabanus' reign he was unable to maintain control of the Parthian kingdom and indeed lost his throne for a while. In 35 A D, shortly after his return to power, the Greek city of Seleucia, one of the principal mint-cities of the empire, declared itself independent, being tired of the anarchy of Parthian rule. Seleucia maintained its independence for seven years. During this time Artabanus died and once again there were two rival claimants for the throne. These two continued to fight each other until 47 A D, when Gotarzes was finally triumphant, though he had to face another pretender only two years later. The much-damaged victory relief, carved next to that ascribed to Mithradates II at Bisitun, records Gotarzes' triumph over the latter, one Meherdates by name. The relief showed three knights in armor: the king in the center, crowned by a winged victory, is charging Meherdates with leveled spear. Gotarzes, identified by the Greek inscription above, is followed by his page. That Hellenistic influence was still strong is illustrated both by the use of Greek for the inscription and by the winged victory or Nike motif. This Hellenism was perhaps consciously reversed by Vologases I, who acceded c. 51 A D and who reigned until c. 76 or 77 A D.

Parthia was again able to meet the Roman challenge during the long and comparatively successful reign of Vologases I. Despite a serious challenge by the competent Roman general Corbulo, Vologases maintained the Euphrates frontier, though Armenia, after a long struggle, finally fell into the Roman instead of the Parthian sphere of influence. The Armenian king Tiridates, himself a brother of Vologases, actually traveled to Rome to receive his crown from the hands of the Emperor Nero.

We know little of what was happening in the east, though considerable areas of formerly Parthian territory must have been lost to the Kushans, another tribe of

Victory relief of Gotarzes (c. 49 A D) at Bisitun, much damaged by weathering. Gotarzes, in the center, is charging Meherdates, a challenger to the Parthian throne. Above the king is a Nike or winged victory motif; behind him is his page.

Iranians who had established a flourishing empire in northwest India and Afghanistan (see the following chapter). In the north too the Parthians faced a serious threat when the nomad Alani poured over the Caucasus passes and ravaged much of Media Atropatene and Armenia in 72 A D. Fortunately for the Parthians they retreated back over the Caucasus when sated with plunder.

Seleucia again declared its independence early in Vologases' reign, though it soon capitulated, and this continuing Greek-inspired rebellion perhaps encouraged Vologases to promote an Iranian renaissance. Certainly the first positive evidence of developed Parthian architecture dates from his reign, though this may be archaeological chance rather than historical fact. Strong Parthian influence is shown in Level II at Seleucia, which is dated c. 60–120 A D. The palace contained a number of courtyards, the principal features of which were great *iwans*. Spectacular Parthian structures were also found at approximately contemporary Parthian Assur (Labbana as it was then called). And the most magnificent doubtless still await discovery at the new commercial center

Vologascierta, which Vologases founded near Seleucia and which is frequently mentioned in Palmyrene inscriptions.

Greek by this time was probably rarely spoken, for during his reign the Greek names of cities were dropped in favor of their local equivalents. The Greek inscriptions on the Parthian royal coinage had become so debased that they were incomprehensible and these too were replaced by Aramaic lettering. Another change on Vologases' coins was that the standard motif on the reverse of the official Parthian coinage, the figure of an archer, was replaced by the motif of a fire altar – and this is taken as evidence of Vologases' interest in and support for the Zoroastrian religion. According to later Zoroastrian tradition it was Vologases who collected the surviving manuscripts and oral traditions of the *Avesta*, the Zoroastrian "Bible."

In the last years of Vologases, as had happened so often before, a pretender began to strike coins, and Parthia was again plunged into a long period of civil conflict between rival contenders for supreme power – but by this time the Roman policy of détente with Parthia was nearly at an end. Roman emperors dreamed of emulating Alexander and conquering the Orient.

Archaeological evidence. The years of greatest prosperity of the Parthian empire were those from the reign of Mithradates II (124–87 BC) to the end of the 1st century AD, after which Parthia's economy was in trouble, partly because of the rise of the Kushans in the east. While we have an outline of the political history of the western edge of the Parthian empire, thanks in the main to Greek and Latin sources, our knowledge of internal and eastern affairs is still sketchy in the extreme. This section attempts to trace the architectural and artistic achievements of the Parthian empire during this time of prosperity. Archaeological chance has resulted in many major monuments of these years being discovered in Mesopotamia, though excavations in southwest Iran, both recently completed and still continuing, may redress this uneven distribution of evidence in the future.

How widespread Mesopotamian Parthian architectural traditions were in the empire cannot as yet be ascertained: we do not know whether there was a standard Parthian plan for the palaces and mansions of vassal kings and nobles or whether these varied from area to area. The building material would certainly change according to what was available – for instance mud brick and baked brick in the alluvial plains of Mesopotamia and perhaps rubble masonry in the mountain areas. Certainly the pottery varied from area to area: glazed wares were popular in Mesopotamia and the Susa plain and these were often shaped into elaborate animal forms, such as the crouching hare found at Hilla, which is now in the British Museum. Throughout the Zagros a distinctive hard red ware, known as "Clinky ware" because of the characteristic sound when sherds are tapped against each other, occurs on mounds of the Parthian period.

The archaeological picture is further complicated by the virtual autonomy of some of the Greek cities within the empire, such as Seleucia-on-Tigris. Excavations undertaken there in the 1930s distinguished three levels which

Glazed pottery vessel of the Parthian period from Hilla in the form of a crouching hare. Length 24·7 cm. British Museum.

Conflict in the West | 55

Above: "Clinky ware" bowl. When tapped together, sherds of this ware make a distinctive clinky sound. They are widely distributed on Parthian sites in the Zagros and help to trace Parthian occupation.

provide a fascinating record of the gradual Parthianization of this Greek city. In the earliest excavated level, Level III, the complex consisted of several similar units of rooms grouped around open courtyards with halls on the southern side: leading into the halls were two-column porticoes between *antae*. This plan clearly reflects a combination of Greek and Babylonian ideas – the *megaron* and the Babylonian courtyard. Level III was dated by the excavators to approximately 140 BC to 69 AD and it was therefore built after Mesopotamia had been conquered by the Parthians but at a time when Seleucia was basically an independent Greek city within that empire. Level II was built in the middle of the 1st century AD shortly after the city's capitulation to the Parthians. The column as an architectural element was abandoned, though it continued

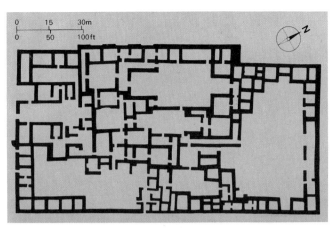

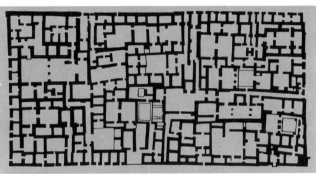

Above: Seleucia-on-Tigris as excavated in the 1930s. The upper plan shows the earliest level, Level III (c. 140 BC to 69 AD) when the city was still more or less independent within the Parthian empire. The lower plan shows Level II, the monumental Parthian palace built c. 120–200 AD.

Below: marble figurine of a reclining lady found at Seleucia. She is wearing only a necklace and sandals. Baghdad Museum.

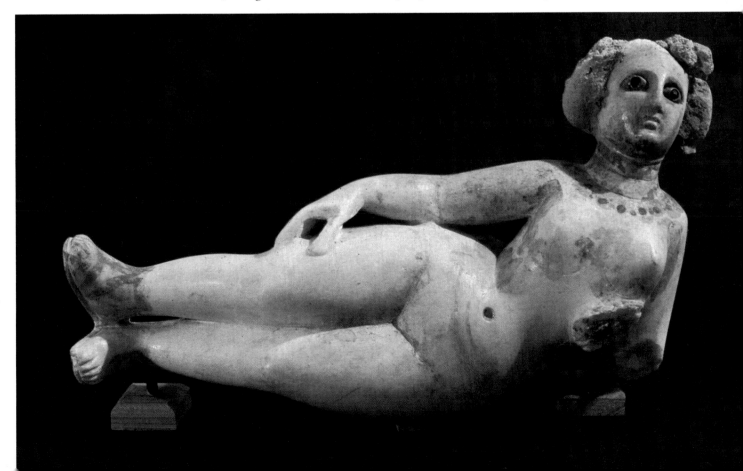

View of part of the great *tell* or mound of Assur/Labbana on the Tigris.

to be used as a decorative element, engaged in the walls. The columned porticoes were replaced by open halls or *iwans*, roofed according to the excavators by barrel vaults. Although detailed technical evidence to support this statement was not actually found at Seleucia, it did occur in contemporary Parthian buildings at Labbana (Assur). In Level II, which continued in use until the early 2nd century AD, the barrel-vaulted *iwan* is used both as an entrance to the complete palace complex and as the principal feature in a courtyard setting. It was only, however, in the final period of occupation at Seleucia, Level I, which is dated c. 120–200 AD, that the Parthian palace there became a monumental structure with huge courtyards, the dominant architectural features of which were the massive vaulted *iwans*.

The palace at Labbana. Parthian Labbana, built on top of the ruins of the Assyrian capital Assur, was located on the banks of the Tigris at a point controlling important caravan routes leading from Babylonia and Iran to the Khabur valley and to the city of Nisibis. Assur had been abandoned from the fall of Assyria until its reoccupation by the Parthians, perhaps because the subsistence of its citizens depended on irrigation sponsored by the state.

Labbana/Assur had a relatively short life: the more important structures were built during the peace and prosperity of the 1st century AD. The city was partly destroyed in 116 AD by the Roman emperor Trajan who reversed Augustus' policy of maintaining the *status quo* in the east. Repaired and enlarged, the city was again destroyed in 198 by Septimius Severus. It continued, in an impoverished state, until 257 AD when it was finally sacked, this time by the Sasanian king Shapur I. The two principal Parthian levels belong therefore to the 1st and 2nd centuries AD.

The principal feature of the palace at Labbana/Assur is the central courtyard, which is more or less rectangular and has a great *iwan* dominating each of its four sides. This four-*iwan*, or *iwan*-cross, plan has continued in use to the present day. The facades of the palace courtyard were lavishly decorated with stories of blind architecture, consisting of slender engaged columns with debased Ionic or Doric capitals, framed arches, niches or blind windows. Each of the three registers was separated from the next by friezes of stucco plaques decorated with stylized naturalis-

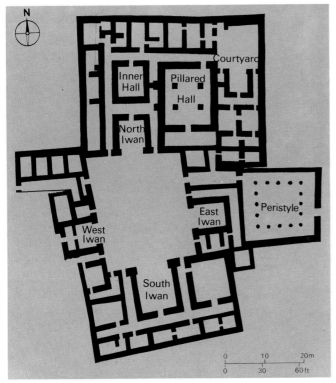

Above: a reconstruction of the richly decorated brick facade of the *iwan*-cross courtyard at Assur. Each of the three registers was separated from the next by friezes of decorated stucco.

Left: plan of the Parthian palace at Assur/Labbana.

tic and geometric motifs. The purpose of this decoration was entirely visual and had no structural significance: it was used to break up an otherwise plain surface and to balance the great voids of the *iwans*. The idea of decorating a facade in this way is related to Roman architecture. However, the Romans may have adopted a Hellenistic tradition which had itself been evolved in the Orient, for there was a long tradition in Mesopotamia, stretching back to the third millennium BC, of relieving plain brick facades with alternate buttresses and reveals. This system was still in use at Seleucia on walls facing the streets. Elaborate stucco decoration is also well attested in Hellenistic Babylonia for fragments were found in the Greek theater at Babylon and stucco decoration occurred in the buildings of all three periods at Seleucia. In typical Parthian manner the Assur facades were thus a combination of the Babylonian concept of the use of light and shadow and of Hellenistic architectural elements. The effect of this rich tapestry of stucco would have been dramatically increased by the brilliant sunshine.

The *iwan* did not only occur in the principal palace courtyard but was widely used elsewhere in the palace, in temples and in private houses. In houses *iwans* were placed in one or more sides of the courtyard, and houses of this type are still common in Syria today. The German architect Oscar Reuther described the *iwan* as "a real living room planned, if it opens to the north, to provide shade but admit the cooling breezes in summer, or, if it faces south, to permit the slanting rays of the welcome winter sun to enter, while it gives shelter from the cold north winds. The *iwan* is not used merely as a living room for work or sleeping, but rather as a parlour in the exact sense, in which the guests are received and friends gather for conversation."

Thanks to Andrae's exceptional recording, full details have been preserved of the method by which the great span of the *iwans* was roofed without the aid of columns and even without scaffolding. In a land where timber was scarce, often of poor quality and expensive, this was a major technical breakthrough, which was made possible by a new brick lay set in a different mortar. The importance of this mortar, gypsum mortar, was that it made a strong bond extremely quickly, holding the bricks in position almost as soon as they were laid. It was thus possible to build the vault without scaffolding. After the side and back walls of the *iwan* had been built, the bricks of the barrel vault were laid vertically in half-circles, beginning at the back wall and working towards the front. Only the vault required the use of expensive fired or baked bricks: the side and back walls could be constructed of the usual mud bricks.

Vaults were widely used throughout the palace, both for spanning rooms and for corridors. In one room there was an interesting development in vaulting technique. This large room (Pillared Hall) contained four massive pillars which, instead of being used to support wooden beams as in the past, were employed to carry barrel vaults. The main vault was carried only on the pillars, from which subsidiary vaults also sprang to the walls. These pillars thus enabled a wider space to be roofed and also divided the room into three aisles. Such a feature was noted at Nysa, where, however, the unit formed a separate building instead of being incorporated into the palace precinct. Another unit which at Nysa had been independent was placed next to the aisled hall at Labbana/Assur. This was a square room with an ambulatory, similar to the "tower" complex at Nysa. Corridors isolating architectural units are a regular feature of Parthian architecture – the north and south *iwans* of the Assur palace are similarly surrounded – and E. J. Keall has recently suggested, when writing of a Parthian building at Nippur, that these corridors may have been structural, acting as "buttressing agents to the main vaulting system."

The unusual Parthian vertical brick lay was not only used to build vaults – it was also employed between courses of regular horizontally laid bricks on some walls as well as to form columns, as in the peristyle courtyard. This courtyard again illustrates the Parthians' ability to borrow and adapt ideas to their own ends, for at Assur the Hellenistic peristyle courtyard is used simply as an entrance tacked on to the palace precinct instead of as an integral part of the plan.

Parthian skill in absorbing and adapting can again be seen in the sacred precinct located in the northeast area of the city where a number of temples were excavated, each built to a different plan. One, Temple A, was an exact replica of the much earlier Assyrian temples below and consisted of an antechamber leading into the shrine. This Mesopotamian plan continued to be widely used in the 1st century AD, examples occurring at Dura Europus and Warka. Another Assur temple, called the Peripteros, combined Mesopotamian, Parthian and Hellenistic elements. An *iwan* entrance was added to the basic Mesopotamian plan of antechamber and shrine, which was surrounded on the other three sides by a row of columns. A third temple plan was purely Parthian and consisted initially of two *iwans* placed side by side with additional rooms behind. Later a third *iwan* was added to the north. This distinctively Parthian plan was built, however, on the site of the old temple to the Assyrian national god Assur, who continued to be worshiped in the new temple.

This diversity of plan may well reflect the many religions flourishing within the Parthian empire. The Parthians themselves were Zoroastrians but they left their subjects free to worship as they wished. The old Mesopotamian pantheon continued to be worshiped together with the newly arrived Olympians and with the cult of the deified kings and queens. Jews had long formed an important section of the community and this was the century of the birth and death of Jesus Christ and the rise of Christianity. The western version of the worship of Mithra – an interpretation in many ways at variance with his Iranian origins – had also begun and a western-style Mithraeum was found at nearby Dura Europus. Meanwhile in India and Afghanistan Buddhism flourished and the constant caravan traffic between east and west spread ideas as well as goods.

Hatra. While Assur with its palace, temples and private houses was essentially a Parthian city, another rich trading city, Hatra, only a day's march, some 50 kilometers, away was an amalgam of Parthian and Hellenistic or Syrian-Roman characteristics. The princes of Hatra were Arabs, only recently settled, who became loyal Parthian vassals. The city's fortunes were closely linked with those of Assur, though Hatra was more successful in resisting Roman sieges; it had a strong natural position in semi-desert lands which were unable to support an enemy force for long. Hatra withstood both Trajan's siege of 116 and that of Septimius Severus in 198, even though on that occasion the Romans successfully breached the walls. It was finally devastated by the Sasanian king Ardashir in the 230s by which time Hatra had become an ally of Rome.

The buildings at Hatra were constructed in fine limestone masonry on a rubble core and this use of stone rather than the brick of nearby Assur is clear evidence of western influence, perhaps from Palmyra. Indeed it suggests the employment of a sizable body of Syrian stonemasons. Not surprisingly many architectural elements were western in origin, although there was a major debt also to Parthian architecture, for the *iwan* was the dominant feature of many buildings.

The massive walls of Hatra were more or less circular in plan and were reinforced with rectangular buttresses. This type of defensive wall is considered to be characteristically Parthian, occurring at such Parthian foundations as Ctesiphon, Darabgird and Merv, among other sites. The earliest Sasanian city, that built by Ardashir at Firuzabad probably in the last years of the Parthian empire, was also enclosed within circular walls.

Aerial view of Hatra: the massive outer walls are more or less circular in plan. The outline of the rectangular walls of the sacred precinct is clearly visible in the center.

The principal public buildings at Hatra were set in an enormous rectangular enclosure located almost in the center of the city. The enclosure was itself divided into three: a large forecourt leading into two smaller courts at the western end. The wall separating the western area into two actually ran through the principal building, which initially consisted of two *iwan* structures placed side by side. At Hatra an *iwan* structure was usually formed either of three *iwans* the same size or of a large central *iwan* flanked by two smaller ones. An additional range of rooms was sometimes added behind the *iwans* and occasionally a columned portico was tacked on in front.

The main palace or temple in the rectangular enclosure is usually identified as the Temple of the Sun, the riches of which were famed. The two large central *iwans* ran right to the back of the building, while the smaller flanking *iwans* were divided into smaller units on two floors. The building was later enlarged: the familiar Parthian square room and ambulatory were placed behind the southern *iwan* unit and two single *iwans* with a room behind were added to the northern unit. These additions were somewhat haphazard; for instance the main axis of the square unit was not aligned to that of the southern *iwan* and this was apparently only discovered after the door

from the square unit had been cut through into the main *iwan*. It was seen to be off center, was filled in and recut in the center of the *iwan*.

The decoration of the facades was both larger in scale and simpler than that employed at Assur, which was doubtless the result of working in stone rather than malleable stucco. The facade of the Temple of the Sun was decorated with engaged columns with Corinthian capitals which rose the full height of the building to the parapet. The *iwan* arches and door lintels were embellished with sculptured friezes. The subject matter of much of the relief sculpture was the human figure: the friezes around the *iwan* arches were formed of rows of complete figures, busts or just heads, placed side by side and carved in high relief. An unusual decorative feature was the application of carved human heads, arranged in pairs or threes, to the inner walls of the *iwans*. Another favorite motif was the griffin: small griffins with curving backs and gathered hind legs were placed on the wall below the springing of the arch and pairs of heraldically opposed griffins decorated door lintels.

Right: part of the facade of the Temple of the Sun at Hatra: the *iwan* arches had fallen in but have now been restored.

Below: reconstruction of the sacred precinct at Hatra, 2nd century AD, after Walter Andrae.

Parthian jewelry. The widespread fashion for sculpture in the round in the 1st to 3rd centuries AD was also followed at Hatra and a vast quantity of statuary has been found both by Walter Andrae and by the Iraq Department of Antiquities, who have been working and skillfully restoring there for a number of years. Lifesize statues were carved representing the deities, the princes and their families, the warriors and the merchants of Hatra. They are shown calm and confident, richly dressed in the Parthian manner and elaborately bejeweled. Much of the information we can glean of Parthian jewelry comes from a study of the sculptures and coins of the time, for relatively little has yet been found in controlled excavations. At this period jewelry was worn by both men and women in great profusion and, as traces of paint still adhering to some Palmyrene sculptures prove, was highly colored. The best illustration of the wealth and love of ostentation of the time is provided by Palmyrene sculptures, but even the less bejeweled princess of Hatra is

Left: detail of the facade of the Temple of the Sun at Hatra. Note the decoration of busts around the *iwan* arch.

Below left: part of a well-preserved *iwan* arch from Hatra, decorated with busts of the kings; at the apex is the eagle of Hatra. Baghdad Museum.

Below: masks placed on a buttress at Hatra: an unusual decorative feature.

Above: mask of a lady(?) on the walls of Hatra. Note the snake entwined in her hair.

Left: Sanatruq, lord of Hatra, 1st–2nd century AD. This limestone statue, some 2·20 meters high, is typically late Parthian in both stance and dress. Baghdad Museum.

shown wearing a high jeweled hat, covered with chains, long heavy earrings, no fewer than four necklaces, one of which is hung with heavy pendants, thick twisted bracelets on both arms, and rings on her fingers.

The Hatrene princess's twisted bracelets were clearly popular, being shown on Palmyrene sculpture and found in burials at Dura Europus. The Durene examples were made of alternating bands of plain and beaded (pseudo-granulate) silver wires. One of the finest jewels found at Dura was a fibula or brooch, similar to one worn by a Palmyrene lady known as the "Beauty of Palmyra." An elaborate golden setting embellished with garnets and blue-green glass cabochons framed an oval green stone which was carved with a design illustrating Narcissus, a subject entirely Roman in inspiration. However the technique of cutting is inferior when compared with similar Roman gems and the excavator suggested that the jewel was made at Dura. This piece typifies the problem of Parthian jewelry: it was found in a Parthian level on a Parthian site and might thus be considered to be Parthian. However it is clearly a jewel completely in the Hellenistic tradition and may well have been cut for a Greek citizen of Dura. On the other hand, this localized Hellenistic style of jewelry may have been that current in Parthian Mesopotamia. Many of the earrings found at Dura were made in this style, for instance a gold earring in the form of a clumsy amphora with volute handles, a type of earring with a long history in Greece and Rome; other earrings decorated with female heads were derived from Hellenistic types decorated with the heads of Maenads, although the schematized features were a local in-

terpretation. Other types include complete bodies both of nude women and of Eros figures, again motifs Hellenistic in origin but showing evidence of local manufacture. Such earrings have been found on many sites in Mesopotamia, including Babylon and Seleucia, and remained popular for a long time.

Two small hoards of jewelry were discovered at Seleucia-on-Tigris and the excavator suggested that they were concealed prior to the advance of Trajan during his campaign of 115/6 AD. A jar buried under a floor contained eight golden jewels, including a pair of "amphora" earrings, a ring set with a garnet engraved with a peacock, and a pair of elaborate gold chain bracelets, their ends embellished with garnets and turquoises. Buried under another floor was a pair of delicate golden earrings which consisted of oval disks set with garnets from which hung pearls on twisted wires. A partially similar pair of golden, garnet and turquoise

Left: the Lady Ubal of Hatra (left) and her daughter, 2nd century AD, 1·70 meters high. Baghdad Museum. The profusion of jewelry worn by both men and women at this time attests to the wealth of the late Parthian period.

Below: gold earrings from Nippur showing schematized versions of the Hellenistic Eros figure. Ht. 2·05 and 2·15 cm. British Museum.

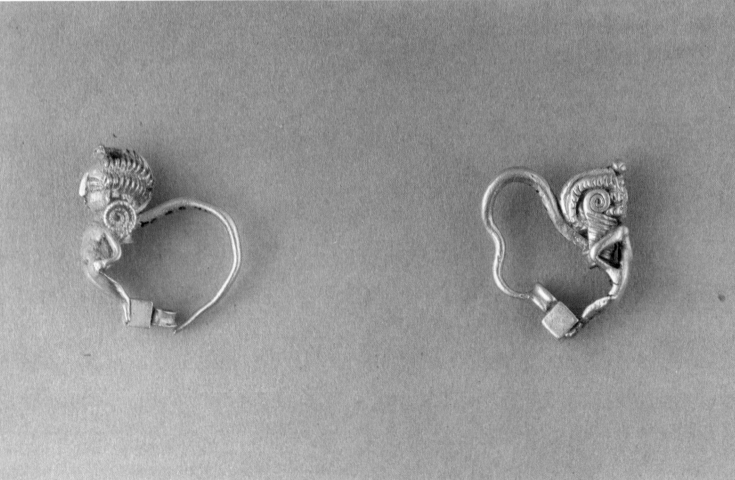

earrings was discovered in the 19th century in a tomb at Nineveh, which is dated to the early 2nd century AD. Some tombs there were opened by Layard's assistant, Hormuzd Rassam, and among the objects recovered were two masks with crude stylized features made of sheets of thin beaten gold, as well as a number of gold "spectacles" and mouthpieces, designed to cover the eyes and mouth of the dead. The latter was a Hellenistic practice, though there are no certain parallels for the masks. Other funerary gifts included glass bottles. The art of blowing glass had been discovered in the 2nd or 1st century BC and had revolutionized the use of glass vessels, for production was easy, cheap and rapid.

Burial practices. The burials at Nineveh were in stone-lined tombs sealed with slabs of stone. Similar tombs, though built of bricks, have been found elsewhere in Parthian Mesopotamia. Many different burial customs were practiced within the empire, reflecting the varied religious and ethnic composition of the population. Bodies were often interred in pottery coffins, either simple "bath tubs," a well-known form of burial in ancient Mesopotamia, or in the distinctive Parthian slipper coffin with an oval opening at one end closed by a lid. These coffins were sometimes covered with an attractive blue-

Gold funerary mask found by Layard's assistant, Hormuzd Rassam, in a Parthian tomb at Nineveh. Ht. 16·5 cm. British Museum.

Above: silver drachm of Orodes II (c. 57–38 BC). His torque ends in an extraordinary creature with the foreparts of an animal and the tail of a fish. Jewelry is often carefully delineated on Parthian coins. British Museum.

Below: a silver bracelet of twisted wires found at Dura Europus, similar to those worn by the Lady of Hatra. Yale University Art Gallery.

green glaze and decorated with designs in raised relief, usually arranged in compartments, the designs of which included warriors, goddesses and dancers. The lid of a fine glazed coffin from Susa was decorated with a schematized human face. Pottery or wooden coffins were buried in the earth or in a brick-lined pit, though richer families placed their dead in specially constructed burial vaults, some of which continued in use for a number of years.

At Assur and Babylon these vaults consisted of more than one room and were sunk into the ground, though the tops of the vaulted roofs may have been visible above ground. At Hatra, however, a new idea, western in inspiration, was combined with that current in Parthia. The dead were placed in stone towers, two stories high, erected both inside and outside the city walls. These were clearly derived from the towers of Dura Europus and

A Parthian relief carved on a freestanding block of stone at Hung-i Nauruzi in SW Iran. 1st century AD?

Palmyra. Palmyra's great stone necropolis, a real city of the dead, was built in a nearby valley.

Frontality in Parthian art. A glance at ancient Oriental sculpture suffices to prove that heads were usually represented in profile. In some Achaemenian sculptures this had resulted in uncomfortable poses such as the body being shown frontally while the head faced one way and the legs the other. However in the early years of the 1st century AD there was a total abandonment of this tradition which was replaced by a new orthodoxy of frontality. This fashion spread widely and rapidly and in a few decades had become standard. In Mesopotamia and Iran it only lasted until the fall of the Parthians, though in the west it was absorbed into early Christian art, continuing until the early Renaissance.

This new convention affected many different art forms. Relief sculpture from Palmyra, Hatra, Assur and Masjid-i Sulaiman adhered rigidly to this canon, as did Parthian rock reliefs, most of which are located in southwest Iran. The poor quality of many of the latter is both disappointing and surprising in view of the technical competence of movable statuary. One relatively competent rock relief, probably to be dated to the early 1st century AD, for it shows figures represented both frontally and in the old profile view, was carved on a free-standing block of stone at Hung-i Nauruzi, not far from Shami. The king on his prancing horse confronts four men. The diademed king and his attendant are shown in profile

Above: detail of a fresco from the Mithraeum at Dura Europus thought to show Zoroaster. Yale University Art Gallery.

Below: a Parthian "slipper coffin" in the Baghdad Museum: the cover is missing.

while the four nobles stare straight out at the onlooker. The scene probably represents the king conferring the status of vassal king on the leading noble, who is considerably larger than his three followers.

Frontality also affected the composition of the frescoes which decorated many public and private buildings. A fascinating series of paintings was recovered from buildings excavated at Dura Europus by Yale University. Religious paintings included those on the walls of rooms used for worship by Jews and Christians, as well as in the Mithraeum and in the earlier temple dedicated to the gods of Palmyra.

It was during the 1st century AD that Parthian art and architecture achieved their own intrinsic character, the vigor, variety and eclecticism of the early years of empire having given way to a distinctive Parthian style. The technical revolution in roofing techniques made possible a new style of architecture dominated by the great vault of the *iwan*. These powerful units so dominated courtyard facades that they required vigorous decoration to achieve a reasonable balance and for this the Parthians used a tapestry of carved stucco. This same formula was still being used in Safavid Iran more than 1,000 years later, though by that time facades were decorated with brilliant glazed tiles rather than with carved and painted stucco. The new artistic canon of frontality revolutionized sculpture, painting and the minor arts during the later Parthian era; in the west it continued to dominate the Christian tradition for a millennium.

But Parthian achievements were not purely material. Despite the all too frequent squabbles over the succession, Parthian subjects enjoyed long periods of peace and prosperity, clearly linked with wise local administration as is proved by the considerable increase in irrigated agricultural land. And furthermore they were ruled by tolerant men who, though themselves Zoroastrians, still permitted their subjects to worship as they pleased.

The Castle at Qaleh-i Yazdigird

Local legends identify the ruins at Qaleh-i Yazdigird as a refuge of Yazdigird, the last king of the Sasanian dynasty, but recent work there by the Royal Ontario Museum has suggested that the castle was built more than 400 years earlier. The excavator, E. J. Keall, considers that the site was probably occupied only for some 50 years towards the end of the Parthian period at a time when central authority was weak. He sees it as the luxurious mountain retreat of an independent robber baron, plundering the caravans traveling along the Great Silk Road.

The castle at Qaleh-i Yazdigird is situated not far from the Zagros Gates, the pass where the main east-west highway begins its long descent to the plains below. Located in an elevated tableland with strong natural defenses, it was further strengthened by massive fortification walls. In this spacious and secure mountain retreat, with an upper castle sited on an inaccessible crag (*below*), the lord of Yazdigird built himself a sumptuous palace decorated with a riot of ornate painted stucco.

Work has only just begun at Yazdigird and the incredible quantities of stucco being found will make its excavation a slow and laborious task. But the discoveries made so far have already revolutionized our understanding of late Parthian art.

Above: detail of a stylized bud-and-tendril motif from a niche in Room 5 of the royal pavilion (1 on the plan).

Above left: still in the royal pavilion, this view of Room 1, which measured 10 meters a side, shows the continuous frieze of interlocking swastika and rosette designs set 4 meters above the floor. Above this a complex series of panels included such elements as busts of a Parthian noble (like the one shown *left*) and a possible Dionysiac scene showing reclining figures reaching for grapes, winged youths playing with felines, and Eros figures.

Left: the lord of Yazdigird from Room 1. This bust is typically Parthian in its frontal representation, in the bushy bunches of hair framing the face and in its enclosure within a decorated roundel. A similar bust, but in stone, has been found at Hatra.

Below: on this plan of the site note 1 Royal pavilion, 2 Palace garden, 3 Stronghold, 4 Upper castle, 5 Defensive wall, 6 Gorge, 7 Look-out post.

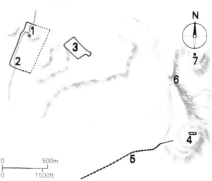

Above: one of the richly decorated niches from Room 5 of the royal pavilion. The sides of this inner hall, some 13 meters long, were decorated with a series of such niches, each flanked by engaged columns. Many other figured panels and Corinthian-style column capitals were also found in this room.

Left: excavation of the royal pavilion. It was built of vertically laid, baked bricks. Only parts of three rooms have so far been revealed. The plan appears to be similar to part of the Parthian palace at Assur: an *iwan* leads into an inner hall with a square room to one side.

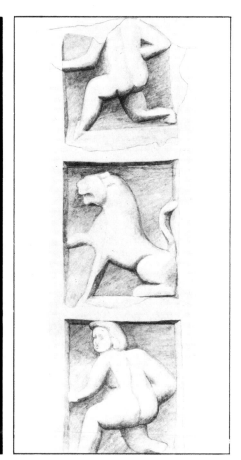

Above: fragment of an engaged column found in the debris of Room 5. Painted green, the column is decorated with a series of naked hunters attacking wild beasts, perhaps lions, each figure set in a panel. Note how the hunters' spears pierce the frame of the panel – a typical Iranian trait. Modern drawings help to elucidate the detail.

Left: unique faceted columns were set along the walls of Room 11, which was perhaps the entrance *iwan*. These columns were brightly painted and decorated with figures, all set in panels, the borders of which were embellished with a scroll design. Here we see a clothed male who, in his tunic and trousers and high pointed hat, is very much Parthian in inspiration and pose.

Above: two other figures from the faceted columns from the walls of Room 11, a naked dancer and (*above right*) a Pan figure, the latter clearly western in inspiration. As in all the stuccos from Yazdigird, the iconography is mixed.

Below: entwined beasts from Room 1 of the royal pavilion. These winged mythical creatures, heraldically knotted, belong to an old Near Eastern tradition.

Above: the fragmentary head of a female.

Above: an engaged column capital from Room 1, painted red. A nude female holds a pair of dolphins with voluted tails. The use of such figural motifs on capitals was popular at the time, and capitals with female heads framed by stylized leaves occur at both Warka (*top right*) and Seleucia.

Center right: an Eros figure leaning on a pedestal, Hellenistic in origin, from Room 1.

Bottom right: a winged griffin, also from Room 1. The distinctive pose clearly foreshadows that of the Sasanian *senmurv*, a favorite motif composed of beast and bird and frequently represented on silks, silver and stucco.

4. Rebellion by Ardashir

And what if she had seen those glories fade,
Those titles vanish, and that strength decay;
Yet shall some tribute of regret be paid
When her long life hath reached its final day.

WORDSWORTH

The 2nd century AD was one of relentless pressure on all Parthian frontiers and this resulted in a significant decline in Parthian power. Parthia was squeezed between Rome on the west and a dynamic new power in the east, the Kushans, while in the north the nomads were as always ready to take advantage of any weakness. Yet despite being surrounded by powerful enemies the Parthian empire was not finally overwhelmed by any of these external forces but by an enemy from within, the vassal king of Persis, Ardashir the Sasanian.

The Parthian collapse was caused by many different factors which included three devastating Roman campaigns in Mesopotamia, a disastrous epidemic of plague and an economy in serious trouble. In the early years of empire Parthia had controlled a considerable area of the Central Asian steppe, certainly up to and including the Merv oasis and probably even beyond. There they had come in contact with the expansionist western Han empire of China and from this had resulted the development and organization of east-west trade, with Parthia well placed to levy taxes and customs. Nearly all goods had been funneled through Mesopotamia, even though the Great Silk Road divided in Bactria, one branch continuing west overland through Parthian territory, while the other

Commanding the road to Shiraz, the palace/fortress of Qaleh-i Dukhtar at Firuzabad, built by Ardashir I, the founder of the Sasanian dynasty, probably before he rebelled against his Parthian king.

crossed the Hindu Kush into northern India, whence it transferred to ships which sailed up the Persian Gulf to Spasinu Charax. However, even before the 2nd century AD this advantageous position had been lost to another group of Iranian tribes who, like the Parthians before them, had invaded, settled and founded an empire.

The Kushans. This new Central Asian power was formed by nomads who, like many tribes before and after them, had gradually been pushed westward from the Gobi desert area. Following the Iranian Saka, whom they displaced, they entered Bactria via the Ferghana region in the second half of the 2nd century BC. The Greco-Bactrian kingdom had been swept away by that time – indeed the city of Ai Khanum had been savagely sacked – but considerable Hellenistic influence still lingered on and this was absorbed by the Kushans, who adopted the Greek alphabet. The various tribes of the Yueh-Chih, as they were known in Chinese records, were unified by a prince of the Kuei-shang (Kushan) tribe about 100 years later and they then began to expand southwards.

The real founder of the Kushan dynasty was Kajula Kadphises and during his reign in the 1st century AD he succeeded in capturing the Gandhara region from the Saka kings of the Indo-Parthian dynasty. Kushan territory at this time probably extended from Sogdia and Bactria in the north across Afghanistan into northwest India, and thus effectively straddled the Great Silk Road, completely controlling the trans-Afghan branch. This in itself need not have been a serious economic loss to the Parthians provided that the old trade pattern of funneling goods through Mesopotamia to the west was maintained. But by this time the Romans had fully developed the sea route to India and Ceylon, using the monsoon winds, and it was therefore both possible and practicable for goods to travel across the Indian Ocean via the Red Sea to Alexandria in Egypt, entirely cutting out the Parthians. One of the Chinese annals proves that this was something the Romans had long wanted to achieve, while the Parthians had striven to prevent it: "[The Roman emperors] always desired to send embassies to China, but the An-hsi [Parthians] wished to carry on trade with them in Chinese silks, and it is for this reason that they were cut off from communication."

One of the results of the *Pax Romana*, established by the Emperor Augustus, had been a massive increase in the Roman demand for Oriental luxuries, which were mostly paid for in gold bullion, and this became a serious drain on the Roman exchequer. In 75 AD Pliny wrote that Rome's imports of silks, muslins, gems and pepper cost more than 100 million sesterces a year, "so dearly do we pay for our luxuries and our women." Although a considerable volume of trade continued to be transported through Parthia, the Parthian loss of revenue is well illustrated by the prosperity of the Kushans. The superb Kushan gold coinage was probably struck on gold specie sent from Rome, and quantities of Roman artifacts have been found at sites in the Kushan empire such as Taxila and Begram (ancient Kapisi).

Kajula Kadphises established close commercial and political relations with Augustus, who recorded visits by a number of Indian missions. Direct Romano-Kushan exchanges continued from this time until the Kushans were defeated by the new power of Sasanian Iran in the 3rd century AD. As relations between Parthia and Rome worsened and internal conditions in Parthia deteriorated in the later 2nd century, the attractions of this direct maritime trade must have been increased – to the further detriment of the Parthians.

The greatest of the Kushan kings was Kanishka, who ruled for 23 years probably during the first half of the 2nd century AD. An indication of his importance is that the Kushan era began from an event in his reign, probably his accession. However one of the major problems of Kushan history and archaeology is that it has not yet proved possible to correlate the Kushan and the Christian eras and the dates of Kanishka himself are hotly debated. The date most generally accepted for the beginning of the Kushan era, and therefore probably for the accession of Kanishka, is c.110–120 AD, though dates range between 78 and 144 AD.

The full extent of the Kushan empire is not known, though it doubtless bounded the Parthian empire along the Kushan western frontier. The limit of Kushan dominance to the east is less certain for it is not possible to determine the relationship between the various groups of the Yueh-chih. Some, known as the Lesser Kushans, had not migrated as far west as the Great Kushans and may still have been living in the Tah Sin oasis on the main route east. They may have acknowledged Kushan suzerainty for a time or may have been allies, permitting frequent and direct contact with Han China. As a pledge of Chinese friendship Kanishka received 30 Chinese "hostages" of whose welfare he was careful. He took them with him as he traveled between his various capitals at Purushapura (near Peshawar), Mathura and Kapisi (Begram in the Kabul valley). The Kushans, like other originally nomadic dynasties such as the Medes, the Persians and the Parthians, retained an essentially migratory pattern of life even after the accession of empire, palaces and untold wealth.

Like the previous great Indian emperor Asoka, Kanishka was converted to Buddhism and became an energetic patron and builder of Buddhist stupas and, following the Hellenistic and Parthian traditions, of dynastic shrines. Sculpture, both secular and religious, flourished. A superb example of secular carving is the great stone statue of Kanishka himself which is inscribed across the front of the tunic and coat with his titles "the Great King, King of Kings, the son of God, Kanishka," and which shows a typical Iranian warrior king. This was found in the Kushan dynastic shrine near the city of Mathura and is representative of the output of the Mathura school of carving.

During Kanishka's reign the Fourth Buddhist Council was held in Kashmir when the schism between the Hinayana and Mahayana sects was recognized. The Mahayana sect became dominant in India and missionaries traveled extensively in Central Asia and China, successfully introducing Mahayana Buddhism. By this time the Buddha himself was represented in human form and numerous statues were carved of him and of the Boddhisattvas, those who had chosen to help others rather than to attain *Nirvana* (enlightenment) themselves. Many scholars consider that the finest works of the Gandharan school of sculpture, which was almost entirely devoted to Buddhist themes, should be dated to the reign of Kanishka.

Kanishka probably died fighting in Central Asia. His successors continued to rule for a further century, but the era of Kushan expansion was over and that the Kushan dynasty lasted so long is perhaps more a reflection of Parthian weakness than of Kushan ascendancy. After the Sasanian takeover of the Parthian empire they were soon forced to recognize Sasanian supremacy.

Kanishka the Great. An inscribed stone statue, found in the Kushan dynastic shrine at Mat. 2nd century AD. Ht. 1·63 meters. Mathura Museum.

Parthian decline. The 2nd century AD presents an extraordinary paradox within Parthia as far as we can tell from our present inadequate and frequently biased sources: it should not be forgotten that Romano-Parthian relations are known to us only from the Roman point of view and the propaganda element must not be overlooked. Politically the 2nd century was disastrous; there were frequent squabbles over the succession to an increasingly shaky throne, and there was a change for the worse in the balance of power with Rome, with Parthia forced onto the defensive. The old frontier along the Euphrates which had been held for more than 250 years was lost, the new one was shifted significantly eastwards and the great Parthian winter capital of Ctesiphon on the Tigris was sacked three times. Economically, too, the situation was difficult and the coinage, reflecting this, was seriously debased in both metal and artistic merit. Much of the east-west trade, on which profit margins were extremely high (the Chinese recorded that the merchants of Roman Syria made a tenfold profit), had been lost to the Kushans. And Roman and Chinese records report a disastrous epidemic of plague in the second half of the century. Although we have no internal records of the epidemic, the Parthian population must have been substantially reduced by it. Yet despite this political and economic gloom, the renaissance of art and architecture which had begun in the preceding century was consolidated with magnificent buildings at cities such as Assur and Hatra.

It was the emperor Trajan who actually reversed Augustus' policy of halting Roman expansion in the east, though his predecessor Domitian had already been planning a Parthian campaign. The pretexts for the war were probably the usual ones, Armenia and a frontier dispute. While these were the overt reasons, the real motive "was a desire to win renown" as well perhaps as a conscious wish to emulate Alexander. According to Dio Cassius, Trajan, when standing on the shores of the Persian Gulf, said, "Were I yet young I would not rest till I too had reached the limits of Macedonian conquest" and on his return Trajan visited Babylon "because of Alexander, to whose spirit he offered sacrifice in the room where he had died."

Trajan set sail from Rome in the autumn of 113 and began campaigning in 114, first conquering Armenia, which he turned into a Roman province. He spent the winter of 114/5 in Antioch, which was shaken by a severe earthquake, from the effects of which he only narrowly escaped. Dio writes, "First there came, on a sudden, a great bellowing roar, and this was followed by a tremendous quaking. The whole earth was upheaved, and buildings leaped into the air . . . The crash of grinding and breaking timbers . . . was most frightful; and an inconceivable amount of dust arose, so that it was impossible for one to see anything or to speak or hear a word."

The following spring Trajan crossed the Euphrates and,

having erected a triumphal arch at Dura Europus, continued down the Euphrates. His boats were then hauled across the narrow space separating the two rivers to the Tigris, and Ctesiphon fell almost without resistance. Trajan captured the daughter of Osroes, one of three "kings" of Parthia, as well as his famous golden throne. An effective response to this major Roman invasion of Parthian territory was prevented by the long-drawn-out struggle for the Parthian throne between Pacorus II (c. 75–115), Osroes (c. 89–128) and Vologases III (c. 105–147).

Trajan withdrew in the spring of 117 and because of illness was returning to Italy, when he died in August of that year. His prolonged campaign had achieved little, for Mesopotamia was already in revolt even while Trajan was there, and his siege of Hatra, undertaken as he withdrew, was unsuccessful: "This city is neither large nor prosperous," wrote Dio, "and the surrounding country is mostly desert and has neither water (save a small amount and that poor in quality) nor timber nor fodder. These very disadvantages, however, afford it protection, making impossible a siege by a large multitude, as does also the sun god, to whom it is consecrated . . . And whenever they [the Romans] ate, flies settled on their food and drink, causing discomfort everywhere."

Trajan's appointee to the Parthian throne was rejected and he was already planning another campaign when his failing health forced him to return to Italy. He was succeeded by Hadrian, who reversed Roman foreign policy once more. The Euphrates again served as the frontier between the two empires and a Parthian nominee ruled Armenia. But while in the west, by courtesy of Rome, Parthia had regained her original position, the situation elsewhere was far from satisfactory, with considerable losses in the east to the Kushans, probably at this time ruled by Kanishka. The Parthians had to face another major challenge in c. 136 when the nomad Alani invaded Media Atropatene and Armenia. After desperate fighting the Parthians were defeated but the Alani returned to their homeland and Parthia was reprieved.

Parthia's last revival. The last Parthian revival occurred in the second half of the 2nd century when Vologases IV (c. 148–192) succeeded to the throne without any major dispute and was able to rule until his final years without serious internal challenge for the throne. During his reign he felt strong enough to challenge the *status quo* with Rome and for a while it looked as if he might restore Parthian power, although by the end the balance had once again tilted in favor of Rome. His long-planned campaign began in 161 with an initial success in Armenia and the placing of a Parthian nominee on the Armenian throne. This was followed by resounding defeat of a Roman army, which left the way open into Syria: the Parthians crossed the Euphrates and were warmly welcomed by the Syrians. This sudden Roman reverse threatened control of her eastern provinces and the co-emperor Lucius Verus was sent east to restore the situation. He tried to make peace with Vologases IV but was rebuffed. The Roman forces were in poor shape but after a period of retraining were able to reoccupy Armenia in 163 and two years later were campaigning in Mesopotamia itself. Dura Europus fell after a fierce struggle and remained thereafter in Roman hands. The Romans then moved south and took both Ctesiphon and Seleucia, but were forced to retreat not by a Parthian counterattack but by the dreaded ravages of plague. The epidemic was so fierce that many soldiers died on their way back and much booty had to be abandoned. According to Ammianus, the survivors carried the disease "from the frontiers of Persia all the way to the Rhine and to Gaul."

The Parthians rapidly reclaimed the invaded territory, though the state of war between the two empires continued, resulting in a Parthian loss of territory. The next king Vologases V (c. 191–206/7) became involved in an internal Roman dispute and backed the loser, Pescennius Niger. The victor was Septimius Severus who, provoked by the Parthians' support for Pescennius, and by their attempt to regain territory in northern Mesopotamia, retook the disputed area in 195 but then had to return to Europe to quell a revolt in Gaul. The exhausting struggle was resumed in 198 when Severus campaigned extensively in Mesopotamia, sacking Assur (Labbana), Seleucia and, after a struggle, Ctesiphon. Like Trajan, however, his attempts to subdue Hatra failed and his campaign achieved little of value for Rome, though it must have weakened Parthia still further.

The feudal Parthian state depended for its cohesion on the personal authority of the king and this must have been seriously damaged by the Roman invasions – Ctesiphon had been sacked twice in 30 years. The independence of some of the vassal kings is illustrated archaeologically: the kings of Elymais commissioned a series of rock sculptures while the warlord of Qaleh-i Yazdigird in the Zagros built himself a luxurious mountain palace-fortress, well sited both for maintaining his independence and for the exacting of tolls from the nearby east-west highway, the great Khurasan road. At this critical period, with internal anarchy and a serious external Roman threat, there were once again two claimants for the throne, Vologases VI (c. 207–227?) and Artabanus V (c. 213–224 or 226), both minting coins until 222 when Artabanus finally achieved sole power. But it was too late. While the Arsacids had been fighting each other, the Sasanian prince Ardashir had acceded to the kingship of Persis and had steadily built up his strength to a level where he could challenge and overthrow his suzerain.

The rise of the Sasanians. Ardashir was the younger son of Papak, high priest of the Temple of Anahita at Istakhr. Papak was the son, or perhaps the protégé, of Sasan, from whom the dynasty takes its name and who probably ruled

Detail from the jousting scene commissioned by Ardashir I to commemorate the defeat of his Parthian suzerain c. 224 AD and carved beside the Sasanian road at Firuzabad. Shapur, son of Ardashir, is shown unhorsing Darbendan, Grand Vizier of Parthia.

Persis in the time of Vologases IV. When Papak became king he was able to take advantage of Parthian weakness and united much of the province of Fars. After his accession to the kingship of Persis in c. 209, Ardashir conquered Kerman, Isfahan and finally the kingdom of Elymais. By this time he had amassed sufficient wealth to found a city at Gur, modern Firuzabad, where he built himself a strong fortress on a mountain top, and a magnificent palace, as well as laying out a great circular city defended by strong walls. But to overthrow the Parthians single-handed was still too great a task for the newly emerging Sasanian forces and Ardashir formed an alliance with the kings of Adiabene and Kirkuk. At a great battle in c. 224 AD at Hormizdegan Artabanus V, Great King of Parthia, was defeated and killed, an event which is dramatically recorded in an 18-meter-long frieze placed beside the Sasanian road high up a mountainside at Firuzabad.

But although the battle of Hormizdegan resulted in the defeat and death of the Parthian king, it did not end all resistance in former Parthian territories. While some of the great feudal families submitted, others did not. Ardashir finally succeeded in defeating all his opponents except for the Arsacid king of Armenia. We do not yet know the full extent of Ardashir's conquests: in the east he certainly controlled the oasis of Merv, to which he appointed a member of his family as governor, and he may also have conquered the Kushans. According to Roman sources, Ardashir's aim was to re-establish the Achaemenian empire: "he boasted that he would win back everything that the ancient Persians had ever held, as far as the Grecian Sea, claiming that all this was his rightful inheritance from his forefathers" (Dio). This desire, maintained throughout the 400 years of Sasanian rule, not only provided a frequent cause for war but, when finally achieved in the 7th century, led to the overextension and rapid downfall of the empire.

Ardashir first challenged the Romans towards the end of the 220s and was initially successful. As Dio saw it, "The danger lies not in the fact that he seems to be of any particular consequence in himself, but rather in the fact that our armies are in such a state that some of the troops are actually joining him and others are refusing to defend themselves. They indulge in such wantonness, licence, and lack of discipline that those in Mesopotamia even dared to kill their commander." In 230 Ardashir besieged Nisibis and his forces raided deep into the Roman province of Syria. A Roman peace initiative failed and the Romans prepared a counterattack in 232, which was sufficiently successful to merit a triumph in Rome. Ardashir returned to the Mesopotamian front towards the end of the 230s and succeeded in taking both Carrhae and Nisibis c. 238. He also broke the defenses of Hatra, which had withstood sieges by Trajan, Septimius Severus and a previous attempt by himself. After its sack Hatra was abandoned and the role of the Hatrene princes as "lords of the desert" was transferred to the Lakhmid dynasty at Hira.

The reforms of Ardashir. The old Parthian empire had failed for a number of reasons, one of the most significant of which was the lack of strong central government, and this Ardashir was determined to remedy. He appointed members of his family to be governors in key provinces and employed a large bureaucracy. His other major innovation was the establishment of a formal state church instead of the Parthian policy of religious *laissez-faire*. This led to a rigid division into social classes, based on that laid down in the *Avesta*. The classes of the *Avesta*, designed primarily for a nomadic society, consisted of priests, warriors and workers and this was adjusted to the needs of an empire by the addition of the bureaucracy, placed after the warriors and above the peasants and craftsmen. Both reforms were probably instigated not only to overcome the near anarchy of the late Parthian period but also to be a focus for the revival of Iranian nationalism. The Seleucids and the Parthians were described as foreigners, and the rise of the Sasanians was portrayed as a return to the glories of Iran's Achaemenian past. Ardashir thus gave his empire a moral and spiritual *raison d'être* as well as a military one.

Another urgent reform was that of the coinage which had become seriously debased under the late Arsacids. There are many novel elements in Ardashir's coinage: he struck no fewer than eight different types. He was initially shown either full-face or in profile in a high rounded *kolah*, decorated with various motifs. This headgear was closely similar to that worn by the mighty Parthian king Mithradates II and was perhaps an allusion to the successful conquests of that king. Ardashir then evolved a new form of head covering – a simple skull cap surmounted by a "globe" of hair covered in a silken gauze. This globe, or *korymbos*, became a hallmark of the dynasty as did the adoption of distinctive personal crowns by each king. These crowns, which later became so elaborate and heavy that they could no longer be worn but were suspended from the ceiling on a chain, can be accurately charted from the coinage and they have enabled scholars to attribute not only the huge rock reliefs to the relevant kings but have also made possible the dating of such items as seals, stucco and the characteristic Sasanian silver and gilt dishes, when the king is represented.

By the end of the 230s Ardashir was an old man and in 240 he associated his son Shapur directly with himself in a period of joint rule, as was indicated on coins showing their two heads. Ardashir wore his own distinctive crown while Shapur was shown in the high round helmet or *kolah* of the nobility: he only assumed his own mural crown after his coronation. The exact date of Ardashir's death is not certain but must have occurred some time early in the 240s. His military conquests had restored to Iran the advantageous position of middleman on the east-west trade route and this was jealously guarded and extended by later kings. Secure militarily and economically and with a strong central government, Ardashir's empire was to last for 400 years until the fervor of a new faith, Islam, overwhelmed the long-lasting Zoroastrian kingdom.

Gold dinars of Ardashir I, showing him first (*top*) wearing the jeweled Parthian crown of Mithradates II, and second (*below*) in the distinctive crown he devised for himself. This consists of a simple skull cap, tied around the brows with a diadem, the hair gathered in a high silken globe or *korymbos*. British Museum.

Archaeology of the Kushans.

The archaeological picture of the Kushans has been transformed by recent work, particularly by that at the site of Surkh Kotal near the modern town of Pul-i Khumri in northern Afghanistan. This was discovered as a result of a road-widening scheme in the 1950s and excavations were undertaken there by the late Professor Daniel Schlumberger, Director of the Délégation Archéologique Française en Afghanistan. The site, located in the southern part of the Bactrian plain, proved to be a Kushan dynastic shrine. There were two religious complexes, the principal shrine on top of a steep hill, and a smaller shrine on the valley floor. Five flights of stairs rising 51 meters led to the walled hill-top shrine. The shrine, set in a courtyard, consisted of a square sanctuary surrounded on three sides by an ambulatory. This structure was enclosed by a row of columns and the whole was set on a raised platform. Among the finds were the remains of five stone statues as well as fragments of stucco statues, architectural units and some inscriptions. One of the last recorded that the shrine was founded by Kanishka and it is probable that the broken statue of a Kushan king found at the site represents him. Furthermore, the Surkh Kotal sculpture, though damaged, is similar to the Mathura statue of Kanishka and to effigies on his coins. Compare for instance the proportions, the costume and the distinctive splay-footed pose. This pose, which is relatively unusual, also occurs on a sculpture recently discovered at distant Bard-i Nishandeh in southwest Iran, as well as on some statues found at Hatra. Ideas and craftsmen, as well as goods, traveled along the well-used trade routes.

In the 1930s the French delegation were working near the village of Begram in an area which contains extensive ruins of a number of cities of different periods. The excavations concentrated on the ruins of the Kushan city and the nearby shrines at Paitava and Shotorok, which may have been the chief places of worship of the Kushan aristocracy. Certainly large numbers of statues of worshipers have been found at both sites. The city proved to be ancient Kapisi, the summer capital of the Kushan kings, and the major French discovery was a treasure which had been stored in two rooms, subsequently sealed. This hoard was associated with coins ranging from those of Kanishka himself to a later Kushan king, Vasudeva, and the assemblage presumably dates therefore from the 2nd to the early 3rd centuries AD. The treasure included Hellenistic bronze figurines and vessels, Syrian and Alexandrian glass, and stucco medallions with Classical subjects which served as models for metal objects, from the west; from the east came Chinese lacquer; and from within the Kushan empire itself superb ivory carvings. This wide-ranging collection serves as an illustration of the strategic position of the Kushan empire connecting east and west.

Kanishka was converted to Buddhism and one of the stupas he built was at Peshawar, the Kushan capital of Purushapura. This great stupa, one of the Buddhist "wonders of the world," was described by Chinese pilgrims and apparently consisted of a high multi-storied tower made of wood and rising to a height of some 210 meters. The site of the stupa was identified and excavated in 1908. All that remained was the high square plinth on which the tower had been constructed. The plinth had projections on each side which gave it a cruciform shape. The identification of these ruins with those of Kanishka's stupa was established by the discovery of a bronze reliquary inscribed with the king's name in the center of the ruins of the plinth. Measuring some 20 centimeters in

Found in the treasure at Begram, an elaborate dark blue glass vessel, flecked with gold and entwined with glass "ribbons," imported from the west. 1st century AD. Ht. 17 cm. Kabul Museum.

height, the reliquary is crudely made and its crudity has long been a puzzle, for it was during Kanishka's reign that the superb sculptures of the Gandharan and Mathura schools flourished.

Gandharan and Mathura sculpture. Although contemporary, the styles of these two schools are entirely different. That from Mathura, of which the Kanishka statue is a fine example, followed Indian traditions, while Gandharan sculpture was strongly influenced by Hellenistic and/or Roman art. Exactly where this Classical influence came from has long been disputed, for it could either have been a legacy of the Greco-Bactrians – a theory reinforced by similarities between Greco-Bactrian Ai

Khanum and Kushan Surkh Kotal – or the result of Kushano-Roman contacts made both diplomatically and commercially, or it could of course have been a mixture of both. Classical influence is undeniable on the style and technique of Gandharan sculpture, although the subjects were entirely Indian and mainly represent episodes in the life of Buddha and his followers. The first representation of Buddha in human form is credited to the Gandharan school and this in itself reflects Hellenistic influence, for deities were always seen anthropomorphically in the Classical world. Buddha's head was closely modeled on that of Apollo with the addition of distinguishing characteristics such as his elongated ears and third eye. As well as single statues of the standing or seated Buddha, or of Boddhisattvas, there were many small panels of relief sculpture, principally devoted to illustrations of the life of Buddha. The sculptures were carved in the readily available blue schist and green phyllite, although the stucco tradition which had already occurred at Ai Khanum and in Kushan Surkh Kotal, was also used and later almost replaced stone carving. Both stone and stucco works were originally brightly painted and decorated with gold leaf.

The Gandharan school, which was mainly located in the Peshawar valley, only lasted a relatively short time and was probably brought to an end by the invading Sasanians, although a few more distant outposts escaped destruction. The internal chronology of the many beautiful sculptures discovered there is unfortunately almost entirely based on stylistic evidence, for the few dated examples are of an unknown era. Although the major site of Hadda on the Afghan side of the Khyber pass has been excavated, it has yielded only stucco sculpture. Situated on a major road, its site was still occupied in the early 7th century; how early its Buddhist stupas and viharas were cannot yet be closely settled.

While the Gandharan school was essentially a phenomenon of the Kushan dynasty, the sculptures of the Mathura school were rooted in an earlier indigenous tradition and continued after the fall of the Kushans, finally developing into the superb Gupta style. The Kanishka statue referred to above was one of a number of royal Kushan statues found in the ruins of a dynastic shrine at Mat near the city, and they are rare examples in Indian carving of portrait statuary. Like other works of the Mathura school they are carved in a poor-quality red sandstone and must presumably have been covered with a plaster finish and brightly painted and gilded. As well as royal statues, the Mathura school carved statues of Buddha, the earliest example of which is dated by an inscription to the third year of Kanishka. Although the idea of the anthropomorphic representation of Buddha had presumably traveled to Mathura from Gandhara, the style of sculpture is entirely local. In fact the easiest way to see the difference between the two styles is to compare the soft flowing lines of the Gandharan seated Buddha from

95

Opposite: a stone "pillar railing" from Bhutesar. Kushan period. The *yakshi* or fertility spirit is offering wine to the loving couple above. Mathura Museum.
Below: an Indian ivory statuette of a *yakshi* found with the Begram treasure. Ht. 56 cm. Kabul Museum.

Above: seated Buddha from Katra, carved in the more stylized Mathura manner. 2nd century A D. 69 cm high. Mathura Museum.
Above left: seated Buddha from Takht-i Bahi, carved in the more flowing lines of the Gandharan school. 2nd century A D. 52 cm high. Staatliche Museum, Berlin.

Takht-i Bahi with the more abstract representation of the same subject from Katra. The Katra Buddha is clothed in the Indian *dhoti* as opposed to the Gandharan version of the toga.

Older Indian motifs continued to flourish at Mathura under the Kushans as is illustrated by the beautiful pillar railings which once surrounded relic mounds. These uprights were usually carved in high relief with the sensuous figure of a *yakshi* or fertility spirit and they exemplify the Indian ideal of womanhood – "Broad, plump and heavy hips to support the girdle, and navel deep, large and turned to the right, a middle with three folds and not hairy; breasts round, close to each other, equal and hard . . . and neck marked with three lines, bring wealth and joy" (Varahamihira). Similar female figures were carved on ivory plaques found at Begram.

The late Parthian period. Archaeological evidence of the final years of Parthian rule is only just beginning to be found. Parthian Hatra continued to flourish to the end of the dynasty and for some 15 years thereafter, and its sculpture and architecture illustrate the traditions current in late western Parthia. But we do not yet know whether there was any overall uniformity of plan and design throughout the empire in the later Parthian period, although new information which may answer this problem is being collected year by year. Recently surveyed and planned, though not yet the subject of excavation, is a small *iwan* structure at the remote mountain site of Qaleh-i Zohak, between the modern towns of Maragheh and Mianeh. This *iwan* unit formed only a small part of a large fortified complex which was built in a commanding position on top of some precipitous rocks. Interestingly enough the walls of the *iwan* are built in the same unusual vertical brick lay with occasional horizontal layers already seen at Assur and employed on other Parthian sites. The bricks were then plastered and the springing of the vault marked by an ornate plaster molding.

This same vertical brick lay also occurred in the palace pavilion at the mountain stronghold of Qaleh-i Yazdigird in the Zagros (pp. 67–72), a site being excavated by the Royal Ontario Museum. The site occupies some 24 square kilometers of an elevated tableland which was naturally fortified on three sides – the fourth side was defended by a massive wall strengthened by square towers and built in a rubble and gypsum mortar masonry. "In this type of construction the stones are not really built up like masonry, but are simply piled on top of each other, without any bond, the walls being modelled, as it were, in the rapidly setting mortar, and the stones packed in only as a filling. Were it not for the mortar, the walls would immediately tumble into a shapeless heap," wrote the

The remote Parthian mountain fortress at Qaleh-i Zohak: the remaining standing monument, an *iwan* structure, built with rows of vertically laid bricks.

German architect Oscar Reuther, when describing this method of building – a method also used in many Sasanian structures. At Qaleh-i Yazdigird the vertical bands of plaster marking the shuttering could be clearly seen.

Within the heavily defended enclosure were a number of buildings including what will probably turn out to be an upper castle, a central castle and a paradise with a palace pavilion at one end. The brick-built palace pavilion had been decorated with an unbelievable wealth of stucco ornament, much of which has only begun to be revealed in the excavations which took place in the summer of 1976. Decoration was both architectonic, that is copying real architectural units, and figural. Among the former were engaged columns and pilasters of many different shapes, round, fluted and even faceted, and niches decorated with elaborate imposts and friezes of griffins. The wide range of figural ornamentation included many human figures, men and women, clothed and naked, dancers, warriors and musicians. Among the animal repertoire was the extraordinary dog-bird or *senmurv* motif, so widely used in the Sasanian period, as well as winged horses and other winged beasts entwined together on the capitals of engaged columns. The lord of the manor himself was probably depicted on a bust enclosed within a decorative roundel. The hair was arranged in great bunches in typically Parthian manner on either side of the face, which stared straight out at the onlooker. This riot of ornament was deeply carved and brilliantly painted in vivid blues, reds, yellows and greens – the effect must have been overwhelming. Fragments of mosaics, found on the ancient dump, suggest that the palace may also have had mosaic floors.

The sheer mass of stucco preserved at Qaleh-i Yazdigird makes excavation there a slow and laborious task. But over the years we can expect to see unearthed one of the most spectacular monuments of this otherwise almost unknown period. Furthermore this magnificent mountain fortress can be closely dated: it was probably occupied only for some 50 years towards the end of the Parthian period and will therefore illustrate the final development of Parthian art and architecture. The whole complex, in the words of its excavator E. J. Keall, "makes sense as the home of a feudal lord, thumbing his nose at the King of Kings, and maintaining himself in his gardened enclosure with the luxuries afforded by plundering the highroad at will without fear of reprisal."

This same spirit of independence is shown in the rock reliefs of the king of Elymais. These were carved on free-standing rocks in a high valley at Tang-i Sarvak in the Zagros Mountains, and they date to the final years of the Parthian period. The reliefs were designed to glorify the Elymaean kings with no reference to their Parthian suzerains. They show the ruler reclining on a couch with eagle feet and holding in his hand the ring of authority, worshiping before an altar, and fighting a lion on horseback. He is accompanied by rows of courtiers and the representation of all these figures conformed to the strict late Parthian canon of frontality. The Elymaean reliefs are of interest mainly because of their novel narrative content, which may have influenced Sasanian rock relief art. Technically, however, the Tang-i Sarvak sculptures are little more than crude drawings in stone. This is surprising in view of the widespread fashion for statuary, current as close as Masjid-i Sulaiman, as was proved by the recent discovery of a late Parthian relief of a worshiper: the Masjid-i Sulaiman statue is infinitely superior in execution to the Tang-i Sarvak sculptures.

The buildings of Ardashir. When Ardashir conquered the Parthian empire he was in a very different position from that of the nomadic Parthians and Kushans, for he and his forebears had been living in an empire with a developed art and architecture. Ardashir could well have expressed his imperial power in the same terms but, as is shown by his coins, he was as dynamic artistically as he was militarily and he evolved a new and distinctively Sasanian style.

Ardashir had founded his new city and palatial structures at Ardashir Khurra (the glory of Ardashir, later abbreviated to Gur), modern Firuzabad, even before he defeated Artabanus, so strictly they are late Parthian foundations. However, in spirit and even at this early phase of Ardashir's reign, they are already Sasanian in style. Probably his first structure was the strongly defended fortress sited on top of a mountain and commanding the road to Shiraz (p. 73). To those driving through the narrow defile at sunrise the great buttressed walls of the castle high above the road present an unforgettable image of golden masonry against an azure sky. The fortress-palace formed the apex of a large fortified area with its own integral water supply, achieved by a well cut down to the river winding along beside the road below. The fortress-palace, known as Qaleh-i Dukhtar or Maiden Castle, was built on three levels and was entered from the lowest level from which a spiral ramp led to the main courtyard of the middle terrace. The courtyard was surrounded on three sides by rectangular vaulted rooms – the fourth side led to the upper terrace on which stood the main palatial structure. Its facade was dominated by a great barrel-vaulted *iwan* flanked by two smaller ones. The great *iwan*, 14 meters wide and 23 meters long, led into a square central chamber roofed in a new way, with a dome. This domed chamber was flanked by additional rooms, all of which were contained within a circular outer wall.

Parthian architects had used barrel vaults which, when they joined at right angles, were linked by simple arches. There is no evidence that they constructed domes, although these occurred on contemporary Roman buildings, principally baths. Roman architects had solved the problem of placing a circular roof on a square room either by resting the dome on stone slabs in the corners or

Numerous late Parthian reliefs were carved on a huge freestanding rock in the valley of Tang-i Sarvak. *Above*: the principal scene shows the ruler of Elymais reclining on a divan and holding in his right hand the ring of authority; *below*: the ruler is offering a sacrifice at an altar (top left in shadow).

Above: reconstruction of Ardashir's palace/fortress at Qaleh-i Dukhtar, Firuzabad. Late Parthian or early Sasanian. After D. Huff.

Below: plan of Ardashir's palace in the Firuzabad plain. Early Sasanian.

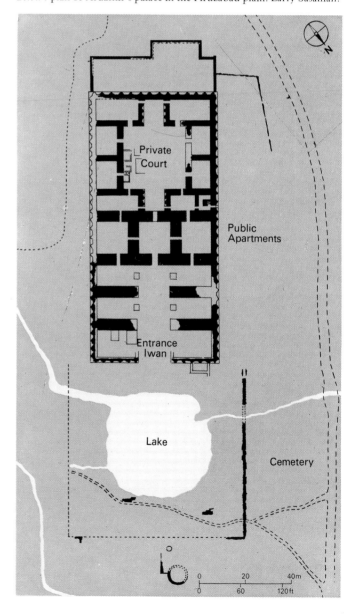

by gradually corbeling out the bricks or stones in an increasingly circular form. Sasanian builders solved the same problem in a different way, one which is still standard in Iranian architecture today. The earliest example may be the domed room at Qaleh-i Dukhtar. The dome was set onto the square room by means of cone-shaped "squinches" built up from each corner until a circle was formed; the circle was then gradually closed.

In contrast to the rich stucco of late Parthian facades, the decoration of both Qaleh-i Dukhtar and of Ardashir's palace, which he set where the mountains open out into the fertile Firuzabad plain, was almost stark. External walls were relieved by stepped buttresses or engaged columns on *torus* bases, and doorways were enhanced by a simple stucco molding, the design of which was copied from old Achaemenian doorways at Persepolis.

Ardashir's palace was built facing a circular lake and was almost certainly surrounded by a luxuriant garden or paradise. The building was a long rectangular structure, divided into a reception area and a residential suite. A long *iwan* led into a high domed room, presumably the principal chamber of audience, which was flanked on either side by similar square domed rooms. To the south a smaller *iwan* led out into the inner courtyard with another *iwan* opposite. Barrel-vaulted rooms opened out of the courtyard. The palace walls were built in the same manner as most of the structures at Qaleh-i Yazdigird, rough stones held together with gypsum mortar. Although this method of construction is somewhat crude, it lasts well and much of Ardashir's palace is still standing today, even to the second story.

Ardashir built his great city in the plain some distance away from his palace across the river. The layout was strictly symmetrical and geometrical for the walls formed a perfect circle and were described by the Arab geographer Ibn al Balkhi as "if drawn with compasses." These walls, pierced by four gates, consisted of double ramparts of clay and a moat and enclosed an area some 2 kilometers in diameter. The city was divided exactly in four by two main axes, crossing at right angles in the center, and the four quarters were then further subdivided.

Ardashir's rock reliefs. Ardashir's palaces and city at Firuzabad continued to use many Parthian concepts, but used them in a novel manner. He did the same with the sculptures he carved on the cliffs of Fars, creating an entirely new "official art" to proclaim the supremacy of the Sasanian king of kings. Nearly every king for the next

Right: distant view of Ardashir's palace at Firuzabad. Much of it remains standing today.

Below: view of Ardashir's palace, showing the lake in front of the building.

150 years carved a rock relief, after which the tradition lapsed until nearly the end of the Sasanian era.

Ardashir's first two reliefs were carved at Firuzabad, beside the Sasanian road: one, the dramatic jousting scene, commemorated the defeat of his Parthian suzerain, Artabanus V, at the battle of Hormizdegan, and thus the physical foundation of the empire, while the other illustrated the spiritual justification for his seizure of power, showing him receiving the ribboned diadem from the hands of Ahuramazda, the supreme god of the Zoroastrian pantheon (pp. 87–90).

The joust illustrates the unequivocal victory of three Sasanian knights over their Parthian opponents. The three Sasanian chargers are in full gallop with legs extended. The two leading riders have struck their opponents with their lances and have overturned the Parthian horses. The last Sasanian has swept his enemy off his horse and is grappling with him. All the knights are fully protected by armor and identified by heraldic crests, foreshadowing medieval European chivalry. The leading pair represent Ardashir and Artabanus, the second Ardashir's eldest son, Crown Prince Shapur, and the Parthian grand vizier, whom Shapur is said to have slain, while the third Sasanian was Ardashir's loyal page, who is shown on all his reliefs. The whole is a dramatic record not of the mêlée of battle as it was fought, but of its most significant events. An entirely new spirit breathes out of this relief: the self-important merchants and petty kings of the later Parthian period who stared straight out are gone; they are replaced by stirring action recorded in the traditional profile view. Not only is the bold composition original, but also the technique of carving. Although carved in low relief, only some 6 centimeters, this depth is fully used to model both the figures and details of dress, harness and chain mail.

The jousting scene was never completed and neither was the crude investiture scene beside the river. For his next two reliefs Ardashir left Firuzabad for the environs of the city of Istakhr. He placed one investiture scene in the grotto of Naqsh-i Rajab, and carved a scene combining the twin themes of investiture and triumph on the great cliff of Naqsh-i Rustam. This last sculpture is an official proclamation as well as a superb work of art and shows the king and Ahuramazda, each mounted, heraldically opposed to each other. Ardashir raises his hand in respect and submission to the Great God from whom he receives the ribboned diadem. The king is thus shown as Ahuramazda's representative on earth and himself divine. Both god and king are shown effortlessly triumphant over their enemies: the unfortunate Artabanus is trampled by Ardashir's horse, while Ahuramazda's horse stands beside the prone figure of Ahriman, the Zoroastrian embodiment of evil. His evil is subtly indicated by a diadem ending in snakes' heads wound around his head.

The Naqsh-i Rustam sculpture achieves a three-dimensional quality almost unsurpassed in Sasanian sculpture. Both in its overall composition and in its detail this relief proves that the craftsmen concerned could truly claim to be sculptors, while their predecessors were little more than calligraphers. The composition is strictly heraldic: the figure of Ardashir's fan bearer is balanced by the god's billowing cloak. The monumental effect is achieved by a minimum of fussy detail combined with a considerable depth of relief, varying between 4 and 33 centimeters (some elements are nearly in the round). The dramatic effect was heightened by the finish: the strongly modeled figures were polished to a shine while the background was deliberately left rough in contrast.

This magnificent and austere representation of the triumph of good over evil, of the power of the new state church, and of Ardashir's indisputable right to rule, a right achieved by conquest and consecrated by the supreme god, is a fitting monument to the brilliant founder of the Persian renaissance: soldier, politician, patron of the arts.

The principal reception room of Ardashir's palace. Note the squinch in the corner, by which the architect was able to place a round dome on a square room.

Rock Reliefs of the Sasanian Kings

The early Sasanian kings commemorated important events, such as their investiture or a major victory against an enemy, with great carvings on the cliffs. These were nearly all lifesize, if not larger, and were usually sited near the king's favorite city and close to water – a river, spring or pool.

There are about thirty Sasanian rock reliefs, nearly all of which are located in the province of Fars, ancient Persis or Pars, and belong to the first 150 years of the dynasty. They provide a fascinating record of changing styles and fashions, and mirror the preoccupations of the king. Ardashir I, who rebelled against his Parthian sovereign and seized power for himself and his family, recorded his investiture by Ahuramazda no less than three times, and his defeat of the Parthian Great King twice. His son, Shapur I, recorded his victories against Rome four times, while Bahram II, who was notably unsuccessful politically and militarily, showed himself with members of his family or his court.

In addition to their historical interest, the reliefs also provide information about dress, jewelry and hairstyles, and in the jousting scenes about armor and weapons.

Below is part of the 18-meter-long jousting scene of Ardashir I at Firuzabad. Sited beside the Sasanian road high up the mountain, the relief shows three pairs of Sasanian knights defeating their Parthian opponents. Below is Ardashir I unhorsing Artabanus III.

Left : drawing by the French artist, Eugène Flandin, of the jousting scene at Firuzabad. Three separate contests are shown : in the lead are Ardashir I and Artabanus III, Great King of Parthia, while in the center is Ardashir's son Shapur and the Parthian Grand Vizier Darbendan. The impact of the Sasanian lances has caused the Parthians and their horses to fall. Ardashir's hair, gathered into a bunch above his head to form the Sasanian *korymbos*, has lost its covering and is shown streaming out behind (*opposite below*). Shapur's hat, which ends in an animal's head, is that assigned to the crown prince. In addition to their headgear, the Sasanians can be identified by the crests shown on their horses' caparisons. In the last fight a Sasanian knight has swept his opponent off his horse (*center left*). *Below left :* a detail of the Parthian Grand Vizier Darbendan, thrown by Shapur.

Below : there is no doubt about the overwhelming Sasanian victory in the Firuzabad joust. In another jousting scene at Naqsh-i Rustam carved in the late 3rd or 4th century the outcome is less certain. The opponent, shown here, is about to be unhorsed – the king's lance can be seen thrusting against his shoulder.

At his coronation every Sasanian king was invested with the right to rule by his favorite deity, usually Ahuramazda, though Anahita and Mithra were also sometimes chosen. This was symbolized sculpturally by the god handing the king a diadem. *Top*: at Naqsh-i Rustam, Ardashir I receives the diadem from Ahuramazda. Beside the king's horse is the corpse of the Parthian king; beside the god's horse is the corpse of Ahriman (*above*), the spirit of evil.
Left: investiture of Bahram I by Ahuramazda at Bishapur. The damaged area across the relief was caused by a water channel built against the cliff. The corpse below the king's horse was a later addition and may perhaps represent Bahram's grandson, deposed by Narseh.

Above: investiture of Shapur I by
Ahuramazda at Naqsh-i Rajab, a small
grotto near Istakhr.

Left: investiture of Ardashir II by
Ahuramazda at Taq-i Bustan. Behind the
king, offering a second diadem, is Mithra
standing on a lotus.

In two huge reliefs on opposite walls of the Bishapur gorge Shapur I epitomized his major triumphs against Rome. These he recorded in the central scene of each sculpture. A single scene, however, was no longer considered sufficient to convey the magnitude of Shapur's victories, so these are framed with additional registers

showing Sasanian cavalry and tributaries
(*below*). The central scenes of the two
reliefs are identical except for the spacing
and the style: kneeling in front of the
king is Philip the Arab; standing at the
horse's flank, his hand grasped by Shapur,
is Valerian; while the king's horse
tramples the corpse of young Gordian.

While the subject and composition of
the two reliefs are closely similar, there
are significant variations between the two
which suggest that not only were they
carved by different hands, but that they
were probably carved by craftsmen of
different nationalities. The left-bank relief
(*right*) is carved in the standard Iranian
manner and to the usual large scale, while
that on the right bank (*opposite*) is only
half-lifesize and shows more western
concepts of style and design. It was
perhaps carved by captured Roman
craftsmen. Details from it include
(*opposite center*) Sasanian cavalry, (*opposite
below*) Valerian's captured chariot,
(*opposite top right*) tributaries.

Detail from a relief attributed to Shapur II in the Bishapur gorge. Despite its apparent technical inferiority, this relief is important for it may well provide the clue for the decline of the genre. The rock surface was deliberately left rough so that "plasterer's scrim," traces of which still remain, would adhere. The surface was then plastered and presumably painted.

One of the most famous Sasanian rock reliefs carved on the great cliff of Naqsh-i Rustam, which, over the centuries, has been variously identified. The huge figure of the king has been considered to represent Samson or the Persian national hero, Rustam; it actually shows Shapur I celebrating his Roman triumphs.

5. The Persian Renaissance

So it hath been from of old; the o'erthrowing of strong towers
   Is the birthright of the Persian, god-appointed to his trust,
And the thunder of the horsemen and their gladness, it is ours,
   And the trampling of cities in the dust.

AESCHYLUS

Ardashir's son Shapur had had a long training to prepare him for kingship. He had fought beside his father at Hormizdegan and been shown ratifying an alliance with him on a relief carved at Shapur in Azerbaijan. As his father grew old, he had been appointed co-ruler and the transfer of power was, therefore, effected peacefully. Shapur was as able a warrior and ruler as his father, and during the 30 years of his reign inflicted a series of major defeats on the Romans, as well as completing the conquest of the Kushans.

Shapur's Roman campaigns. There is at last in Shapur's reign a record of Persian campaigns seen from the Persian rather than from the Roman side, for Shapur had a long inscription commemorating his deeds carved on the stone walls of the Achaemenian tower known today as the Ka'aba-i Zardusht (cube of Zoroaster) at Naqsh-i Rustam. This was written in three languages, Sasanian, Parthian and Greek, and it is one of the major historical documents of the Sasanian period. It began by giving the king's full titles: "I am the mazda-worshiping divinity Shapur, King of Kings of Aryans and non-Aryans, who is of the stock of the gods, son of the mazda-worshiping divinity Ardashir, King of Kings of the Aryans . . ." The difference between Shapur's and his father's titles is illuminating for Ardashir was only called King of Kings of the Aryans, while Shapur was also king of the non-Aryans and this must indicate that he had conquered extensive areas not considered to be "Aryan."

Much of Shapur's inscription describes his battles with Rome, whom he considered to be his only worthy rival. He began with his first triumph against two Roman

Above: the pleading figure of the Roman emperor, Philip the Arab, from Shapur's investiture/triumph relief at Bishapur. c. 244 AD.

Previous page: the priest and king-maker Kartir, from a relief of Bahram II at Naqsh-i Rustam.

emperors, Gordian III and Philip the Arab: "Then when firstly I was established over the empire Gordianus Caesar from all of Rome, of Goth and German kingdom, assembled a force and came against Assyria upon the Aryan empire and us. And at the frontier of Assyria at Meshik a great frontal battle took place. Gordianus Caesar was killed. The Roman force was destroyed. And the Romans made Philip Caesar. Then Philip Caesar came to us to sue for terms and having given us 500,000 dinars as ransom for the life (of his friends) became tributary to us." The propaganda element of such a proclamation is immediately evident for it is unlikely that the Romans would have agreed that they were "tributaries." This same factor has to be remembered when trying to reconstruct the history of the period from purely western sources.

The battle took place in 244 in Sasanian territory not far from Ctesiphon and this is an indication of how much territory the Persians had lost in the reverse they suffered shortly after Shapur's accession when the Romans had retaken the much-fought-over cities of Carrhae and Nisibis. This slight reverse was, however, more than avenged in 244 when the Roman forces were decisively defeated, when one emperor died, perhaps after rather than during the battle, and when his successor had to sue for peace by paying a swingeing ransom.

Shapur commemorated this major Persian triumph with a rock relief, which was carved on the walls of the river gorge adjoining the site of his new capital city, Bih or Wih Shapur (the excellence of Shapur). Like his father's sculpture at Naqsh-i Rustam, on which it was obviously modeled, the relief recorded both his recent triumph and his divine investiture. New was the figure of a kneeling Roman placed between the horses. His hands were held out in supplication to the king and he has been plausibly identified as Philip the Arab "suing for terms," while the corpse trampled by the king's horse is considered to represent the young emperor Gordian.

As in the Parthian period, control of Armenia continued to be a frequent pretext for war. Shapur probably connived at the assassination of the Armenian king, who was an Arsacid and a bitter enemy, and the Armenian's son fled to Rome. Another confrontation between the two powers therefore became inevitable. This campaign, which took place in 256, resulted in another resounding Persian victory: a Roman army of 60,000 men was destroyed, Armenia was conquered and Persian forces raided deep into Syria. They captured many cities, including Dura Europus and Antioch-on-the-Orontes, capital of the Roman east and known as the "fair crown of the Orient." By this time the Persians had

The Sasanian bridge-dam at Shushtar, built by Roman prisoners.

learned siegecraft from the Romans, and they constructed "a ram of great size" to raze the walls of Antioch. This they dismantled and brought back with them to Carrhae where it lay until it was reassembled and used against them a century later by Constantine!

The third and last of Shapur's Roman campaigns was the most successful and is best described in his own words: "In the third war when we attacked Carrhae and Edessa and were besieging Carrhae and Edessa, Valerian Caesar came upon us having with him . . . a force of 70 thousands. And on that side of Carrhae and Edessa with Valerian Caesar a great conflict took place. And Valerian Caesar himself with our own hand we made captive. And the rest, the pretorian prefect, senators and generals, and whatever of that force were officers, all we made captive and away to the Persis we led . . . In the Aryan's empire in Persis, Parthia, Khuzistan, Assyria, and others, land by land, where our own and our father's and our grandfather's and our forebears' foundations were, there we settled them."

The defeat and capture of Valerian and his army left Syria and Cappadocia at the mercy of the Sasanian armies. The citizens of Antioch, who had presumably been confident of Valerian's ability to contain the Persian menace, were strolling around the streets or watching a

play when the Persians struck. Ammianus relates that an actress performing on the stage suddenly cried, "'Is it a dream, or are the Persians here?' Whereupon all the people turned their heads about and then fled in all directions to avoid the arrows that were showered upon them from the citadel. Thus the city was set on fire . . . and the enemy, laden with plunder, returned home without the loss of a single man."

These victories Shapur commemorated in a new series of reliefs which showed him triumphant over all three Roman emperors, Gordian, Philip the Arab and Valerian, in a single scene. These reliefs therefore epitomize Shapur's triumphs against his principal rival. The two figures seen in his earlier sculpture, the corpse of Gordian and the pleading Philip, were repeated, and to them was added the standing figure of Valerian, the Roman's hand firmly grasped by Shapur who thus illustrated visually his written description of the capture of Caesar.

The vast numbers of prisoners taken by the Persians in these campaigns and settled throughout the empire formed a considerable pool of cheap and often technically experienced labor. The remains of their endeavors are plentiful in Khuzistan, where also the ruins of their towns, laid out like Roman camps, can still be seen today. Particularly impressive are their bridges, the piers of some of which are still in use. One of these was built over the Karun river and measures some 516 meters in length. It is supported by 41 piers with cutwaters typically Roman in style. The piers of the bridge at Shushtar (500 meters long) were set close together, for this barrage was also intended to act as a dam. It winds its way across the river, the builder having set the piers wherever he could find stone outcrops in the riverbed. The Shushtar bridge/dam was one of many Sasanian state-sponsored irrigation works which were carried out on a massive scale right across the empire.

The Prophet Mani. Both Shapur and his father were remembered as builders of cities. Among the many cities Shapur founded was his favorite, Bishapur, and a new town in Khuzistan, later known as Gundeshapur, in which many prisoners were resettled, including the Christian bishop of Antioch. Shapur had the reputation of being a liberal and tolerant man, who allowed the many religious minorities, Christians, Jews and Buddhists, to practice freely within his empire. He was himself an active supporter of the Prophet Mani, who began his ministry at the time of Shapur's accession. Mani converted two of the king's brothers, Mihrshah and Peroz, who became powerful patrons. Shapur himself, although remaining a Zoroastrian, was deeply impressed by Mani's message, which claimed to be a fulfillment of Zoroastrian, Christian and Buddhist beliefs. Perhaps hoping to find a religion that would unify all his people, Shapur gave Mani permission to travel and preach throughout his empire. Of his audience with the king Mani wrote "King Shapur was solicitous on my behalf and wrote letters for me to all

magnates in the following terms: 'Befriend and defend him, that none shall transgress or trespass against him'."

According to Mani, Shapur died at Bishapur. The date is disputed; it was probably either 270 or 273, by which time he must have been an old man. He and his father in their 50 years of conquest and consolidation had fully restored Persian greatness and had ruled with a light hand. Under their three successors, each called Bahram – I (c. 273–276), II (276–293) and III (293) – much territory was lost and religious minorities were savagely persecuted.

Kartir the priest. This reversal of the policy of religious toleration was probably instigated by one of the most remarkable characters in Sasanian history, the priest Kartir. Kartir had begun his career in the reign of Ardashir and had continued to promote Zoroastrian orthodoxy against the Manichaean heresy throughout Shapur's reign. His chance came under the Bahrams, when the Prophet Mani was soon imprisoned and done to death. Kartir proudly proclaimed in inscriptions carved near the royal rock reliefs how he persecuted Jews, Christians, Manichees, Mandaeans, Buddhists and Brahmans: for the first time Zoroastrianism had become a fanatical and persecuting religion. Within the Zoroastrian faith Kartir enforced strict uniformity, upholding the doctrines of good and evil, of heaven and hell and of rewards and punishment.

Shapur I: the head of the enormous statue (8 meters high) of Shapur carved from a stalactite in a cave near Bishapur: one of the few examples of Sasanian statuary in the round. Late 3rd century AD.

Silver drachm of Bahram II with his queen Shapurdukhtat and one of the crown princes. Note the high bonnets of the queen and the prince, both of which end in animals' heads. British Museum.

Kartir's considerable powers probably derived from his ability as a politician. It was perhaps thanks to his intrigues that Bahram I was succeeded by his son Bahram II rather than by his brother Narseh, officially next in succession, if, indeed, Narseh should not have preceded Bahram I. Kartir was amply rewarded for his help by Bahram I and II and his spectacular rise to power is illustrated by the titles conferred upon him by the different kings he served. To Shapur he was "the priestly schoolmaster," while under Bahram I he was appointed "Ahuramazda's magus-master," and under Bahram II he not only became "Bahram's soul-savior" but also had conferred upon him "the rank and dignity of the grandees." He had achieved the almost impossible feat in Sasanian society of changing social classes – from priest to noble.

Kartir's considerable influence over Bahram II is attested not only by his receiving the highest honors from that king but also by his appearing on all but one of Bahram's numerous rock reliefs. These abandoned the standard formulae of investiture or triumph and attempted new subjects with an emphasis on internal affairs: Bahram is shown with members of his family and/ or courtiers, and in one remarkable scene he is depicted protecting his wife, Queen Shapurdukhtat, from attack by a lion. The king and queen are also shown side by side on some of his coins, accompanied sometimes by one of

the princes, and the same group is to be found on a unique silver cup discovered in Georgia and now in the Tiflis Museum. Bahram's preoccupation with his family may have reflected a fashion current in Rome, or perhaps his determination to secure the succession of his son. It may even have been brought about by a desire to overlook the external humiliations inflicted on Iran during his reign: in 283 the Emperor Carus sacked Ctesiphon and in the subsequent peace treaty much of northern Mesopotamia was lost to the Romans. In the east too Bahram faced a challenge – a revolt of the Sakas, Kushans and the people of Gilan led by his brother Hormuzd. This Bahram successfully crushed, but in 288 he failed to respond to the placing of a Roman nominee on the throne of part of Armenia.

Narseh, the last of Shapur's long-lived sons, revolted against Bahram III after he had ruled for only a few months. Narseh, as we know from his long inscription carved on a commemorative tower at Paikuli in Kurdistan, was supported by many nobles and successfully deposed the young king. On his accession Narseh was determined to regain the territory lost to Rome under the Bahrams. He was initially successful against Galerius but was defeated in 298 and his family captured. In the following peace treaty northern Mesopotamia and parts of Armenia once again became Roman and the Romans insisted that all trade must be funneled through the Roman frontier fortress town of Nisibis.

Somehow or other Kartir survived the change of kings, but his policy of persecution did not. Manichaeans were tolerated, which may reflect either a return to more liberal policies or a subtle move to secure the support of Manichaeans in the Roman empire – they had been proscribed in an edict of 297. Religion was to play an increasingly important part in the formation of foreign policy, for in 312 the Emperor Constantine was converted to Christianity, and he was followed by the king of Armenia. With Christianity the religion of the Roman empire, persecution of the Christian community in Iran was inevitable and they were harshly treated by Shapur II. Shapur II was the grandson of Narseh and, according to legend, was crowned while still in his mother's womb. "A royal bed on which the queen lay in state was exhibited in the midst of the palace and the diadem placed on the spot which might be supposed to conceal the future heir of Artaxerxes" (Gibbon).

The reign of Shapur II. Initially under the control of the nobles, on attaining manhood Shapur gathered power into his own hands. He ruled for 70 years from 309 to 379, during which time Iran recovered lost ground. Among his early successes he re-established Sasanian control over the Kushans in the east and also campaigned in the desert against the Arabs – he is supposed to have filled their wells with sand to force them to submit. His main effort was, however, once again directed against the Romans but here the situation on the ground had changed. Diocletian and Constantine had erected a strong system of fortresses in Roman Mesopotamia and in the Syrian desert. These fortifications were defended by a force of well-trained troops able to move rapidly along a system of roads, wells and caravansarays to wherever danger threatened. Even though the Sasanian army was probably better organized and disciplined than ever before, Shapur II was unable to repeat the sweeping victories of his namesake and great-grandfather.

We are fortunate in having a vivid eyewitness account of some of the many campaigns fought by the Persians and the Romans. It was written by the soldier Ammianus Marcellinus, a Greek born in Antioch-on-the-Orontes, who fought in Mesopotamia in the 350s and again with Julian the Apostate in 363. He described the appearance of Shapur II and the enemy forces as follows:

"And when the first gleam of dawn appeared, everything so far as the eye could reach shone with glittering arms, and mail-clad cavalry filled hill and dale. The king himself, mounted upon a charger and over-topping the others, rode before the whole army, wearing in place of a diadem a golden image of a ram's head set with precious stones, distinguished too by a great retinue of men of the highest rank and of various nations.

"The Persians opposed to us serried bands of mail-clad horsemen in such close order that the gleam of moving bodies covered with closely fitting plates of iron dazzled the eyes of those who looked upon them, while the whole throng of horses was protected by coverings of leather. The cavalry was backed up by companies of infantry, who, protected by oblong curved shields covered with wickerwork and raw hides, advanced in very close order. Behind these were elephants, looking like walking hills, and, by the movements of their enormous bodies, they threatened destruction to all who came near them, dreaded as they were from past experience."

In 359 Shapur finally succeeded in capturing some towns and this resulted in a major Roman counterthrust organized by Julian the Apostate, which reached the very walls of Ctesiphon. Both sides fought with unrelenting ferocity as Ammianus Marcellinus, who was there, recorded:

Hormuzd II (303–309) defeating an unidentified enemy. The composition of this jousting scene, carved at Naqsh-i Rustam, is obviously derived from that of his great-grandfather Ardashir at Firuzabad. The style and technique, however, are entirely different. Maximum size, c. 3·60 × 8 meters.

"So, when both sides were near enough to look each other in the face, the Romans, gleaming in their crested helmets and swinging their shields as if to the rhythm of the anapestic foot, advanced slowly; and the light-armed skirmishers opened the battle by hurling their javelins, while the earth everywhere was turned to dust and swept away in a swift whirlwind. And when the battle cry was raised in the usual manner by both sides and the trumpets' blare increased the ardor of the men, here and there they fought hand to hand with spears and drawn swords . . . Meanwhile Julian was busily engaged in giving support to those who gave way and in spurring on the laggards, playing the part both of a valiant fellow soldier and of a commander. Finally, the first battle line of the Persians began to waver, and at first slowly, then at quick step, turned back and made for the neighboring city with their armor well heated up. Our soldiers pursued them, wearied though they also were after fighting on the scorching plains from sunrise to the end of the day, and following close at their heels and hacking at their legs and backs, drove the whole force with Pigranas, the Surena and Narseus, their most distinguished generals, in headlong flight to the very walls of Ctesiphon."

Fortunately for Iran, Julian died from wounds sustained in battle and his craven successor Jovian was tricked into giving away all the Roman gains in order to secure a safe conduct for himself and his men. The treaty gave the Persians not only much of northern Mesopotamia but also Armenia.

The wars in the west were not the only ones. A new tribal horde had arrived in the east, the Chionites or Huns, and wars with these ferocious fighters were to preoccupy Shapur's weaker successors. Shapur II, however, succeeded in controlling them and even persuaded the Chionites to help him in his battles with the Romans. Another frontier requiring constant vigilance was the northern one, particularly the Caucasus region, and it may have been during Shapur's reign that the famous Wall of Darband was built in the Caucasus to try and keep the invaders at bay. Control of this frontier was vital both to the Sasanians and to the Romans and the western empire frequently made a contribution to the expenses of its defense, even when east and west were at loggerheads elsewhere.

To pay for his army Shapur had to raise more taxes, and an obvious target was the Christian community, which had been actively persecuted since the Roman empire had officially become Christian. Taxes on Christians were doubled and not surprisingly there was trouble. The Christians of Susa – Khuzistan was one of the centers of Christianity in the Sasanian empire, together with Adiabene and Ctesiphon – revolted against Shapur and shut the gates of the city. This revolt the king savagely crushed, using his formidable force of elephants to flatten the walls and houses of the city, evidence of which was found by Ghirshman when excavating at Susa.

Zoroastrian orthodoxy was given a new impetus in Shapur's reign, when the Great Mobad, Adhurbad, submitted to an ordeal to prove the efficacy of the "good religion." There were a number of ordeals, both "hot" and "cold," and Adhurbad is supposed to have submitted to, and survived, the terrible ordeal of having molten metal poured onto his chest. He is highly regarded in Zoroastrian tradition and some of his writings have survived.

The city of Bishapur. Shapur I sited his favorite city, Bishapur, where the river Shapur cuts through a gorge and opens out into a fertile plain. The steep walls of the gorge formed an ideal site for rock reliefs and the high hill dominating the city made a strongly defensive site for the fortress he built there. The rolling wooded hills around were rich in game and provided a natural hunting ground, thus satisfying a favorite pastime of all Sasanian kings. The climate too is pleasant except in summer.

The rectangular layout of Shapur's city is still visible on the surface today, as are many of the strongly built rubble and mortar structures. According to literary sources, the city had a relatively short life, and this is helpful from the archaeological point of view for the major structures are likely to date from early in the Sasanian period, the time of its foundation. The city flourished until the 5th century, when Peroz transferred some of its inhabitants to Kazerun, then only a village. Bishapur continued in use, although by the 10th century it was declining and it had been abandoned by the 12th century. The population moved to Kazerun, which is still a prosperous town today.

Excavations undertaken at Bishapur in the late 1930s by Georges Salles and Roman Ghirshman revealed some of the principal buildings within the royal enclosure. Recently work has been resumed by the Iranian Center for Archaeological Research under the direction of Ali Sarfaraz. The main emphasis has been on a large-scale program of conservation of the exposed monuments, although Sarfaraz has also made many significant discoveries while working there.

The French excavations uncovered a large area of the royal quarter, although many structures within it still remain to be revealed. It was probably walled and provided with spacious gardens, as were the houses of the nobility. The most imposing building consisted of an enormous square hall or courtyard, in the center of each wall of which was a great *iwan* – the *iwan*-cross plan first seen at Parthian Assur. The walls of this hall, built of rubble and mortar, were immensely thick and the excavator suggests that they once supported an enormous dome some 25 meters high, although other scholars consider that the structure was not roofed. Around the walls were niches set within rectangular frames and decorated with painted stucco patterns in a simple geometric design.

The most lavishly decorated structure in the royal

quarter was a triple-*iwan* building to the east of the great hall. It opened out onto a courtyard, the limits of which have not yet been revealed. The floor of the principal *iwan* was paved with slabs of stone and decorated at the sides with a border of superb mosaic panels. The designs for these panels were derived from patterns current in Roman Syria, although adapted to conform with Iranian taste, and they must have been laid by some of the Roman prisoners Shapur had taken in his western campaigns. The principal scenes showed women, either standing, dancing or reclining luxuriously on cushions. They plaited garlands, held flowers or plucked at the strings of harps. The holding of flowers clearly had some distinct iconographic meaning for both men and women are regularly shown doing so. These scenes were framed with panels of complex geometric designs and linked one to the other by friezes of heads. These heads, arranged in groups of three or four, are cut short at the chin and recall the stone "masks" carved at Hatra. They showed men and women, old and young, in a variety of positions. Another panel showed a delightful pair of birds walking towards each other along the branches of a tree.

In addition to the mosaics on the floor, the walls of this *iwan* may have been decorated with stucco panels,

Right: plan of the palace area and temple at Bishapur.

Below: the ruins of the city of Bishapur seen in spring time from the fortress.

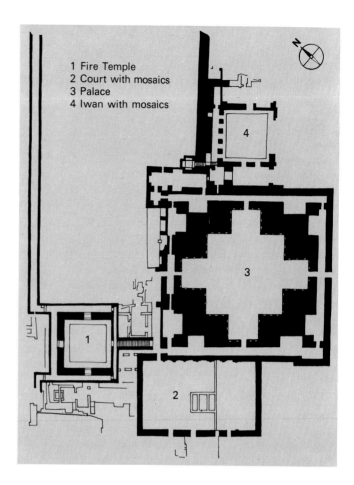

1 Fire Temple
2 Court with mosaics
3 Palace
4 Iwan with mosaics

although those found *in situ* are considered to be late in style, dating to the end of the Sasanian period or early in the Islamic era. They presumably replaced earlier ones.

Another important structure in the royal quarter, and the one noted by the early travelers, was built of finely dressed stone masonry as opposed to the more usual rubble and mortar construction, and this may again be an indication that it was built by Roman prisoners of war. Like a small domed room behind the triple-*iwan* building, it was semi-subterranean. A covered stairway of 20 steps led steeply down into a narrow corridor which surrounded the single square room. The corridors, only half the height of the central chamber, were vaulted, although the sanctuary itself may have been roofed with beams. Some of the supports for the beams, in the form of bulls' forequarters (an echo from Persepolis), still stand on top of the 15-meter-high northwest wall. The stone paved floor of the sanctuary is on two levels, with a higher pavement running around the walls. This is pierced by water channels which Ali Sarfaraz has recently proved are directly linked to the river, as is the covered basin in the center of the floor.

The purpose of this enigmatic building has been frequently debated: it has been considered to be a fire temple, or a temple dedicated either to Anahita or to Mithra, or to be a cool subterranean summer living room – the tradition of living underground during the broiling summer months is still followed today in some parts of Iran. However, this particular plan of a square *cella* and ambulatory has a long history, having occurred frequently throughout the Parthian period, as well as earlier, and its occurrence in the sacred precinct at Hatra suggests that it was used as a temple there. If it was indeed a temple, as its antecedents suggest, then Sarfaraz' important recent discovery of the water-circulating system within the building lends weight to the theory that it was a temple dedicated to Anahita, the goddess of fertility and water.

Since only part of the royal enclosure has been excavated to date, it is not yet possible to understand the overall plan of what was clearly a monumental and luxurious complex. At Firuzabad the plan of the palace was both logical and symmetrical: the principal chamber or chambers of audience were entered after walking through a monumental *iwan* entrance. At Bishapur, however, the great *iwan*-cross hall has no such dramatic entrance, and the principal *iwan* of the triple-*iwan* structure with five doors in its back wall leads only into a corridor going nowhere particular. More excavation is required before we can hope to understand the architecture of Shapur's capital city, although what is already visible illustrates the power and wealth of the empire, and the many artistic currents influencing the decorative arts.

The two main avenues of the city met in the center at right angles and the governor of Bishapur erected a

The monumental *iwan*-cross hall of Shapur's palace at Bishapur. The niches lining the walls were decorated with geometric friezes.

monument in honor of the king at this intersection in 266 AD. This monument consisted of three stone bases on two of which stood monolithic columns with Corinthian capitals, a type of monument entirely Roman in inspiration and probably also the work of prisoners of war. The inscriptions on the shafts, written in Pahlavi, are a valuable guide to the chronology of the early Sasanians and also record that a statue of the king formed part of the monument. This statue, which was probably set on the third pedestal, doubtless resembled the colossal image of Shapur carved in a cave near Bishapur, though it must have been considerably smaller. The statue in the cave, located on top of a mountain some 6 kilometers away, was carved out of an enormous stalactite and was still standing in the 14th century when it was described by the Persian geographer, Hamd Allah Mustawfi of Qazvin. By the 19th century, however, it had fallen down, though it has recently been somewhat clumsily re-erected near the mouth of the cave. The colossal statue originally stood

Looking down into the sanctuary of the Temple of Anahita, Bishapur, which is partly subterranean: The central area of the sanctuary could be flooded by water running through channels connected to the river: the opening of one such channel can be seen in the raised pavement in front of the door.

some 8 meters high: the *korymbos* surmounting the king's crown was carved into the roof of the cave while the feet were cut into the stone floor. In appearance the king is shown much as on the rock reliefs: he wears a similar cross-over tunic, softly molded to his body. His sword is slung at his hip. The whole presents an image of imperturbable majesty and absolute power.

Rock reliefs. Shapur I carved some six or seven reliefs which can probably be dated either to his first decade in the 240s or to his last one after his capture of Valerian in the 260s. His remarkable achievement in actually capturing Caesar alive seems to have provided a fresh sculptural impetus. However, even though the earliest and the latest reliefs were possibly separated by more than 10 years in their time of carving, all Shapur's sculptures were worked in a distinctive personal style entirely different from his father's austerity. There is an emphasis on flamboyant detail and considerable sculptural play with fluttering ribbons, which were always shown in motion though stirred by breezes blowing in opposite directions. This baroque quality is already apparent in what may have been Shapur's first relief, his investiture scene in the little grotto at Naqsh-i Rajab, and is readily visible when that relief is compared with the simple monumentality of Ardashir's sculpture at Naqsh-i Rustam.

Similarity of style is, however, all that unites Shapur's early and late reliefs, for the two late sculptures commemorating his victory over three Roman emperors, which were carved in the Bishapur gorge, break new sculptural ground. They abandon both the heraldic composition of the earlier reliefs and the use of a single scene. The principal panels of these victory scenes still form the *raison d'être* of the sculpture but they are flanked by in the one case two and in the other five more registers. These illustrate serried ranks of the invincible Sasanian cavalry lined up behind the king and rows of tributaries or infantry in front of him. The principal panel shows the mounted figure of the Persian king victorious over three Roman emperors. Young Gordian is being trampled by Shapur's horse, while Philip the Arab pleads eloquently on his knees before the king, as in Shapur's earlier investiture triumph. New is the figure of Valerian standing by the horse's flank, his wrist firmly held by the king. Shapur's triumph is subtly emphasized by the winged Nike or Victory offering him a ring.

While these two late reliefs share much in common – the arrangement into registers, the subject of the principal panel and the introduction of the Nike – there are also important differences between them. The two-register relief on the left cliff is in the usual Iranian idiom of massive size and has the figures spaced out to avoid too large an empty area. Those in the relief with five registers are unique in being less than half-lifesize. Although the relief is entirely Sasanian in content and iconography, the design and execution are not: the figures are placed closer together and show much more "movement." All these factors suggest that this relief was the work of some of the captured Roman craftsmen while the other was carved by Iranian sculptors who were not familiar with the complexities of the composition.

The same flamboyant style was used by Shapur's son, Bahram I (c. 273–276), in his only relief, which, predictably enough, illustrated his divine investiture. Many scholars consider this relief to be the highpoint of early Sasanian sculpture. Indeed the traveler and writer James Morier described it as "exquisite; the proportions and anatomy of both horses and men were accurately preserved, so that the very veins and arteries in the horses' legs and belly were most delicately delineated."

Beside his relief Bahram I placed an inscription recording his name, titles and lineage. In an ancient forgery his name was erased and replaced by that of his brother Narseh, who came to the throne only after Bahram's son and grandson. This erasure reinforces the impression that the Bahrams usurped the throne of Narseh, perhaps with the aid of the ambitious priest

Kartir. It was probably Narseh too who added to the relief another figure, which was only discovered by Ali Sarfaraz in 1974. With somewhat morbid humor, Narseh had carved below the king's horse the corpse of a Sasanian prince, which may perhaps have represented Bahram III, whom Narseh deposed.

Bahram II (276–293) carved a number of sculptures which were entirely novel. Although his first relief, carved next to his father's at Bishapur, was identical in style and was probably cut by the same sculptor or sculptors, the subject was different. In it the king on his horse receives an Arab delegation bringing gifts or tribute of horses and camels. Another of Bahram's reliefs, carved on the mountain at Sar Mashhad, depicts the king on foot slaying a lion, which was shown twice, first leaping at him and then lying dying at his feet. Behind the king stands Shapurdukhat, his queen, who was also shown on his coinage. The king protectively holds her back with his left hand, though slipped in between the king and the queen is Kartir, the *éminence grise* of the Sasanian court.

The scene on this relief is variously interpreted. Some see it as an actual event: the lion was indigenous to Iran and Mesopotamia and the slaying of these predators was a task which the kings and the nobility, the only people with

One of the commemorative inscribed columns at Bishapur, erected by the governor in 263 AD.

adequate weapons, were expected to undertake, as they had been over the millennia. Others see it as symbolic, illustrating the triumph of good over evil; and some see in it reflections of the worship of Mithra. However that may be, technically the sculpture is of considerable interest. The subject is new in Sasanian art and the figures of the king and the lion form a taut and effective composition to which the followers add nothing. The style too is original – the depth of relief is considerably lower and because of this the amount of detail was correspondingly reduced.

Not surprisingly, when Narseh finally won the throne in 293, he rejected Bahram II's new sculptural style and recorded his divine investiture in a style based on Shapur's florid and fluttery technique while the composition reflected an early and unsuccessful relief of Ardashir's. What is unusual about his relief, though, is that he is shown being invested not by Ahuramazda, but by Anahita. This may perhaps have reflected his distaste for the persecution carried out in Ahuramazda's name by Kartir under the Bahrams.

Middle Sasanian architecture. One of the few closely dated architectural monuments of the middle Sasanian period, i.e. the 4th and 5th centuries, belongs to Narseh's reign. He built a tower, now ruined, at Paikuli in Iraqi Kurdistan, the purpose of which was purely commemorative: it was built to carry a long inscription listing Narseh's supporters in his campaign against Bahram III and it was also decorated with busts of the king.

Carved on the mountain at Sar Mashhad, a relief showing Bahram II defending his queen against an attacking lion. Between the king and Shapurdukhtat stands Kartir, the priest.

The tower, sited at the top of a hill, was solid: the core of rubble masonry was faced with finely cut stone blocks, on some of which Narseh's inscription was carved. Square in plan, the corners were embellished with engaged columns and the cornice was crenellated in typical Parthian and Sasanian fashion. In the four busts, one of which was placed on each wall, Narseh was shown full-face, wearing his own personal crown with a fluted decoration, which is considered to be an attribute of Anahita. Anahita is also mentioned in the inscription on the tower and this emphasis on the goddess rather than Ahuramazda both at Paikuli and in Narseh's sculpture at Naqsh-i Rustam confirms his preference for her. Unusually his hair was arranged in ringlets rather than the bushy curls of kingship, and his arms and chest were represented by a convention of stylized curves frequently seen on busts on silver vessels and seals.

Although Paikuli is securely dated to Narseh's reign and could therefore be a convenient peg to help reconstruct a history of Sasanian architecture, it is unfortunately only of limited value for its plan is unique. The problems of trying to establish such an architectural history are well summed up by Oscar Reuther in the *Survey of Persian Art*: "The divergence of opinion and insecurity in dating Sasanian buildings are shown by the fact that one scholar formerly

Reconstruction of Narseh's commemorative tower at Paikuli in Iraqi Kurdistan. The stone tower, now ruined, once carried four stone busts of the king and a long inscription. Late 3rd century AD.

classed as Arsacid the Taq-i Girra . . . and believed that a relatively early dating for it must be conceded, but now this same scholar considers it late Sasanian. The Taq-i Kisra, the vast ruin of the royal palace of Ctesiphon, is attributed by some to the reign of Shahpur I . . . while others identify it as the iwan built by Khusraw I Anushirwan . . . How difficult it is, under these circumstances, to discuss Sasanian architecture can best be realized by imagining how the history of Greek architecture would be written if the dating of the Parthenon varied by two, three or even four hundred years."

This confusion continues today. The stone platform and associated temple at Kangavar were long considered to be Seleucid or early Parthian. However, recent research by the Iranian excavator Kambaksh Fard has suggested that the structure as seen today was the result of a major late Sasanian reconstruction of the earlier temple, traces of which have still to be found in earlier levels.

Shapur II, having flattened much of the city of Susa with his elephants after the Christian revolt, founded a new town not far away on the banks of the Kerkha, so the buildings there should presumably be considered to be mid-Sasanian. Rectangular in plan, the town measured some 5 × 1 kilometers and was built in brick. Plans of two buildings attributed to Shapur II have been recovered.

One was a familiar "Parthian" three-*iwan* structure, the walls of which had been richly decorated with frescoes. The other building was entirely different and consisted of a long rectangular hall which was divided into three: the square central area was domed, while the side wings were vaulted in a novel way. They were spanned by five wide arches, the spaces between which were vaulted transversely. The side walls between the arches were pierced with windows, which must have made the building pleasantly light and airy.

A somewhat similar method of roofing, though developed one stage further, was employed in two rooms in the palace at Sarvistan. Dates proposed for this delightful building, much of which is still standing, vary between the 4th and 6th centuries. It was once set in extensive gardens, the plan of which can still be seen from the air, and, as befits a garden pavilion, has many ways in and out. The plan is pleasantly irregular: the main west facade at first sight appears to consist of the familiar triple-*iwan* structure, but the left *iwan* is actually a small domed room. This innovatory element is strong at Sarvistan: for instance the smaller domed room at the rear, which had

Reconstruction of a hall at Iwan-i Kerkha near Susa, probably built in the reign of Shapur II. Novel is the system of vaulting the wings: five arches were thrown from wall to wall and the spaces between vaulted transversely. After Reuther.

direct access to the garden and to the inner courtyard, contained a balcony running around the walls and supported on four columns. What is of particular architectural interest at Sarvistan is the method of roofing two long rooms, which appears to be a development of that of the side-halls at Iwan-i Kerkha. At Sarvistan the wide arches spanning the room rested on pairs of columns set along the walls rather than on the walls themselves. The space between these arches was then filled in, as at Iwan-i Kerkha, with transverse barrel vaults. With the many niches and the intersecting arches breaking up the walls, which were then presumably plastered and painted, these rooms must have been attractive and have given a great impression of space.

Architectural decoration. At Sarvistan, Bishapur or Firuzabad all we have left in the main are the huge bare bones of these monumental buildings. Only fragments remain of the decoration which transformed them from skeletons into palatial residences. The most complete idea of the probable appearance of a Sasanian palace has been preserved in an *iwan* not built of brick but cut out of the rock at Taq-i Bustan near Kermanshah. This *iwan* formed the last, and also the most ambitious, stone sculpture of the Sasanian dynasty and was probably commissioned by Khusrau II (591–628). It was lavishly decorated both on

Above: the long hall at Sarvistan: detail showing the columns and niches. The arches spanning the room rested on the columns.

Below: reconstruction of the mid-Sasanian palace-pavilion at Sarvistan. After Reuther.

Above: the ruins of the palace of Sarvistan which were once surrounded by extensive gardens. Mid-Sasanian period.

Right: the palace at Sarvistan: interior of the great dome currently being restored.

the facade and on the side and back walls and this decoration probably reflects that of a late Sasanian palace.

Excavations at Kish, principally a Sumerian site in Babylonia, also uncovered two "villas" of the Sasanian period, the walls of which had been embellished with numerous stucco plaques. This stucco can be dated to the mid-Sasanian period for it included busts of a Sasanian king which had been keyed into the walls. This king, with great bunches of curls on his shoulders and wearing a mural crown, has recently been identified with Bahram V (420–438), known as Bahram Gur and famed in Iranian legend as a mighty hunter of onager. The Kish stucco can therefore be dated to the early 5th century.

Rich stucco collections have also been found in a palace at Tepe Hissar/Damghan and in the ruins of the great Sasanian capital city of Ctesiphon. The Damghan palace consisted of a monumental *iwan* entrance leading to a domed room with a smaller chamber behind. The *iwan* entrance was not, however, simply vaulted, for the vaults rested on thick pillars near the walls, as in the long rooms at Sarvistan. Such a columned *iwan* is also a feature of a late Sasanian palace at Qasr-i Shirin, built by Khusrau II (see next chapter). The date of the Damghan palace is disputed: it was probably built some time before that at Qasr-i Shirin, and after the palace at Sarvistan.

The stucco collections from Kish, Damghan and Ctesiphon, despite probable differences in the date of manufacture, are in many ways closely similar and some panels are indeed almost identical. For instance, figured panels from Kish, such as those showing the bust of a woman and others with moufflon, are closely paralleled at Damghan and at Ctesiphon. The actual arches of the Kish *iwans* were outlined with a pattern representing the diadem tied around the king's crown with its long fluted diadem ties, though on the *iwan* it was untied and the ribbons flutter up on the facades to either side. This form of *iwan* decoration may well have been standard, for stucco fragments have also been found at Damghan and at Ctesiphon. A similar untied diadem also outlined the *iwan* arch at Taq-i Bustan.

The repertoire of motifs was large and varied, and the panels were of course also brilliantly painted. The Kish stucco consisted of an almost endless variety of motifs, including more than 40 variations of geometric and floral patterns, which were repeated to form continuous flowing designs. Other panels were more defined and depicted

people and animals, as well as occasional epigraphic and elaborate floral designs. At Damghan motifs included browsing deer and the heads of wild boars set in roundels. Furthermore the thick columns in the entrance *iwan* were encased in a flowing stucco design. Fragments of wall paintings were also found. One of these showed parts of a horse and rider, who was probably hunting. Fragments of just such a hunting scene, securely dated to the 4th century for it was found on the wall of a house at Susa destroyed by Shapur II, showed two mounted huntsmen shooting deer. Ammianus Marcellinus, describing a "pleasant and shady dwelling" by which the Romans camped in 363, wrote that there were paintings in every part of the house "representing the king killing wild beasts in various kinds of hunting; for nothing in their country is painted or sculptured except slaughter in diverse forms and scenes of war." Painted rooms were also found at Ctesiphon.

From the available evidence it seems probable that the art of stucco decoration flourished in the middle and late Sasanian periods. It is entirely different in spirit from the restrained stucco found at Firuzabad and Bishapur and its full development and exploitation in the later 4th century may well explain why the Sasanian kings ceased to carve rock reliefs. There is a remarkable absence of rock reliefs from the time of Shapur III (383–388) until Khusrau II commissioned his *iwan* at Taq-i Bustan, which itself was as much a building as a sculpture. It seems probable that during this time the art of the stone-cutter was replaced by that of the molder and carver of stucco.

Stucco bust of a king from Kish of the early 5th century AD, once keyed into the wall of a Sasanian villa excavated there. Identification of the king is not certain; the bust is currently considered to represent Bahram V. Ht. 46·5 cm. Ashmolean Museum, Oxford.

Stucco panels from Ctesiphon showing (*below*) a cock in a roundel and (*opposite*) a leaping bear. The cock is 30 cm high, the bear 28·5 cm. Metropolitan Museum of Art, New York.

Applied arts. A similar flowering to that in stucco can also be observed in the applied arts in the 4th century, particularly on the marvelous silver and golden vessels. Favored motifs on these naturally included representations of the king both at the hunt and relaxing at court. When hunting, he is shown both mounted and on foot, fighting a wide variety of game including lion, boar, moufflon and deer, with either the bow or the sword. Many of these animals also occur on vessels on their own when they probably represented deities: thus the wild boar is usually considered to represent Verethragna, god of victory; the lion, Mithra, lord of the contract; the horse, Tishtraya or Sirius, the benevolent god of the Iranian pantheon; the cock, the spirit of good fortune, and so on. Another protective genius which was frequently represented was the *senmurv*, the famous Sasanian mythical creature which was half-bird and half-beast. The voluptuous figures of lightly clothed dancers, often shown between arcades, were another favorite motif.

It is possible to suggest dates within the 400 years of the Sasanian period for some of these vessels, particularly if the king was represented, for he can often be identified by his personal crown. Prudence Harper of the Metropolitan Museum of Art, New York, has been working for a number of years on this vexed problem, which has been complicated because few vessels have been found in secure archaeological contexts and because, among those circulating on the art market, there are many excellent forgeries. A further problem is that "Sasanian" silver continued to be made after the fall of the dynasty. Despite this, Dr Harper has succeeded in proposing a basic classification of the vessels into three groups, an early group, a central group and a late group. Her earliest group is decorated only with a single central bust enclosed within a roundel. This bust usually portrayed an important noble or his lady, presumably the person who commissioned the vessel. A late example of this type is the silver cup found in Georgia, which was decorated with four busts showing Bahram II and members of his family. By the reign of Shapur II, however, Dr Harper suggests that private patronage had been banned and that the state had secured a monopoly of silver production. Typical vessels of this group are those decorated with the king hunting. Interestingly the composition of the metal of these vessels

does not vary much, while that of the earlier group changes considerably from vessel to vessel. Dr Harper's third group is late Sasanian and early Islamic and by this time the subjects have become somewhat stereotyped with little internal development. There is evidence both of copying earlier designs and of harking back to past glories by the depiction of the feats of earlier kings. Consequently the crown type is no longer a sure guide to dating.

There are vast numbers of Sasanian seals in museums and private collections and again the dating is extremely difficult unless either they are inscribed or they illustrate a king, as in the famous British Museum seal showing Bahram IV (388–399). Wearing his characteristic crown and the distinctive apron skirt of the later 4th century, the king, spear in hand, stands triumphantly on the corpse of a fallen enemy. Many seals, however, just show a bust, an animal motif, or the family device or crest.

The years of empire from Shapur I to the early 5th century were a time of internal peace and prosperity. This led to a real flowering in art and architecture, which developed in many different ways. There was a deliberate attempt to lighten the massive halls of the palaces, breaking them up with columns and niches, and covering the walls with a textured mass of painted stucco and fresco, as opposed to the simple monumentality exhibited in Ardashir's building. By the late 4th century, developed stucco designs had replaced the official art of the rock relief and had reached a new height of artistic achievement. And the state takeover of silver production gave fresh impetus to precious metalworking. Silks and jewelry must have echoed this flowering, but of these there is as yet distressingly little firm evidence.

Above: Shapur III (383–388 AD) killing a leopard: a silver dish, partially gilded, in the Hermitage Museum, Leningrad. On the reverse is a Sogdian inscription, probably of the 5th century. Diameter 27·6 cm.

Below: stamp seal and impression showing Bahram IV (388–399 AD) standing on a defeated enemy. The apron skirt came into fashion in the late 4th century. 3·1 × 1·9 cm. British Museum.

Takht-i Sulaiman:
The City of the
Warriors' Fire

The focal point of the Sasanian city of Shīz or Ganzak, as Takht-i Sulaiman was then known, was the great lake at its center, apparently bottomless, from which water has never ceased to flow. This water is exceptionally rich in minerals which are deposited wherever it runs. Thus, over the millennia, the water has formed for itself a stone basin with sheer sides over 40 meters deep, and has made numerous stone channels down the hillsides.

Much of the area enclosed within the buttressed outer walls is occupied by the sacred precinct, for the purpose of this city with its inexhaustible lake was religious: it housed the Fire Temple of the King and of the Warriors (Atur Gushnasp). The site was an important religious center long before the Sasanian period – traces of both Parthian and Achaemenian occupation have been found in tests made below the Sasanian floors. Earlier still a

shrine was built around the Zendan-i Sulaiman nearby. This great stone basin also once contained a lake but, the side cracked and the water rushed away.

The ruins visible today at the Takht mostly belong to the Sasanian period, for the strongly constructed rubble-and-mortar buildings survived the sack by Heraclius in 624 AD and many still stand to a considerable height. The very durability of the buildings – the vaulted and domed roofs did not crash down and seal the floors – enabled the site to be thoroughly plundered. The great temple treasures were of course carried away by Heraclius, but long after this, when the site was occupied by squatters, the buildings continued to be emptied of anything useful. The Takht is therefore exceptionally rich in architecture, with nearly all the plan of the sacred precinct already recovered, but poor in objects.

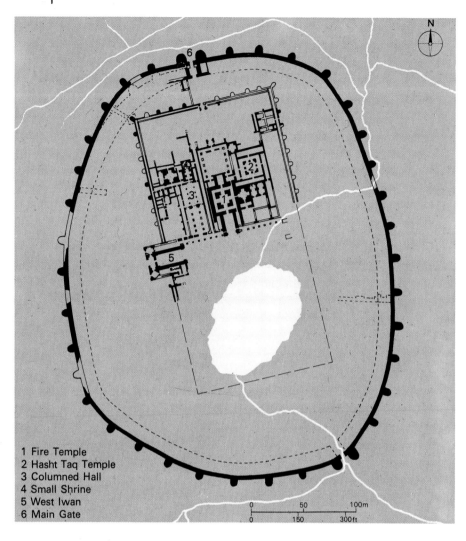

1 Fire Temple
2 Hasht Taq Temple
3 Columned Hall
4 Small Shrine
5 West Iwan
6 Main Gate

Above and right: the southern gate, with a decorative motif in the form of a row of Sasanian keyhole arches. The defensive buttresses flanking the gateway have been restored. A water channel runs under the arch.

Left: plan of the late Sasanian city. The sacred precinct was enclosed by the rectangular walls. The site was bisected by a Processional Way which ran straight from the main entrance at the north (6 on the plan) to the shrine of the Fire Temple (1), and on to the lake. The second axis of the site connected the great palace *iwan* at the west (5) to the corresponding one opposite, now only a heap of rubble.

Below left: morning roll call: men whose names have been checked walk off to their trenches. The hard stony surface, under which lies the southern wall of the sacred precinct, was formed by the lake waters when they flowed uncontrolled over the site.

Opposite above: the buttressed city walls of Shiz from the north. These were wide enough for a sentry's walk along the top.

Opposite below: workmen carrying a large carved block of red sandstone across to the dig house. The block originally belonged to a Mongol palace but had been reused by squatters.

Left: the sanctuary of the Fire Temple. Two of the four great brick piers which carried the dome can be seen, as well as the door leading out to the North Iwan (*below left*). On ceremonial occasions the fire altar would have stood in the center of the sanctuary in a direct line between the main entrance and the lake. The Fire Temple was the only building on the Takht constructed of baked bricks, with which the floor was also paved: this pavement has been covered with soil to protect it.

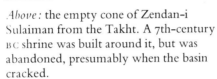

Opposite: the lake and West Iwan from the south on a windy morning.

Below: the stony edge of the lake: channels cut in the sides lower the water level. In the background, the West Iwan.

Above: the empty cone of Zendan-i Sulaiman from the Takht. A 7th-century BC shrine was built around it, but was abandoned, presumably when the basin cracked.

Left and right: the fortunate find of a hoard of clay *bullae*, or labels stamped with seal impressions, proved that the Fire Temple at the Takht was indeed Atur Gushnasp, or the Royal Fire.

Left: a doorway in the Fire Temple showing the characteristic Sasanian keyhole form. This enabled the arch to be economically built on centering balanced on the imposts.

Far left: the north facade of the Fire Temple, showing the foundations of the large entrance *iwan*.

Right: one of the four massive pillars in the Fire Temple.

Left: the "Hasht Taq" or Eight Arches Temple. Built of fine masonry, the shrine was surrounded by four long magazines or storerooms. The Zendan can be seen in the distance.

Center left: the ruins of the West Iwan from the north. The niches in the facade are a Mongol feature added to the Sasanian structure.

Below: part of one of the vaulted rooms beside the West Iwan.

Left: the columned hall to the west of the Fire Temple. This may have been the palace of Khusrau: the door in the back wall leads through into a small shrine with an altar. When the roof showed signs of collapse the builders tried to shore it up by adding the two square columns in the center.

6. Khusrau of the Immortal Soul

I saw a ruined palace towering high
    Where monarchs once in splendour ruled supreme
Now on its walls a mournful ring-dove sat
    And softly murmured cooing, "Where? Where? Where?"

OMAR KHAYYAM

Dominance of the east. New tribal movements in Central Asia caused widespread disruption in the civilized world at the end of the 4th and during the 5th centuries. Shapur II had defeated the Chionites and had even persuaded them to help him in his Roman wars, but after his death Huns had ravaged Armenia, Syria and Cappadocia, as well, probably, as parts of northern Iran. Who exactly these Chionites, Kidarites, Huns who called themselves Kushans, and White Huns were is not made clear in the predominantly western sources. Shapur's successors succeeded in holding the eastern frontier and Bahram V (421–439) was victorious in his eastern campaigns. However, his son Yazdigird II (439–457) died without having obtained peace on the eastern frontier and this was the beginning of a decisive change in the balance of power between Iran and a formidable new enemy, the Hephthalite Huns. The Hephthalite Huns had established themselves in Bactria in the middle of the 4th century and were at the height of their power from c. 460 to 530, controlling an extensive empire centered on Afghanistan.

On Yazdigird's death his two sons fought for the throne: the younger one Peroz or Firuz (457/9–484) was ultimately successful, but he only won with the help of the

Above: desert landscape near Yazd.

Previous page: Khusrau I, or his father Kavad, on a silver dish in the Hermitage Museum: seated on a throne supported by winged horses, the king is attended by four nobles. Diameter 26 cm.

Hephthalites. Despite this debt, Peroz renewed war in the east in the 460s but his campaign was a total failure and he himself was captured in 469. He was forced to agree to pay a large ransom and had to leave his son Kavad as a hostage in the Hephthalite court until it was paid. This military disaster coincided with a terrible drought and consequent famine that lasted for seven long years. This drought was vividly remembered in the great Persian national epic, the *Shahname* or Book of Kings, compiled by the poet Firdausi early in the 11th century AD: "the air dried up and water in the channels became scarce as musk . . . because of the drought no man was left with sufficient food. The mouth of the atmosphere became dry as the dust and in the channels water was rare as theriac." To try to help his people Peroz "lifted all tax and levies from the world, and wheresoever he had a hidden granary in a town he gave away what it contained to small and great."

Hephthalite control of Central Asia and Afghanistan

probably caused interruptions to the overland east-west trade route, and this may have forced Peroz once again to challenge his powerful eastern neighbor. He began this campaign in 484 – and led the flower of Sasanian chivalry into a terrible trap. The Hephthalite king had prepared a deep concealed ditch, filled with sharp stakes, which ran right across a plain except for a narrow channel in the middle. The Sasanian forces were decoyed there by a group of Hephthalite cavalry apparently retreating. As the Hephthalites fled, carefully crossing the bridge, the Sasanian knights spread out across the plain and charged their quarry at full speed. They crashed headlong into the ditch. Those behind were following so fast and so closely that they fell in on top of those who had already fallen. Nearly the whole army was utterly destroyed and the king died with his men.

After this overwhelming disaster peace was made, but Iran had to agree to pay a heavy annual tribute to the Hephthalites. By this time the monarchy had again lost power to the nobles, who first elected Peroz' brother Balash or Valgash (484–488) and then deposed him after a reign of only four years in favor of Peroz' son, Kavad. He too was deposed and imprisoned in 496 but succeeded in escaping and fled to his former hosts, the Hephthalites, who restored the Sasanian throne to him in 498/9, presumably preferring to have their own protégé as king of Iran.

The condition of the people within Iran at this time must have been appalling with the combined effects of the prolonged drought, heavy taxation to meet the cost of the annual tribute and internal near anarchy. This prompted the rise of a new prophet, Mazdak, who was probably originally a Zoroastrian priest but one with a distinctively new message. Mazdak's doctrine consisted of a call against violence coupled with a form of primitive communism which had an obvious appeal to the starving and desperate people. He told them that "an empty-handed fellow was the equal of any rich man, that no one person should claim superiority over another, since the rich were the warp and the poor the weft. In the matter of possessions, he said, the world must be made equitable; it was unlawful and an evil thing for the rich to have excess. Women, houses and material goods were all to be equitably distributed" (Firdausi). Mazdak succeeded in convincing Kavad by his eloquence and he flourished for much of Kavad's reign, perhaps because the king was using him to try to lessen the power of the nobles. Towards the end of Kavad's reign, however, he and a number of his followers were executed, according to Firdausi by order of the Crown Prince Khusrau. Khusrau was Kavad's youngest son but had been chosen to be his successor some years before Kavad died.

The glory of Khusrau. Iran entirely recovered her former power during the long and glorious reign of Khusrau Anushirwan (of the Immortal Soul), both internally and externally, and any peasant asked today about ancient ruins will readily reply that it was the work of the mighty Khusrau. His first task was a complete reorganization of the demoralized Persian state, which was impoverished, deeply torn by Mazdak's doctrines and threatened on every frontier. To give himself time to undertake this massive task Khusrau made peace with the Romans and continued the payment of the annual tribute to the Hephthalites.

Khusrau's reforms affected every aspect of life. First the land was surveyed and measured, a task which had been begun by Kavad, and all the date palms, vines, olive, nut and fruit trees were counted. Using this accurate assessment of the agricultural potential of his country, on which was based the prosperity of Iran, Khusrau entirely reformed the tax system. The old yearly assessment had resulted in the frequent spoiling of crops, which could only be gathered after the assessor had been. It was replaced by a fixed annual levy reckoned on the average of past harvests. This levy had to be paid in three installments in cash and not in kind. Each farmer was therefore able to plan ahead, knowing his commitments in advance, and the state greatly benefited by having a steady cash income. A head tax was also levied on men between the ages of 20 and 50, although this only applied to the common people – nobles, priests and bureaucracy were exempt.

With an assured annual income Khusrau was able to institute far-ranging military reforms. Instead of expecting all the nobles to equip themselves and their followers and to serve without pay, which had been a standing invitation to disaffection, Khusrau both paid and fitted out the poorer knights – owners of a village rather than of landed estates – and thus in effect created a new class of soldier loyal only to himself. These *dihqans* became an essential part of Iranian society and it was partly through them that Iranian ideas and administration were later transmitted to the conquering Arabs. This new class of soldier greatly increased the efficiency of the army and at the same time lessened the power of the great nobles with their huge private armies.

In a further important reform Khusrau divided Iran militarily into four zones, each of which was commanded by a general: the general of the east commanded Khurasan, Seistan (Sakastan) and Kerman and was expected to hold the northern and eastern frontiers; the general of the south commanded Persis and Susiana including much of the long Persian Gulf coast; the general of the west was in control of Mesopotamia, the richest agricultural area and the one most exposed to Roman attack; while the last general commanded Media and Azerbaijan together with the vital passes over the Caucasus. Khusrau looked to the reinforcement of his frontiers, settling families near them with the duty of defending them, and it was probably he who built the great wall in the Gurgan plain, as well as repairing and rebuilding other defenses and fortresses, particularly those guarding the Caucasus passes. As the Arabs discovered later, Iran's defenses were concentrated on the frontiers: the interior was left empty of warriors.

Khusrau was also concerned with checking the moral malaise of his people, the result of recent hardship and of the Mazdakite excesses. In particular the Mazdakite sharing of women had led to misery. Those women who had left their husbands were restored to them, and those who had been ravished were married to their abusers. A national register was made of widows and orphans, and each received the help that he or she required. The ownership of property, too, was clarified and many ruined villages were rebuilt.

With the organization of state finance Khusrau was also able to carry out massive irrigation works and the various archaeological surveys so far undertaken suggest a vast increase in population, in sophisticated irrigation works including the construction of canals and weirs, and in a much more intensive and widespread use of land in the Sasanian period. One of his state-sponsored works was probably the construction of a large canal, known as the "Cut of Chosroes," which was designed to supplement water supplies in the Diyala river area by bringing some from the Tigris. The importance that Khusrau attached to the prosperity of agriculture is well summed up in his philosophy of kingship, preserved in a text written by the 10th-century writer Masudi:

"Royal power rests upon the army, and the army upon money, and money upon the land-tax, and the land-tax upon agriculture, and agriculture upon just administration, and just administration upon the integrity of government officials, and the integrity of government officials upon the reliability of the vizier, and the pinnacle of all of these is the vigilance of the king in resisting his own inclinations, and his capability so to guide them that he rules them and they do not rule him."

Khusrau spent eight years reorganizing the Iranian state and army and preparing to restore Iran's former military and political position. He then repudiated his treaty with Byzantium and in 540 invaded Syria, primarily in search of plunder: intermittent warfare continued on this front for the next 20 years. The history of these wars has been recorded in detail by Procopius, secretary to Justinian's brilliant general Belisarius, though predictably his outlook is somewhat biased and he painted Khusrau as a treacherous Oriental despot. Khusrau's swift advance into Syria soon brought him before the walls of Antioch, which after a fierce battle fell to the Persians.

"Chosroes commanded the army to capture and enslave the survivors of the population of Antioch, and to plunder all the property, while he himself with the ambassadors descended from the height to the sanctuary which they call a church. There Chosroes found stores of gold and silver so great in amount that, though he took no other part of the booty except these stores, he departed possessed of enormous wealth. And he took down from there many wonderful marbles and ordered them to be deposited outside the fortifications, in order that they might convey these too to the land of Persia" (Procopius).

To house the deported population of Antioch Khusrau built a new city on the outskirts of the Sasanian capital city of Ctesiphon, which he called Veh az Antiok Khusro or "Better than Antioch [has] Khusrau [built this]." It was still flourishing when the Arabs conquered Mesopotamia.

A 50-year peace treaty was finally agreed and signed in 561, though it did not last long. The Persian objective of these wars had been to regain territory east of the Euphrates and they succeeded in making considerable gains. Furthermore, by 579 when Khusrau died, much of Armenia was again in the Sasanian sphere of influence.

Khusrau finally felt strong enough to repudiate the agreement to pay the Hephthalites an annual tribute and allied himself in about 557 with the Turks, who had recently arrived in Trans-Oxiana. Together they utterly defeated the Hephthalite forces and divided the kingdom between themselves: the Turks took the territories north of the Oxus while Khusrau ruled over much of Afghanistan. The exact extent of his new eastern territories is not known, although he probably controlled the important Buddhist community in the Bamiyan valley. More importantly Persian defeats at the hands of the Hephthalites had finally been avenged and Persian honor restored. He issued a coin with the poignant inscription "Iran delivered from fear."

The importance of trade. Revenues from east-west trade continued to be a vital Iranian interest and it was during the reign of Khusrau that Byzantium sought once again to try to break the Sasanian monopoly. From the time of the foundation of the Sasanian dynasty by Ardashir I, the Sasanian kings had been aware of the advantages of promoting maritime trade and, as conditions deteriorated for safe overland transit with the movement of the Huns in Central Asia, so the attractions of maritime trade increased. The punitive expedition which Shapur II had led deep into Arabia early in his reign had been in response to Arab raids in the Persian Gulf and to fears of the possible loss of Sasanian control of the seas. By the reign of Bahram V direct Sasanian rule extended along the Gulf coast to the Indus delta, where the king had been given the port of Daibul (Banbhore) as part of the dowry when he married an Indian princess. But control of the actual ports was only part of Sasanian policy; they also physically prevented western shipping from buying cargoes at ports outside their actual jurisdiction for "the Persian merchants always locate themselves at the very harbors where the Indian ships first put in . . . and are accustomed to buy the whole cargo" (Procopius).

Justinian was determined to try once again to break the Sasanian stranglehold on trade and approached the Christian Ethiopians, proposing that, because of their common faith, they should be allies and suggesting that the Ethiopians should buy silk from the Indians for sale to the Romans so that they "might themselves gain much money, while causing the Romans to profit in only one way, namely, that they be no longer compelled to pay over their money to their enemy." Khusrau was successful in resisting the Ethiopian attempts at expansion into the Yemen and by the time of his death in 579 southern Arabia had become a dependency of Sasanian Iran. Sasanian ships were actually based in Aden, thus effectively controlling the entrance to the Red Sea and finally closing the Indian Ocean to Roman shipping. During the whole of the 6th century Iranian merchants dominated trade with India and Ceylon, in whose ports Sasanian ships were regular visitors. But what is not as yet certain is whether or not Sasanian ships traveled further east in search of their wares.

The Bamiyan valley in Afghanistan, site of an important Buddhist monastery. After the defeat of the Hephthalites this probably formed part of Khusran's territory.

Certainly by the end of the 8th century, after the fall of the Sasanian dynasty, there was direct maritime trade between China and the Persian Gulf, to which the prosperity of such Gulf ports as Siraf bears vivid witness: it may well be that Sasanian merchants traveled further east than Ceylon.

Khusrau has been remembered through the centuries not only for his imperial successes, great though these were, but also for his sense of justice and chivalry, and for his care for the common people. He made sure, Firdausi tells us, that "no villager should be reduced to distress. He that had no seed or cattle when the time came for cultivation was provided with them from the king's treasuries and no ground was left to lie without being tilled . . . The shah covered the face of the earth with his justice; wherever land was deserted he brought it into cultivation. Any man, small or great, could lie down to sleep in the open, and to the water hole there came the ewe

as well as the wolf." Khusrau was also famed for his constant search for knowledge, and many Pahlavi books were written in his reign. Although he enforced Zoroastrian orthodoxy, with its consequent rigid class structure, he did not persecute minorities. Indeed he welcomed Greek physicians and thinkers to his court and founded a university at Gundeshapur. Many stories are told of his wise vizier Buzurjmihr who is credited with the invention of a favorite Persian game, *nard* or backgammon. Another popular game at the time was polo.

Despite this brilliance – Iran was at the height of her glory – the days of the Sasanian dynasty were numbered. A few years before Khusrau I Anushirwan died "on a Monday on the 13th day of the month of Rabi in the year of the Elephant" (c. 570) the Prophet Muhammad was born. The crusading armies of Islam were utterly to destroy Sasanian power a mere 70 years later in two crushing victories at Qadisiya in 636 and Nihavand in 642, but before these disastrous defeats Khusrau's grandson Khusrau II Parviz (the Victorious), was to carry Sasanian arms further west than ever before, to capture Jerusalem and Egypt and even to lay siege to Constantinople itself. This feat is all the more remarkable when it is known that

The golden "cup of Khusrau" in the Bibliothèque Nationale. The rock crystal medallion in the center shows Khusrau seated on a throne supported by winged horses. This is set in a golden frame inlaid with colored glass paste, red, white and green. Diameter 28 cm.

Khusrau II Parviz was not able to achieve it by building on the considerable military successes of his namesake and grandfather. After the death of Khusrau I Anushirwan the Sasanian empire had almost collapsed and Khusrau II owed his very throne to outside assistance – that of Iran's long-time enemy, Byzantium. But how did this amazing double *volte face* in Sasanian fortunes occur?

Khusrau the self-willed. Hormuzd IV (579–590) succeeded his father Khusrau I peacefully and the exhausting struggle against Byzantium continued unabated. Taking advantage of Sasanian preoccupation in the west, the Turks attacked in the northeast and Hormuzd dispatched an army led by the Iranian noble, Bahram Chubin, to contain the Turkish threat. Many stories in Arabic and Persian literature, and of course in the *Shahname*, have been told of this remarkable man, an Iranian warrior *par excellence*, "a general proud as a male lion," a "Pahlavan" with "magnificent stature, ready speech and clear intelligence." Bahram Chubin defeated the Turks and was thereafter also victorious against the nomadic Khazars in the Caucasus and against the Byzantines. Using a later defeat by the Byzantines, Hormuzd IV, who was worried by Bahram's popularity and success, tried to remove him from office, but Bahram revolted and the king found himself surrounded by enemies. He was seized, blinded, imprisoned and later murdered and his son, Khusrau, unable to defeat Bahram, fled to the west. Bahram crowned himself "lord of the world." Had he been a member of the Sasanian royal family instead of the Mihr-ran family of Rayy, Bahram might well have succeeded in holding on to the kingship. Instead, after only a year, Khusrau, with the active military assistance of the Byzantine emperor Maurice, succeeded in defeating him and Bahram fled to the Turks, by whom he was assassinated a year later, probably at the request of Khusrau.

Even though Khusrau II was now king, internal revolt was not ended in Iran. Khusrau tried to punish those who had overthrown his father and supported Bahram, and some of these fled and fostered further trouble. Among these was Khusrau's uncle, who maintained his independence in the Rayy area, minting his own coins, for nearly ten years before he too was murdered. For failing to support him, Khusrau also attacked the king of the Lakhmid Arabs, which vassal dynasty had long served an important role acting as a buffer between the Arabs of the desert, over whom they asserted hegemony, and the rich cultivated plains of Iraq, the granary of the Sasanian empire. Khusrau deposed the Lakhmid king and replaced him with a Persian governor. This was a serious tactical error for it exposed lower Iraq to attacks from the Arabs. Defenses along this frontier were weak, little having been done since Shapur II had built a long canal from Hit on the Euphrates to near Basra, the Khandak Shapur, to act as a deterrent. While the Lakhmids were in control, weak defenses had been unimportant but their inadequacy was soon exposed. In about 604 an Arab alliance decisively defeated Persian forces in the battle of Dhu Qar, thus foreshadowing the downfall of the empire. Khusrau's energies were, however, still directed towards the centuries-old struggle with the west: he failed to recognize the significance of rising Arab power in the south which, when fired with crusading zeal, was to sweep all before it.

Khusrau II had won his throne with Byzantine support and as a result the exhausting state of war between the two empires ceased. But in 602 Maurice was murdered by Phokas, an officer of the Byzantine army in the Balkans, which was in revolt, and Phokas became emperor (602–610). Khusrau was determined to avenge his former patron and from 604 to 610 the Persians won several important victories and conquered much of Armenia, Cappadocia and Syria. In that year Phokas was deposed and executed and Heraclius (610–641) ascended the throne. He tried to make peace with Khusrau but the Persian, fired by dreams of glory and convinced of Sasanian invincibility, rejected his offer and embarked on a career of conquest that briefly recreated the Achaemenian empire. Persian armies overran the Near East: in 612 Antioch, Damascus and Tarsus fell; in 614 Jerusalem was taken and the True Cross brought to Ctesiphon; in 615 much of Anatolia was conquered and in 619 the Persians besieged Alexandria, which soon fell, and all Egypt was occupied.

Many stories are told of this last great Sasanian king and of his stormy career, but they are amazingly contradictory. According to some traditions he was cruel, suspicious, treacherous, cowardly and avaricious, while he has also been described as a champion warrior, tolerant of different faiths, who built around himself a magnificent court, fabled for its luxury and etiquette. This luxury and etiquette were described by Firdausi writing of the preparations for a royal hunt:

"Thus . . . there were brought along 300 led horses with golden trappings. On foot there were 1,160 loyal slaves with javelins in their hands, in addition to whom he had 1,040 wearing cloaks or brocade with armor beneath and carrying staves and swords. Running behind them came 700 falconers with sparrow hawks, lanners and royal falcons. After the falconers came 300 men on horseback all bearing panthers. There were also there 70 lions and leopards attached to chains firmly fastened and wearing coats of Chinese brocade, and there were other leopards and lions trained and muzzled with gold chains. Also there were 700 hounds collared in gold which seize gazelle at the gallop. Accompanying all were 2,000 minstrels ready to play airs on hunting days. Each was mounted on a camel and wore on his head a golden coronet."

Famous musicians, including the minstrel Barbad whom "no one could play like," were attracted to Khusrau's court, and in a well-known text describing the proper education of a page, knowledge of musical instruments was considered to be essential, together with that of rare foods, perfumes and games. But Khusrau's rich and glittering court was achieved at the expense of his people, for as Firdausi wrote, "the king, who had at one time been himself the giver of justice, turned to injustice . . . Always imposing new burdens, his one demand was for fresh treasure. He extorted money from all, ever adding that to this and this to that. The blessings of yore now turned to curses on the king, who, after having been a mild ewe, had turned into a ravening wolf."

No account of this extraordinary king is complete without mentioning that he was also the hero of the Persian love story *par excellence*, the *Romance of Khusrau and Shirin*, which has been told and retold by many poets, including Firdausi and the famous Nizami. The beauty of Shirin, extolled in many verses, rivaled that of the moon. Shirin was a Christian and for most of Khusrau's reign Christianity was encouraged and spread throughout the empire.

The end of Sasanian rule. But Khusrau's comet was short-lived. Although Heraclius had nearly fled from Constantinople, attacked as he was by the Sasanians in the east and by an alliance of the Slavs and Avars in the Balkans, he stayed on and organized a remarkable defense, which was based on Byzantine control of the sea, an advantage the Sasanians had no way of defeating. In 622 Heraclius sailed into the Black Sea and launched a successful offensive behind the Persian front against Armenia. The Persians, unprepared, were defeated and Heraclius won back Asia Minor. The next year he again attacked Armenia and penetrated Persian defenses, invading Azerbaijan. He sacked the great Sasanian sanctuary and Temple of the Sacred Fire of Gushnasp at Ganzak or Shiz (modern Takht-i Sulaiman), to which every Sasanian king made a pilgrimage.

Heraclius again advanced through Azerbaijan in 627 and marched into Mesopotamia, once more defeating the Persians. He sacked Khusrau's favorite palace of Dastagird, where he found prodigious quantities of treasure. After this disastrous series of reverses Khusrau was desperate and recalled all his generals, hunting for a scapegoat. But a revolt broke out and he was murdered. His death marks the end of effective Sasanian rule, though a variety of puppet kings and even one queen, Boran, a learned daughter of Khusrau II, were installed by the nobility and continued nominally to rule until the Arab invasion.

Khusrau's switchback career reflects both the strengths and the weaknesses of the reorganization carried out by his grandfather, Khusrau Anushirwan. With such a precise knowledge of the financial resources of the empire taxes could be, and were, raised to intolerable levels without chance of evasion. The creation of the four military areas under four *spahbads* gave those men overwhelming power, as was shown first by Bahram Chubin's seizure of power and then by one of Khusrau's generals, Shahrbaraz, who also ascended the throne for a while after Khusrau's murder. A third fatal weakness was the Sasanian preoccupation with the west. By concentrating all his energy on the old conflict with Byzantium and by trying to restore the long-lost frontiers of the Achaemenian empire, Khusrau failed to recognize the new danger in the south, the rising strength of which had been illustrated as early as 604. And it was the Arabs not the Byzantines who were to be the new masters of Iran.

The Arab victory over the Sasanian dynasty was complete. After the two decisive battles at Qadisiya in 637 and Nihavand in 642, the last king Yazdigird III fled to Merv where he was murdered in 651. After his death few members of the Sasanian royal family were left alive to raise a revolt, even had they been able to do so. But Sasanian traditions in both government and the arts continued and flourished long after the death of Yazdigird. The new conquerors lacked the administrative machinery necessary to govern their vast new territories and they had to take over not only Sasanian organization but also Sasanian bureaucrats. Among those who escaped the wholesale slaughter of the initial conquest, even important nobles, provided they were "converted," were allowed to continue in positions of power. By this time Zoroastrianism had become stifled by the weight of state sponsorship and had failed to respond to the new religious challenges surrounding it, except by the negative reaction of persecution. Christianity was flourishing throughout the empire. Since Persians were eligible for office if they accepted Islam or even if they were converted to Christianity, many did so and survived. Among these were many of the *dihqan* class, created by Khusrau I, who made themselves indispensable to their new masters. Their survival facilitated the transfer of Sasanian organization and tradition.

The palace of Khusrau I at Ctesiphon. Late Sasanian architecture faithfully reflected the revived glory of the Iranian monarchy in this final century of power. The most famous Sasanian building of all time was the palace which Khusrau I built at Ctesiphon, known as the Taq or Iwan-i Kisra (the hall of Khusrau). The geographer Ibn Khurdadbih (c. 864) described Khusrau's palace as the most beautiful ever built of brick and plaster, while others found its enormous size so impressive that they could hardly believe that it was the work of men not of genies. Other writers, including Tabari (838–922), have recorded details of the throne hall and described the elaborate ritual surrounding an audience with the Great King.

Part of the skeleton of Khusrau's enormous throne hall still stands today, and the complete facade was preserved as late as 1888, when some of it collapsed as a result of a disastrous flood. This facade, with its great central arch opening to the east, formed one side of a huge courtyard, the rest of which has disappeared. Opposite it was a second huge *iwan* facing west, of which only traces remain in the ground. The great parabolic barrel vault of the Taq-i Kisra is nearly 35 meters high with a span of over 25 meters and a length of nearly 50 meters. It is the largest example of such an arch, built without centering, in any facade in the world and it is nearly twice as large as that built by Ardashir some 300 years earlier in his palace at Firuzabad. With no experience of the stresses imposed by building on such a gigantic scale, Khusrau's architects constructed walls of exceptional thickness to be sure that they were

Opposite: aerial view of the palace of Khusrau at Ctesiphon. The outline of the second great *iwan*, which stood opposite the Taq-i Kisra, can be seen in the ground.

Right: detail of the decoration on the facade of the Taq-i Kisra, or Hall of Khusrau, at Ctesiphon.

Below: general view of the Taq-i Kisra. The fallen section (to the right) is currently being reconstructed by the Iraq Department of Antiquities.

able to withstand the enormous thrust, 4 meters at the impost and 7 below. Even the crown of the vault was a meter thick. The plan of the structure was essentially simple – the effect sought was one of massive size – although it was unusual. The great *iwan* was connected to a massive closed hall by a series of small rooms, the whole central unit being flanked by corridors and long vaulted rooms.

As at Parthian Assur the huge void of the *iwan* was compensated for by decorating the facade with blind architecture consisting of engaged columns, entablatures and niches, which was arranged in six stories and topped with the traditional row of crenellations. The internal walls were richly ornamented with the multicolored marble slabs taken from the Christian church at Antioch, and with glass mosaics showing battle scenes such as Khusrau on a yellow horse at the siege of that city, doubtless prepared by captured craftsmen. The floors were made of thick marble plaques which were covered with silk carpets representing gardens with their trees and water channels. The throne was set towards the back of the great *iwan*, placed behind a screen or curtain, which was only drawn back when the king, seated on a cushion of golden brocade on his throne, was ready to give audience. Khusrau wore a tunic of a rich material embroidered in gold thread, doubtless similar to that sculpted on the walls of the *iwan* at Taq-i Bustan (see below). On his head he was apparently carrying an enormous crown made of gold and silver and decorated with pearls, rubies and emeralds. This massive object weighed more than 90 kilos and was far too heavy for any head to carry, so it was suspended from the top of the vault by a long gold chain. The chain was sufficiently slender not to be visible to the mass of the people and courtiers who were kept at prescribed distances from the king. This somewhat theatrical presentation of the remote and glittering figure of the famous King of Kings, Khusrau Anushirwan, epitomized the majesty of the Sasanian king and people fell involuntarily to their knees in awe.

The appearance of the king much as he must have been seen on his throne in the Taq-i Kisra is shown on a rock-crystal medallion set in the center of a famous golden cup now in the Bibliothèque Nationale in Paris and said to be that presented by the Caliph Harun al-Rashid to the Emperor Charlemagne. The king, probably to be identified by his crown with Khusrau, is richly dressed and seated on a superb throne with supports in the form of winged horses. The king's hands rest on his jeweled sword.

Takht-i Sulaiman. It was probably Khusrau who refurbished one of the most important religious centers of the dynasty, the Temple of Atur Gushnasp or the fire of the king and the warriors. Thanks to the recovery of *bullae* inscribed with the name of the temple, we actually know its location: it was built at modern Takht-i Sulaiman (the throne of Solomon), which lies in the mountains to the southwest of Lake Urmia/Rezaieh. In the reign of Khusrau the city was known as Shiz or Ganzak and, according to Ibn Khurdadbih, it was visited by every king after his coronation. Many of them endowed it with great treasure.

Water has long been venerated on the dry Iranian plateau and so it is not surprising that a mound which was itself created by an extraordinary natural phenomenon, the incessant flow of water from its center, was chosen as the site of an important shrine. The rocky mound which the buildings of Takht-i Sulaiman crown was formed over the millennia by the steady deposit of minerals from the water which flowed out of the inexhaustible lake at its center. The sheer walls of the lake grew higher and higher and had formed a hill as early as the Achaemenian period, although this was not allowed to grow much higher in the following centuries for channels cut in the lake sides let the water rush away.

The earliest levels appear to be Achaemenian but there was an older shrine within sight of the Takht built around an even higher conical hill formed in the same way and known as the Zendan-i Sulaiman (prison of Solomon). This 8th/7th-century BC shrine had to be abandoned after an earthquake had cracked the steep sides of the stone basin. The water flooded out and left the deep hollow cone empty and smelling strongly of sulfur. This same overpowering smell is experienced today at the countless bubbling pools of varying temperatures which abound in the area.

There were at least two major phases of construction at the Takht during the Sasanian period. The earlier one surrounded the top of the hill in a massive mud-brick wall and the later one reinforced this by an outer skin of finely cut masonry. These stone walls, largely standing today, are approximately oval in shape and are strengthened by numerous rounded buttresses. The main entrance was through a strongly fortified gate at the north from which a "processional way" ran due south into a walled rectangular inner enclosure or sacred precinct. This occupies most of the space within the city walls: the northern half contained a large complex of religious buildings while the lake fills most of the southern half.

The principal temple, that of Atur Gushnasp, is sited in the sacred precinct on the main north-south axis of the site. It was approached from the north along the "processional way" through a pillared courtyard, the most dominant feature of which was the large *iwan* leading into the shrine. The shrine itself is square in plan and contains four great piers. These carried the dome and effectively formed within the shrine an inner room with an ambulatory – a plan familiar from Parthian times. The fire altar was placed in the center on a paved brick floor. This domed square unit pierced by four arches is the standard form of Iranian fire temple or Chahar Taq (four arches), many examples of which have been found throughout Iran. All that usually remains today are the ruins of the four great piers which supported the dome, for the relatively weak outer walls have disintegrated and left no trace above ground. A particularly well-preserved example of a Chahar Taq was found by Vanden Berghe in an isolated and dramatic mountain setting at Tang-i Chak Chak. In addition to the Chahar Taq with its four great stone piers there was a second enclosed domed chamber nearby, an Ateshqadeh, in which the fire was kept.

There were many fires throughout Iran, both large and small. Nearly every town or village had its own fire, in addition to which there were the important provincial (or Bahram) fires. These were usually founded by the king, though an eminent noble such as Mihr-Narseh in the reign of Yazdigird I could also acquire merit by founding fire temples, which he did in the Farrashband valley near Firuzabad. Each social class had its own fire: while the Gushnasp fire was that of royalty and of the warriors, the priests had the Farnbag fire and the peasants the Burzin-Mihr fire. Only the location of the Atur Gushnasp is known to date.

As in any major shrine, there were many other temples and shrines built close to the principal Chahar Taq. One to the northeast, which was built of cut stone instead of fired brick, shows a unique development of the standard plan. Instead of the usual four pillars the sanctuary has eight and has thus been called the Hasht Taq or eight arches. Four long magazines enclose the shrine, which was clearly a building of some importance, even though it only has a twisting and insignificant entrance. Leading out of the Chahar Taq to the east was a small square room with a deep niche in each wall. There are four of these niched shrines at the Takht in one of which were found the remains of an altar socle.

The lake, the *raison d'être* of the site, was enclosed in a courtyard, of which only the plan of the northern end is yet known. Much of the rest has been sealed below layers of the hard stony deposit of the lake waters, thus making excavation extremely difficult. The dominant feature of the northern facade is, of course, the large *iwan* of the Chahar Taq, which was linked by a colonnaded facade to *iwans* in the east and west. Only the wall footings of the east *iwan* remain above ground, although much of the west *iwan* is still standing. It led into small rooms behind and was flanked by long halls, and is thus reminiscent of the plan of the Taq-i Kisra at Ctesiphon. Forming part of this northern facade and located between the west *iwan* and that of the Chahar Taq were two long columned halls which formed a separate unit within the sacred precinct

The Fire Temple (Chahar Taq) and House of Fire (Ateshqadeh) at Tang-i Chak Chak, an isolated and dramatic mountain site.

and it may be that they were part of the famous palace of Khusrau.

The 20 years of sustained effort which the German Archaeological Institute has put into this remarkable site have uncovered much of the plan of the most important religious city in Iran. But although we now know the form of some of the buildings and temples, we may never know what purpose they fulfilled and to whom the various shrines were dedicated, for unfortunately very little occupational debris or inscribed material of the Sasanian period has been found there. With the site's emphasis on water we should expect to find a temple dedicated to Anahita, although firm evidence is lacking and there is no trace of such an unequivocally water–orientated temple as that attributed to Anahita at Bishapur. Many rooms would have been needed for the storage of the temple treasures and of wood, for the winter at the Takht is bitterly cold. And there would also have to have been living quarters for the priests, as well as adequate accommodation for the king and his court.

Khusrau's city of Shiz was sacked by the Byzantine

Reconstruction of the palace at Qasr-i Shirin, built by Khusrau II, probably for the beautiful Shirin. After Reuther.

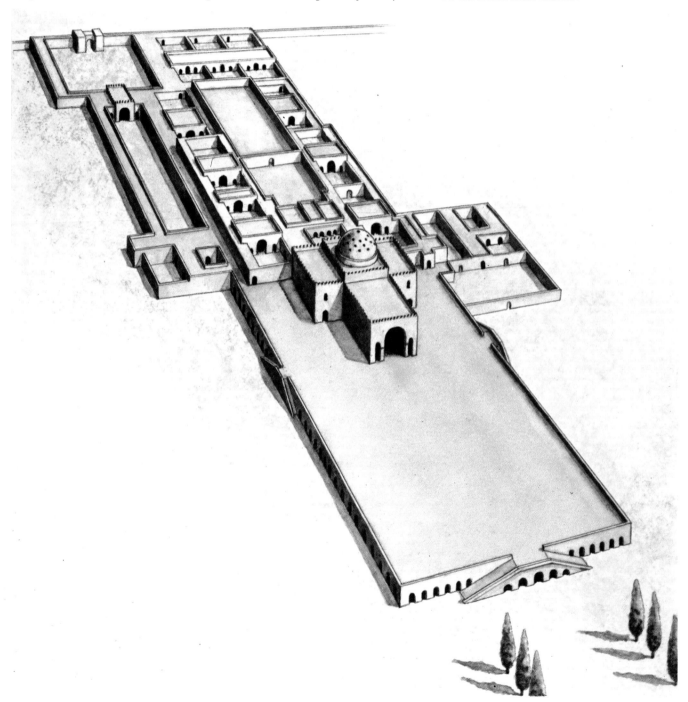

The stone stairs leading to the platform at Kangavar. Late Sasanian.

emperor Heraclius in 624 and all its rich treasures seized. But even after this the strongly constructed buildings continued to be lived in, initially by squatters who built workshops in the temple magazines. The site knew a second phase of royal patronage and glory in the Mongol period when Abaqa Khan (1265–81) is said to have drunk and womanized himself to death in the beautiful tiled palaces he built in the ruins of the Sasanian city.

Khusrau II's palace and sculpture. The buildings of Khusrau Parviz are remarkable more for their size than for architectural innovation or merit, as is well illustrated at Qasr-i Shirin. In an enormous paradise of nearly 300 acres, just where the plains of Iraq meet the great mountain wall of the Zagros, Khusrau built a palace for the beautiful Shirin and a large Chahar Taq with numerous supporting buildings, all of which were watered by an aqueduct taken off the river Hulwan.

Shirin's palace was built on a terrace some 8 meters high and measuring c. 285 × 98 meters, which was approached by a series of double flights of stairs similar to those giving access to the late Sasanian platform at Kangavar. The palace, which was still considered to be one of the wonders of the world by Yaqut in the 13th century, even though it had been sacked by Heraclius in 628, was set well back on the terrace. According to the 9th-century writer Ibn

Rustah, this was paved with marble. As at Firuzabad, the palace consisted of public and private apartments. The official reception rooms consisted of a large domed room, entered through an enormous *iwan*. The parabolic vault of the *iwan* rested on columns rather than on the side walls, a feature also seen in the Sasanian palace at Damghan. Behind the domed room was a pillared courtyard with another huge *iwan*. The private apartments consisted of a series of the traditional courtyard houses, relatively small and simple living units, usually with only a single *iwan* facing east.

Larger private houses of the same type were found at Ctesiphon, though these had from one to four *iwans* in the courtyard. They had been decorated with stucco panels and painted friezes. Brilliant friezes, mosaics and marble revetments had also been used to decorate the bath house, located to the west of the Taq-i Kisra. Water channels, pipes, a warming oven and a platform for resting after the bath prove the importance of bathing in the east as well as in the west at this time.

The most remarkable work attributed to Khusrau Parviz is not, however, the ruins of Qasr-i Shirin, nor even those of his favorite palace at Dastagird, which was also sacked by Heraclius, but is the rock sculpture at Taq-i Bustan near Kirmanshah. This art form, so popular with the early kings of the dynasty, had been abandoned since the 4th century. The initial impression of the Taq-i Bustan sculpture is, as at Qasr-i Shirin, the sheer magnitude of the undertaking, for Khusrau carved a huge *iwan* out of the living rock and decorated all its surfaces, the facade, as well as the back and side walls. The idea of placing a sculpture in an arched cave or *iwan* was not new, for Shapur III (383–388) had carved a small *iwan* out of the rock nearby and had placed statues of himself and his father on a ledge at the back: Shapur's inspiration for this type of monument may well have been Indian in origin.

Predictably the setting for Khusrau's sculptured building was magnificent: it was set beside a spring gushing out of a mountain in a hunting park or paradise. The facade was made to look like that of any Sasanian palace, an impression reinforced by the proximity of Shapur's *iwan*. The actual arch of Khusrau's *iwan* is decorated with an untied diadem, the ribbons at the ends of which flutter up. In the spandrels fly winged Victories, clearly western in inspiration, while lower down is an

The great grotto of Khusrau II at Taq-i Bustan. The arch of the *iwan*, which is carved out of the rock, is decorated with a diadem. Below is an ornate tree of life design. In the upper register on the back wall is the investiture of Khusrau II.

Above: the rich textiles worn by the Sasanian court are carefully recorded in this detail from the boar-hunt relief at Taq-i Bustan. The king's clothes in particular are lavishly decorated with *senmurv* motifs and floral designs. Over the rich and stiff tunic he wears a heavy jeweled collar and belt, as well as bracelets and almost certainly numerous finger rings.

Opposite: Khusrau II shooting a boar, first shown leaping towards him and then dead. Khusrau is accompanied by musicians in a second boat. From the boar-hunt scene.

ornate tree design of twisting branches, leaves and flowers.

Each side wall is covered with a hunting scene, a type of design unique in stone sculpture, although known in stucco and in fresco. The hunts, of boar on the left and deer on the right walls, take place within a huge fenced enclosure or paradise, all four sides of which are represented. Each stage of the hunt is shown in the single scene: mahouts on elephants flush out the boar from their marshy hiding places and drive herds of them across to where the king is waiting in his boat. The king, accompanied by lady musicians, is shown twice, first shooting a boar leaping towards him, and then at rest. Around the boats fishes and birds swim among the water plants. More mahouts collect the slain boars and carry them away at the end of the day. The whole makes an effective composition with the focus of the scene, the king, framed on all sides by a compact mass of animals. The same sequence of events occurs in the unfinished deer hunt on the other side, although there the king, shown three times, is mounted and is accompanied by his courtiers. The musicians are playing on a special stand at the top of the enclosure.

It is the scene on the back wall that was the real *raison d'être* of the sculptured *iwan*. Beneath the actual curve of the arch we see a late Sasanian version of the investiture

scene, so frequently depicted in the first century of Sasanian rule. Three figures are shown, the king standing between Ahuramazda and Anahita, both of whom offer Khusrau a diadem. He accepts the one offered by Ahuramazda but is unable to take that offered by Anahita for his left hand rests on his sword. Below this somewhat unsuccessful scene stands the symbol of the military might of the Sasanian empire – a fully armored knight on his charger. This represents Khusrau himself riding his famous horse Shabdiz, which was considered to be one of the wonders of the world. The king's lance is poised, his shield at the ready, his bow case by his leg. The knight's head and neck are completely concealed: only the eyes can be seen gleaming through slits in the fine chain mail. This unparalleled act of sculptural audacity, that of almost completely hiding the face, was wholly successful, subtly adding to the menace of the figure.

But Khusrau's Taq-i Bustan sculpture is more than just an outstanding work of art, it is also a valuable source of information on many aspects of Sasanian life. It amplifies our scant information of the actual decoration of Sasanian palaces and it is a primary source for our knowledge of Sasanian textiles, jewelry and musical instruments.

The deer hunt on the side wall of the great grotto. The hunt takes place within an enclosure or paradise and the king is shown three times. Musicians are again present, on a stand at the top.

Silk and jewelry. Silk had been woven in Iran from early in the Sasanian period for Shapur I had settled some weavers at Bishapur. Techniques however were relatively crude and Shapur II gave a fresh impetus to silk production when he settled Syrian craftsmen at several centers in Susiana. At this time every thread of silk had to be imported from China and most of it was re-exported still in the raw state for weaving in the west. It was not until the 6th century that the Persians (and slightly later the Byzantines) were finally successful in smuggling out fertile eggs of the silkworm from China and were thus able to initiate their own supply of raw silk. This gave new momentum to the weaving of silks in Iran, which was further increased by the influx of new craftsmen brought back by Khusrau I after his sweeping victories in Syria. Iran began to export locally woven cloths and Iranian fabrics became highly prized in the west.

This gradual development of a highly sophisticated weaving industry is illustrated on the few monuments showing cloth designs: a 4th-century fresco from Susa illustrated a huntsman clothed in a tunic decorated only with a simple lozenge design picked out in gold thread. The king's tunic on the 4th-century relief of Ardashir II at Taq-i Bustan also shows a simple geometric decoration, while the materials illustrated on Khusrau's sculptures carry a complex mass of figurative, floral and geometric designs. For instance the king's hunting coat is entirely

covered with large winged *senmurv* designs allied with floral motifs enclosed in roundels, while many of his attendants wear clothes embroidered with birds, flowers or complex circular motifs. For his investiture even such richly decorated materials were insufficiently magnificent to express his majesty, and Khusrau's coat is almost entirely covered with jewels sewn onto the cloth.

The increasing importance of lavish personal display in the late Sasanian period is reflected in the jewelry worn by Khusrau when compared with that worn by the first kings. Again the principal source of information, in the absence of major finds of jewelry from secure archaeological contexts, is the rock reliefs. The early reliefs show the king wearing a relatively simple crown, light enough to be worn without external support, earrings, a necklace and with the beard held in a ring – a regular attribute of monarchy. The heavy drop-earrings may have been similar in form to, though doubtless much larger than, a pair of gold and pearl earrings recently found in a Sasanian building at the site of Siraf on the Persian Gulf. The junction of the large pearl and the gold ring is subtly concealed by two rows of small beads. The necklace

Below: the armed might of Sasanian Iran, exemplified in this magnificent statue of Khusrau II at Taq-i Bustan. Only the eyes of the massive and menacing figure, a fully armored knight, can be seen gleaming through the helmet (*right*).

shown on the reliefs is usually formed either of enormous round beads or pearls, or of flatter circular stones set in a collar, presumably made of gold. The king's light cloak is held across the chest by a pair of roundels. Just such a pair of golden roundels set with turquoises was found by peasants in the 1930s in a hoard of precious objects near Nihavand. These show an eagle with spread wings gazing out of an enclosing circle. We do not know their date; they may have been made in either the Parthian or the Sasanian periods.

By the 4th century a single necklace was no longer sufficient to express the king's magnificence so a "chest harness" consisting of jeweled straps crossing the chest and going over the shoulders and under the arms was worn as well. Predictably Khusrau Parviz is even more richly jeweled. In the investiture scene he is shown wearing an enormous crown so heavy it would have required suspension from the roof, long earrings, a richly decorated necklace, a chest harness, jeweled belt, sword belt and scabbard, as well as all the huge precious stones sewn onto his robe. Even hunting he wears a large necklace with many pendants, a jeweled belt also embellished with many long pendants and beaded bracelets on each arm.

But too much was spent on personal display and on achieving a refined elegance of court life – the welfare of the peasant and of the land was neglected. And with the defeats of the Persians at Qadisiya and at Nihavand the 400 years of Sasanian rule were finally at an end. However, "Sasanian" art and architecture continued to flourish long after the historical end of the dynasty. Many of its ideas spread and developed independently, according to local traditions, in areas as far distant as western Europe and Japan. The bones of Christian saints were wrapped in

Half of a gold clasp found near Nihavand inset with turquoises showing an eagle and its prey. Partho-Sasanian. British Museum.

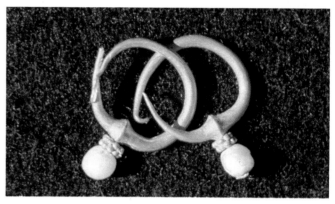

A pair of gold and pearl earrings found in Sasanian levels at Siraf.

Sasanian silks, or in Byzantine silks woven to Iranian designs, and the famous Japanese treasure of Shoso-in, collected and sealed in the 8th century, illustrates some of Sasanian Iran's influence on China. In its country of origin too, Parthian and Sasanian architecture continued to dominate religious buildings through the centuries down to the present day, as did many of their decorative ideas. Superb Mongol stucco was a descendant of Parthian and Sasanian stucco and the Safavid decoration of complete facades with brilliant tilework an adaptation of Parthian facades first seen at Assur. "Sasanian" silver and silks continued to be made in the early Islamic era and the designs were copied in other media such as glass, bronze and pottery. Law, taxes and administration were virtually unchanged under the Arab rulers and the very name Khusrau or Kisra came to symbolize kingship. European chivalry and methods of warfare in the Middle Ages were descended from those evolved by the Parthians and Sasanians – two peoples of Iranian origin, one of the Parni tribe, the other of the Persian. And the Iranians themselves, although apparently utterly defeated by the Arabs, were to rise again to form new dynasties.

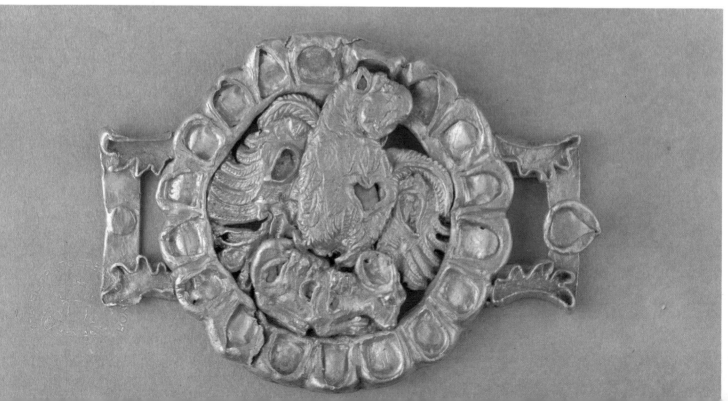

Further Reading

Adams, R. McC., *Land behind Baghdad* (Chicago, Ill., and London, 1965).

Andrae, W., and **H. Lenzen,** *Die Partherstadt Assur* (Leipzig, 1933).

Bivar, A. D. H., *Catalogue of Western Asiatic Seals in the British Museum, Stamp Seals: II. The Sassanian Dynasty* (London, 1969).

Brown, Peter, *The World of Late Antiquity* (London, 1971).

Byron, Robert, *The Road to Oxiana* (London, 1937).

Cambridge Ancient History, vols. 9–12.

Christensen, A., *L'Iran sous les Sassanides* (Copenhagen, 1944).

Colledge, M. A. R., *The Parthians* (London, 1967).

Curzon, G. N., *Persia and the Persian Question* (London, 1892; repr. 1966).

Debevoise, N. C., *A Political History of Parthia* (Chicago, Ill., 1938).

Erdmann, K., *Die Kunst Irans zur Zeit der Sasaniden* (Berlin, 1943).

Frye, R. N., *The Heritage of Persia* (London, 1962 and 1965).

—— "Political History of Iran under the Sasanians," *Cambridge History of Iran*, vol. 3 (forthcoming).

Ghirshman, Roman, *Iran, Parthians and Sassanians* (London, 1962).

Göbl, R., *Sasanian Numismatics* (Braunschweig, 1971).

Herzfeld, E., *Paikuli, Monument and Inscription, of the Early History of the Sasanian Empire* (Berlin, 1924).

—— *Archaeological History of Iran* (Oxford, 1935).

—— *Iran in the Ancient East* (Oxford, 1941).

Lukonin, V., *Persia II, from the Seleucids to the Sassanids* (London, 1971).

Oates, David, *Studies in the Ancient History of Northern Iraq* (London, 1968).

Pope, Arthur Upham (ed.), *Survey of Persian Art*, vols. 1 and 4 (Oxford, 1938).

Porada, Edith, *Ancient Iran* (London, 1965).

Rice, F. M., and **B. Rowland,** *Art in Afghanistan, Objects from the Kabul Museum* (Harmondsworth, 1971).

Rosenfeld, B., *Dynastic Art of the Kushans* (Berkeley, Calif., 1967).

Rostovtseff, M. I., *Caravan Cities* (Oxford, 1932).

Roux, Georges, *Ancient Iraq* (London, 1964).

Rowland, B., *Art and Architecture of India* (3rd edn., Harmondsworth, 1970).

Schippmann, Klauss, *Die iranischen Feuerheiligtümer* (Berlin, 1971).

Schlumberger, D., *L'Orient hellénisé, l'art grec et ses héritiers dans l'Asie non méditerranéenne* (Paris, 1970).

Schmidt, Erich, *Flights over Ancient Cities of Iran* (Chicago, Ill., 1940).

Sellwood, David, *Coinage of Parthia* (London, 1971).

Stein, Aurel, *Innermost Asia* (Oxford, 1928).

—— *Old Routes in Western Iran* (London, 1940).

Stevens, Roger, *The Land of the Great Sophy* (London, 1971).

Strange, G. le, *Lands of the Eastern Caliphate* (London, 1966).

Tarn, W. W., *The Greeks in Bactria and India* (Cambridge, 1938).

Thompson, Deborah, *Stucco from Chal Tarkhan-Eshqabad, near Rayy* (Colt Archaeological Institute Publication, Warminster, 1976).

Vanden Berghe, L., *Archéologie de l'Iran ancien* (Leiden, 1959).

Wheeler, R. E. M., *Rome beyond Imperial Frontiers* (Harmondsworth, 1954).

—— *Flames over Persepolis* (London, 1968).

Zaehner, R. C., *The Dawn and Twilight of Zoroastrianism* (London, 1961).

Much of the material used for this book was drawn from excavation reports and from articles in specialized periodicals, such as *Archaeologische Mitteilungen aus Iran, Iran, Iranica Antiqua, Iraq* and *Syria*. The principal ancient authors are Arrian, Dio Cassius, Justin, Ammianus Marcellinus, Plutarch and Procopius. Also consulted were T. Nöldeke's translation of Tabari, *Geschichte der Perser und Araber* (Leiden, 1879); translations of Firdausi's *Shah-nameh*, and of the inscriptions of the Sasanian kings. Some useful general works are listed above, many of which have extensive bibliographies which should be consulted to expand the present list.

Acknowledgments

Unless otherwise stated, all the illustrations on a given page are credited to the same source.

Aerofilms, London 59, 97, 126
W. Andrae, *Die Partherstadt Assur*, 1933, 47 (top)
Archaeological Museum, Mathura 75, 80, 81 (top right)
Ashmolean Museum, Oxford 110 (left)
Bibliothèque Nationale, Paris 26, 29, 124
Carol and Lionel Bier, New York 73, 85, 102 (bottom), 103, 108 (top), 109, 131
British Museum, London 54, 63 (bottom), 64 (bottom left), 72 (top right), 112 (bottom), 136 (bottom)
Errol Bryant, London 107 (bottom)
M. Le Chevalier Chardin, *Voyages en Perse, de l'Orient*, vol. 3, 1711; by courtesy of Basil Gray 12
John Curtis, London 28 (bottom)
Jane Dieulafoy, *A Suse: journal des fouilles*; by courtesy of the Ashmolean Library, Oxford 88 (top)
E. Flandin, *Voyage en Perse*, 1843–47; by courtesy of the Bodleian Library, Oxford 88 (top)
Ray Gardner, London 28 (top), 50, 51, 64 (top), 78, 99
Roger Gorringe, London 20 (top), 30, 32, 34 (bottom), 35, 37 (top), 38 (bottom left), 55 (top right), 57 (bottom), 68 (bottom right), 84 (bottom), 102 (top), 114 (top left)
Basil Gray, Oxford 18 (bottom)
E. Haerinck, Ghent 55 (top left)
Robert Harding Associates, London 9, 19 (bottom), 48, 90 (top), 92 (center), 120
Georgina Herrman, Oxford 38 (top and bottom right), 56, 60 (top), 77, 86, 87, 88 (bottom), 89 (center and bottom), 90 (bottom), 91 (bottom), 92 (top and bottom), 93, 94, 95, 96, 98, 100, 105, 106, 114 (top right and bottom), 115, 116, 117 (top and bottom), 118 (top and center), 127 (top), 132, 133, 135
E. Herzfeld, *Iran in the Ancient East*, 1941; by courtesy of Oxford University Press and the Ashmolean Library, Oxford 19 (top)
Holle Bildarchiv, Baden-Baden 40 (bottom)
Iran Bastan Museum, Tehran 2, 25, 39, 40 (top)
Kelsey Museum of Archaeology, University of Michigan 21 (bottom)
Lovell Johns, Oxford 10, 52
M. E. Masson, G. A. Pugachenkova, *The Rhytons from Nysa*, 1959; by courtesy of David Bivar 41, 42, 43, 44, 45, 46

Metropolitan Museum of Art, Joint Expedition of the Metropolitan Museum of Art and the German State Museums to Ctesiphon, 1931–32; Rogers Fund, 1932, New York 110 (left), 111
Museé des Arts Décoratifs, Paris 11
Musées Nationaux, Paris 23 (top)
Rudolf Naumann, Affalterbach 117 (center), 118 (bottom)
Novosti Press Agency, London 27, 34 (top)
David Oates, Cambridge 61 (top and bottom right), 62 (right), 63 (right)
Photoresources, Dover, jacket, 15, 112 (top), 119
A. U. Pope (ed.), *A Survey of Persian Art*, vol. 4, 1938; by courtesy of Oxford University Press and the Ashmolean Library, Oxford 21 (top)
R. Ker Porter, *Sketch Book II* (ADD 14.758); by courtesy of the British Library 16, 17
Josephine Powell, Rome 79, 81 (bottom)
Michael Roaf, Cambridge 104, 113, 134
B. W. Robinson, London 20 (bottom)
M. Rostovtzeff, *Caravan Cities*, 1932; by courtesy of Oxford University Press and the Ashmolean Library, Oxford 47
Royal Ontario Museum, Toronto 67, 68 (top and bottom left), 69, 70, 71, 72 (top left, center right, and bottom)
Scala, Florence 55 (bottom), 61 (bottom left), 62 (left), 63 (top)
Klaus Schippmann, Friedland 24, 66 (bottom), 82, 127 (bottom)
The Siraf Expedition 136 (top)
Graham Smith, London 36 (top), 60 (bottom), 84 (top), 107 (top), 108 (bottom), 130
Spectrum Colour Library, London 123
Staatliche Museen Preussischer Kulturbesitz, Museum für Indische Kunst, Berlin 81 (top left)
David Stronach, Tehran 36 (bottom), 37 (bottom)
Transart, Oxford 33
Louis Vanden Berghe, Ghent 31, 53, 65, 83, 91 (top), 129
Yale University Art Gallery (Dura Europus), Connecticut 64 (bottom right), 66 (top)
ZEFA (UK) Ltd, London 23 (bottom)

The publishers have attempted to observe the legal requirements with respect to the rights of the suppliers of photographic materials. Nevertheless, persons who have claims are invited to apply to the Publishers.

Glossary

Achaemenians Persian dynasty which took its name from an ancestor, Achaemenes. They were initially rulers of Fars and vassals first of the Assyrians and then of the Medes. Cyrus II the Great (559–530 BC) united the Medes and the Persians and then conquered an empire which eventually stretched from Egypt to Central Asia and from western Anatolia to northwest India (Greece and eastern Europe were only briefly held). The Achaemenian empire gave its peoples 200 years of peace, relative economic stability and freedom to work and travel anywhere within the empire. The last king, Darius III Codomannus, was defeated by **Alexander the Great**.

Agora Place of assembly or market place.

Ahriman Ahuramazda's opposite number and enemy, the spirit of evil.

Ahuramazda Supreme god of **Zoroastrianism** and *the* power for good. Shown on Achaemenian reliefs as a human bust rising from a winged disk; by Sasanian times represented anthropomorphically.

Alani Nomads from the Caucasus region.

Alexander III, The Great (355–323 BC) King of Macedonia, conqueror of the Persian empire. Son of Philip of Macedon and Olympias, he was a pupil of Aristotle. On his father's death he became commander-in-chief of all the Greeks and invaded Asia. He defeated the huge armies of the Persian king, Darius III, at three great battles: at the River Granicus in 334, which gave him Asia Minor; at Issus in 333, after which he conquered all Syria, Palestine and Egypt; and at Arbela (Erbil) in 331, which left the way open into Persia itself. He spent the winter at Persepolis, the dynastic capital of the **Achaemenian** kings, and burned it before leaving in the spring for Ecbatana (Hamadan). While Alexander was pursuing Darius III, the unfortunate Persian king was murdered by one of his own followers. Alexander continued his campaign to the furthest extent of the Achaemenian empire, conquering Bactria and Sogdia. He married Roxana, daughter of an Iranian chieftain. He crossed Afghanistan, where his horse Bucephalus died, and, despite receiving a severe wound, conquered much of northwest India. His army

then persuaded him to return rather than seek further lands: he divided his forces into two, Nearchos traveling up the Persian Gulf coast by sea, while he and his men undertook a grueling march across the desert lands of southeast Iran, during which many died. His forces reunited at Susa; he celebrated with five days of festivities and with the mass marriage of his soldiers to Oriental women in February 325. His boyhood friend, Hephastion, died at Ecbatana and Alexander was overcome with grief. He continued to Babylon, where he himself died at the age of 32 in 323 BC. During his brilliant career of conquest he founded many cities and dreamed of a fusion of Greek and Oriental cultures.

Alluvium Flat land formed by the gradual deposition of silt by rivers.

Ambulatory Corridor surrounding a room.

Amphora Tall narrow jar with two handles.

Anahita Old Iranian goddess, mistress of the waters, and of fertility.

Andrae, Walter (1875–1956) Brilliant German archaeologist who directed excavations at the great mound of ancient Assur from 1903 to 1914. The results he recorded with minute attention to technical detail, far ahead of his time. His *Die Partherstadt Assur* remains the primary source of knowledge of late Parthian architecture. After the 1914–18 World War he worked in the Berlin Museum, becoming Director in 1928.

Angel, Phillippe 17th-century Dutch painter of still life. Commissioned by Shah Abbas II to draw the ruins, he spent a week at Persepolis and then declared he had wasted his time.

Anquetil-Duperron, Abraham Hyacinthe (1731–1801) Founder of Zoroastrian studies. He traveled to India and, while living in Surat, secured a copy of the Zend-Avesta from the Parsees. This he brought back to France and published its first translation.

Antae Square pilasters on either sides of doors.

Antefix Ornament on the eaves and cornices to conceal the ends of tiles.

Antigonus (died 301 BC) One of **Alexander**'s generals, perhaps an illegitimate son of Philip of Macedon. On Alexander's death he won control of western Anatolia. Engaged in constant war against his fellow generals, he gained several victories, conquering all Asia Minor and part of Syria. He was finally defeated and killed by Seleucus in 301 BC at the Battle of Ipsus.

Antony, Mark (c. 86–30 BC) Bold Roman general and lover of Cleopatra. Friend of Julius Caesar and member of the triumvirate after his death. Antony was assigned Rome's eastern territories which he continued to enlarge. He undertook several campaigns in Parthia without success. He was defeated by Octavian (later **Augustus**) at the Battle of Actium.

Apollo Son of Zeus and Leto. Greek god of fine arts, music, poetry and medicine. Associated with the sun, he was thought to know the future. God of shepherds. Identified by the Iranians with **Mithra**.

Aramaic Northern group of Semitic languages, including Syriac.

Arsacids Name of the Parthian royal family who ruled from the mid-2nd century BC to 224 AD. Their founder was called Arsaces or Arshak, and every king on ascending the throne was known as Arsaces in addition to his own name.

Artemis Greek goddess of hunting identified as Roman Diana, Iranian **Anahita**.

Aryan Indo-European group of languages (Sanskrit, Pahlavi, Persian, Greek, Latin, Celtic, Teutonic, Slavonic, etc.), and the people who spoke them.

Asoka See **Mauryan Empire**.

Assur National god of Assyria.

Assyrians People whose homeland was in a small area of northern Mesopotamia, without many natural resources. Three times they conquered large areas of the ancient Near East, holding their territories by a deliberate "policy of frightfulness." They were finally defeated in 612 BC by an alliance of Medes, Babylonians and Scythians.

Augustus, Caius Julius Caesar Octavianus (63 BC–14 AD) Adopted son and heir of Julius **Caesar**. He was a member of the ruling triumvirate after Caesar's death and was assigned the western part of the empire. He defeated Mark **Antony** at the Battle of Actium and then held the position of Princeps for 44 years: he was emperor in all but name. He changed his name to Augustus, by which title later Roman emperors were also known. During his long and wise rule, he increased the efficiency of the army and of provincial government, reformed the laws and maintained peace within and without the empire, establishing friendly relations with neighboring powers, including the Parthians and the Kushans. This period of peace and prosperity, during which trade flourished, was known as the *Pax Romana* or *Pax Augusta*.

Avesta (or Zend-Avesta) Collection of sayings attributed to the Prophet Zoroaster, and of hymns in praise of various deities. It formed the holy scriptures of the Zoroastrian faith and was handed down orally until perhaps the reign of Vologases I (c. 51–76 AD), who is credited with having it written down.

Barbaro, Josefa Venetian ambassador to Persia in 1472. His *Viagi fatti da Vinetia alla Tara* was published in 1545.

Bas-relief Sculpture in which the figures do not stand out far from the background.

Belisarius (died 565 AD) Celebrated general in the reign of **Justinian**.

Benjamin Ben Jonah Jewish rabbi from Tudela who traveled to Persia from 1164 to 1173. One of the first Europeans to leave a record of his travels.

Brahman Member of the highest priestly caste of the Hindus.

Buddhism One of the most influential world religions. The name Buddhism comes from the Sanskrit *buddha*, meaning "the enlightened one." This title was given to Gautama, the founder of the Buddhist faith, who was born about 560 BC in northern India. He was a member of the ruling caste – his father was a local prince. His new movement, begun at a time of religious questioning, could be shared by all and was not confined to the priestly caste. Moral conduct, especially kindness to others, was important. The aim was a state of perfect selfless tranquillity or *Nirvana*. This message is summarized as the Four Noble Truths. Gautama, who lived to the age of 80, founded the world's first order of monks and nuns, who lived by begging.

Later Buddhism split into two sects, the larger one, *Mahayana* (the Great Way), and the smaller one, *Hinayana* (the Lesser Way). In Mahayana Buddhism, Boddhisattvas are considered to be incarnate individuals who stopped short of a state of *Nirvana* to help other human beings.

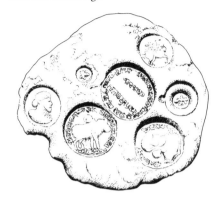

Bulla *with seal impressions.*

Bulla Clay label with seal impressions.

Cabochon Precious stone, often garnet, polished to a rounded, i.e. not faceted, shape.

Caesar, C. Julius (c. 100–44 BC) Successful general and first dictator of Rome. Starting life as a priest of Jupiter, he became High Priest before entering state employment. He was one of the first ruling triumvirate with Crassus and Pompey. Crassus soon died in his unsuccessful war against Parthia (54 BC). Caesar conquered Gaul and twice invaded Britain, before "crossing the Rubicon" and declaring himself dictator. In the ensuing civil war he overthrew Pompey in 48 BC. He used his supreme power to improve conditions, administratively and in the provinces. He was killed by a conspiracy on 15 March.

Caparison Protective covering worn by horses, often emblazoned with the crests of their owners.

Caravansaray Staging post along trade routes, usually sited one day's journey from the next.

Cassius, Dio (*fl.* 200–30 AD). Roman historian and politician. His own experiences colored some of his later history.

Cella Inner sanctuary or shrine.

Chancellor, Richard (died 1556) English traveler. He commanded a ship in Sir Hugh Willoughby's expedition to discover a northeast passage to India. He reached Archangel in 1553 and traveled to the court of Ivan the Terrible. His reports led to the formation of the **Russian and Muscovy Company**. Two years later he revisited Archangel and Moscow but was wrecked on the Aberdeen coast on his return.

Chandragupta See **Mauryan Empire**.

Chardin, Jean or Sir John (1643–1713) French jeweler who traveled to Iran and India, working at the courts of the Great Sophy and Great Mogul, 1664–70 and 1671–77. He published an enthusiastic account of his journeys which was illustrated by G. J. Grelot, the first artist to give an exact idea of the Achaemenian palaces at Persepolis. Chardin was a Huguenot, who had to flee to England to escape persecution in 1681. He became jeweler to the English court and was knighted by Charles II. In 1682 he became a Fellow of the Royal Society.

Cleopatra (69–30 BC) Queen of Egypt and last of the Ptolemaic dynasty. A brilliant and beautiful woman, she captivated Mark **Antony** to further her policy for Egypt. She committed suicide rather than face the ignominy of capture by Octavian after the Battle of Actium.

Column capitals The three principal Classical types of column capitals were the

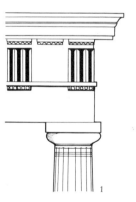

The three orders of column capitals: 1 Doric, 2 Ionic, 3 Corinthian.

Ionic, Doric and Corinthian orders. All three were popular in Iran from Hellenistic times.

Columns, engaged Columns built into the wall so that only half the column was visible.

Corbel Stone or brick projecting from a wall.

Coste, P. French artist and traveler who visited Iran with Eugène **Flandin** from 1839 to 1841.

Cotton, Sir Dodmore Ambassador of Charles I to the Safavid court in 1627.

Crest Important families in Parthian and Sasanian Iran could be recognized by their family crest, which was emblazoned on, for instance, their hats and on the **caparisons** worn by their horses. Cut on their personal seals, it served as a sign of ownership.

Curzon, George Nathaniel, Marquis Curzon of Kedleston (1859–1925) English traveler and statesman with a deep interest in the east. He traveled in Persia as a correspondent of *The Times* and published *Persia and the Persian Question* in 1892. He was viceroy of India 1899–1905, during which time the Durbar of 1903 was held.

Darius I, The Great (522–486 BC) Acceded to the throne of Persia on the death of Cambyses, after having had virtually to rewin the Achaemenian empire: he inscribed an account of his struggles high up on the mountain at Bisitun. This account was written in three languages, Old Persian, Elamite and Babylonian, in the cuneiform script; the translation by **Rawlinson** of the simple Old Persian provided the key to the others. Darius reorganized the administration of the empire, including its laws and taxes, and began to build the Achaemenian palaces at Persepolis.

Dhoti Loin cloth.

Diadem Insignia of royalty, handed to the king by the god at his investiture. It was tied around his crown and the long diadem ties hung down the king's back or flew out behind when he was shown moving. Members of the royal family, vassal kings and nobles sometimes wore a smaller version of the diadem with short ties.

Dieulafoy, Marcel 19th-century French architect and archaeologist, accompanied by his intrepid and delightful wife Jane, who both sketched and photographed what she saw. In 1881 the Dieulafoys began to make a systematic examination of Achaemenian and later monuments. In 1884–86 they began the excavations of the French Délégation at Susa (still continuing today) and uncovered the palace of Artaxerxes; they brought back to the Louvre a superb series of bull capitals and the "Frieze of the Archers" – glazed brick panels depicting archers in brightly colored robes. Dieulafoy's work was published in 1893 (*L'Acropole de Suse*). More entertaining reading is Jane Dieulafoy's diary of their life at Susa: *A Suse: journal des fouilles* (1888).

Dihqan Head of a village or owner of small estates.

Diocletian, Caius Valerius Jovius (245–313 AD) Celebrated Roman emperor who began as a soldier and worked his way up to the rank of general. Appointed emperor, he made his friend and fellow soldier Maximian co-emperor. He enlarged the army and set up a mobile force available for rushing to any area at risk. He reorganized and strengthened the frontiers and greatly improved communications: his formidable defenses effectively checked Sasanian expansion westward. His reforms were financed by heavy taxation: he reformed the currency and imposed price controls to check inflation. He began the last great Christian persecution in 303, for he considered Christianity a subversive force in the empire. After ruling for 21 years, he voluntarily retired to a palace at Split on the Dalmation coast.

East India Company Name of several private trading companies, chartered by European governments in the 17th century for the development of trade in the eastern hemisphere. The British company, chartered in 1600, monopolized the trade with India.

Coin of Musa wearing a diadem.

Entablature Architectural term for the horizontal elements resting on columns: these consist of the architrave, frieze and cornice.

Farr Mystical majesty of kingship.

Fibula Brooch or safety pin.

Firdausi (940–1021) Persian poet who compiled most of the **Shah-nameh** or "Book of Kings," the national epic of Iran, part legend, part historical.

Flandin, E. French artist who traveled in Iran in the middle of the 19th century with P. **Coste**, and drew and planned many ancient monuments.

Gama, Vasco da (c. 1469–1524) Portuguese navigator and explorer, the first man to travel from Europe to India by sea around the Cape of Good Hope.

Gibbon, Edward (1737–94) English historian. He toured Italy in 1764–65 and conceived the idea for his *Decline and Fall of the Roman Empire* while standing in the ruins of the Capitol. The first volume was published in 1776, the last in 1788.

Glyptic Art Art of the seal cutter or gem engraver.

Godard, André (born 1881) French architect and museum director. He was invited to Iran in 1928 by Reza Shah to create an archaeological service and to draw up an inventory of historical monuments. He built the Tehran Archaeological Museum and organized the archaeological service, also training teams of restorers. He stayed in Iran for 30 years and in 1956 published his *L'Art de l'Iran*.

Great Silk Road Principal overland route from China via Central Asia, Iran and Mesopotamia to Syria, whence goods were shipped to Rome. The precise route varied according to political and climatic conditions. The first silk caravan traveled west around 106 BC.

Greco-Bactrians Dynasty founded in the mid-3rd century BC by the rebel Seleucid satrap of Bactria, Diodotus. Diodotus formed an independent Greek kingdom, the most eastern expression of Hellenism, which lasted until c. 130 BC, when it was overwhelmed by the **Saka** hordes.

Hadrian (76–138 AD) Roman emperor who established an efficient administration and stabilized the frontiers. He built the great wall in Britain from Tyne to Solway. Hadrian codified Roman law and was a benefactor and patron of learning. He painted and sang, wrote verse, toured the provinces and visited ancient monuments.

Han Dynasty (202 BC–9 AD and 25–221 AD) Chinese dynasty. Under Emperor Wu Ti (141–87 BC) China rivaled Rome as the world's greatest power.

Heracles Greek god, equated with Roman Hercules and Iranian **Verethragna**. Originally a hero who was deified after death. The first of his 12 labors was to kill the Nemean lion, which he attacked with his club and then throttled: thereafter he always wore the lion's skin.

Heraclius (610–41) Byzantine emperor who saved his empire from collapse. On assuming power he found the Sasanian armies masters of the Near East. Using his superior naval power he struck behind the Persian lines and inflicted severe defeats on them. His successes led to the murder of Khusrau II and the end of effective Sasanian rule.

Herbert, Sir Thomas (1606–82) English soldier. He accompanied Sir Dodmore Cotton's embassy to Iran in 1627, which he described in his *Discription of the Persian Monarchy*, first published in 1634 and subsequently revised.

Hermes Greek god of luck and wealth, the messenger of the gods. Responsible for conducting souls to Hades.

Herzfeld, Ernst (1879–1948) German Orientalist and archaeologist who made major contributions to the study of all periods of Near Eastern art and architecture. He dug at Assur with **Andrae**. Among his many contributions was the first serious publication of Iranian rock reliefs, illustrated with photographs taken by Friedrich **Sarre** (1910), the Sasanian palace at Ctesiphon (1920), the commemorative tower of Narseh at Paikuli (1921) and an intuitive book *Iran in the Ancient East* (1941), in which he drew together his knowledge of Iran from the earliest times to the Islamic era. He conducted many excavations, including a short season at Kuh-i Kwaja in Seistan, where he recorded an important palace/temple of Partho-Sasanian date and uncovered brilliant frescoes. His contributions to other fields, both Achaemenian and Islamic, were fundamental. His papers are in the Freer Gallery of Art, Smithsonian Institute, Washington, D.C.

Horace, Quintus Horatius Flaccus (65–8 BC) Roman poet, born the son of a freed slave. His verse attracted the notice of Virgil. He was given an estate at the age of 32 and was thereafter able to write, free from financial worries. His subjects vary from the ideals and majesty of Augustan Rome, the shame of civil war and the brevity of life to country life, friendship and love.

Huns Large confederation of Central Asian nomad peoples, several groups of which controlled large areas of territory. The Hephthalite Huns formed a powerful empire in Afghanistan from the 4th century and posed a major threat to Sasanian Iran, until they were finally defeated by Khusrau I and the Turks. Other powerful groups moved westward and crossed the Danube into Europe, where they settled in present-day Austria and Hungary. Under the ruthless Attila in the 5th century, they reached the height of their power, controlling territory from the Rhine to the Urals and the Caucasus. Attila nearly defeated the Roman empire but soon after his death in 453 the Huns destroyed themselves by internal quarrels. Small groups of them returned to the Urals.

Isidore of Charax Greek historian of the 2nd century BC who wrote a history and description of Parthia – *Parthian Stations*.

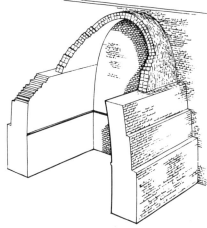

Barrel-vaulted iwan.

Iwan Barrel-vaulted three-sided hall.

Jenkinson, Anthony (died 1611) English merchant, sea-captain and traveler, who was the first Englishman in Central Asia. He commanded the first expedition of the Muscovy Company in 1557 and was well received at the Russian court. He traveled to Astrakhan and Bokhara (1558), returning to England in 1560. His second visit the following year ended in failure. His final attempt to establish trans-Russian trade was in 1577.

Josephus, Flavius (37–93 AD) Jewish historian, born in Jerusalem. He endured the siege of Jerusalem, and after escaping and being again besieged in a cave, surrendered himself to Vespasian. He went to Rome where he was honored by Titus and made a Roman citizen. He wrote many works, including *The Jewish War*.

Julian the Apostate (331–63 AD) Roman emperor, nephew of Constantine the Great. Brought up a Christian, he renounced the faith in favor of paganism. He was appointed Caesar of Gaul by Constans, which he administered well. His soldiers persuaded him to accept the title of Augustus and on the death of Constans in 361 he became sole emperor. He determined to conquer the Persians and advanced into Mesopotamia, burning his boats so that there was no retreat for him or his men. He was victorious and reached the walls of Ctesiphon before he died from wounds sustained in battle. An eyewitness account of his Persian campaigns is given by Ammianus **Marcellinus**.

Justin, M. Junianus Roman historian and Christian apologist of the 2nd century AD, who epitomized the history of Trogus Pompeius.

Justinian I (c. 483–565) Greatest of the late Roman emperors who with his brilliant general Belisarius restored the boundaries of the empire. Justinian revised the Roman laws, both ecclesiastical and civil, and framed a new code of laws. He expected everyone to be Christian: pagans and heretics were persecuted. He brought the famous University of Athens to an end by prohibiting the teaching of law and philosophy at Athens. It was Justinian who first introduced silkworms to the west.

Kolah High hat worn by Sasanian nobles, insignia of their rank.

Korymbos Sasanian royal attribute consisting of a "globe" of hair covered with a fine cloth which rises above a king's crown.

Kushans Group of Iranian tribes, known in Chinese records as the Yüeh-chih, who occupied Bactria in the late 2nd century BC. Unified by a chief of the Kuei-shang (Kushan) tribe, they expanded south over the Hindu Kush. Kajula Kadphises extended Kushan power into the Gandharan region and established direct Kushano-Roman commercial and diplomatic contacts. Greatest of the Kushan kings was Kanishka, who ruled in the early 2nd century AD – the dating of the Kushans is much disputed. The extent of their empire eastwards is not yet established. After their defeat by the **Sasanians**, a dynasty known as the Lesser Kushans, who were subject to the Sasanians, came to power.

Lakhmids Arab dynasty of Yemeni origin, vassals of the Sasanians. They controlled much of Syria from their capital at Hira, near modern Najaf, and acted as a buffer zone between the Arabs of the desert and the Sasanians. They were destroyed by Khusrau II.

Layard, Sir Austen Henry (1817–94) English archaeologist and politician. Born in Paris of British parents, he traveled widely as a child. While working in a solicitor's office in London from 1833 to 1839 he prepared himself for Oriental travel by learning some Persian and Arabic. He traveled widely in Asia Minor, Persia and Mesopotamia and visited the great mounds of the Assyrian city of Nineveh with the French archaeologist Émile Botta, which determined him to start on his career of Assyrian archaeology. Employed by Stratford Canning to travel in Asia Minor, in 1845 he was commissioned by him to explore Nineveh. He began excavation of Nimrud (Biblical Calah), Assur and Nineveh, the results of which he published in brilliantly written and illustrated scholarly and popular works. These books created considerable interest in Victorian England. He published the account of his early travels, *Early Adventures in Persia, Susiana and Babylonia*, in 1887.

Loculus Niche or small chamber for coffins, sarcophagi or burial urns.

Sasanian headgear: korymbos (left) and kolah *(right).*

Loftus, William Kennett (c. 1821–58)
English archaeologist and traveler. Geologist
to Turco-Persian Frontier Commission
1849–52; he excavated at various sites,
including Susa and Warka. He was employed
by the Assyrian Excavation Fund, 1853–55, to
dig at Babylon and Nineveh, and published his
Travels and Researches in Chaldaea and Susiana
in 1857.

Magi Iranian priestly caste, who officiated at
all religious ceremonies.

Mahout Elephant driver.

Malcolm, Sir John (1769–1833) English
diplomat who served in the **East India
Company** in 1782. He was chosen by Lord
Wellesley, the governor general, as envoy to
Persia, 1799–1801, 1808–09 and 1810. He
published his *Political History of India* in 1811
and *History of Persia* in 1818. He later became
governor of Bombay, 1826–30.

Mani (c. 215–c. 273 AD) Prophet who
attempted to combine the best of
Zoroastrianism, Buddhism and Christianity in
a new faith, Manichaeism. He was supported
by Shapur I, who was perhaps hoping to find a
religion that would unite all his people; but
Mani was put to death during the reign of
Bahram I or Bahram II, probably at the
instigation of the chief priest, Kartir.

Manichaean Follower of the Prophet **Mani**.

Marcellinus, Ammianus (c. 330–95 AD)
Roman historian. He was born in Antioch-on-
the-Orontes and served as a soldier in the
Roman army under Constantius, Julian the
Apostate and Valens. He fought a number of
campaigns in Mesopotamia in the 350s and in
363. He retired to Rome and wrote a history in
31 books from the reign of Domitian to
Valens, of which only 18 books remain.

Masudi Arab geographer and historian of the
10th century, two of whose works survive.

Mauryan Empire (c. 320–230 BC)
Chandragupta Maurya was still a boy when
Alexander conquered northwest India, but by
the time Seleucus returned to claim
Alexander's territories, Chandragupta had
succeeded in uniting NW India and forming
the Mauryan empire. Unable to defeat this
new power, Seleucus wisely formed an
alliance with Chandragupta and the two kings
exchanged ambassadors: the Greek
Megasthenes lived at the Indian court for a
number of years.

The greatest Mauryan king was Asoka
(274–232 BC) who conquered most of the
Indian subcontinent. He sent many embassies
to the west and was converted to Buddhism.
During his reign Buddhism became an active
proselytizing religion. The empire did not
long survive Asoka's death.

Mazdak Probably a Zoroastrian priest. The
heretic Mazdak preached a new humanitarian
faith at a time of economic and political failure
in the late 5th century AD. He was put to
death, probably by order of Khusrau I, and his
followers were persecuted.

Medes Iranian tribe, first heard of in the
Assyrian Annals of the 9th century BC, by
which time they were already living in the
Zagros. They formed the first Iranian empire
by defeating the **Assyrians** in 612 BC.
Together with the **Persians**, and led by Cyrus
II the Great, they formed the **Achaemenian**
empire, 550–330 BC. They were famed for
their horses.

Megaron Large oblong hall.

Mithra, Mithraism Mithra was one of the
principal deities of the Old Iranian pantheon
and, despite Zoroaster's attempt to suppress his
worship, he continued to be prayed to. In the
hymn dedicated to him, Mithra is described as
lord of the contract (i.e. of justice); he was
associated with the sun (he was said to go
before the sun's chariot), and responsible for
the wellbeing of cattle and pastures.

The cult of Mithraism was widely followed
throughout the Roman empire and Mithraea
have been found from Dura Europus to
Britain (but not yet identified further east).
This secret cult was subterranean and
associated with the god's slaying of a bull: an
interpretation totally at variance with Mithra's
Iranian origins. His strange transformation in
the west has still to be explained.

Monolithic Made from a single block of
stone.

Morier, James Justinian (c. 1780–1849)
English writer, born at Smyrna. He
accompanied two British missions to Iran,
those of Sir Harford Jones, 1808–09, and Sir
Gore Ouseley, 1811–12. His *Journeys through
Persia* was published in 1812, but Morier is
principally remembered for his Oriental
romances, the best of which was *Hajji Baba of
Isfahan* (1824).

Moufflon Wild mountain sheep with big
horns.

Muhammad (c. 570–632) Founder of Islam.
He began life working with caravans; when
adult, he married Khadija, the rich widow of a
Meccan merchant. When he was about 40 he
went into retirement for a time while his
message was maturing. He used to meditate in
a cave at the foot of a mountain near Mecca.
After a revelation Muhammad was sure he was
intended to be a prophet and went around
commanding that all idols be put away and
everyone should surrender to the will of God.
His message began to be more widely accepted
after 621, the year of the flight to Medina,
from which date Muslims begin their calendar.
The next 18 years were ones of remarkable
expansion for Islam: within ten years
Muhammad had become master of the
Arabian peninsula. His later years were spent
writing his message down in the Koran. A
year after his death the Arabs challenged and
defeated a Byzantine army and shortly
thereafter conquered the Sasanian empire.

Necropolis City of the dead; cemetery.

Nero (37–68 AD) Roman emperor. He began
his reign well but soon proved to be a cruel
and suspicious tyrant who condemned many
innocent people to death. He antagonized
Roman society by his self-display and
licentious behavior. The Senate finally
condemned him to death and he fled and
committed suicide.

Niebuhr, Carsten (1733–1815) Danish
engineer and explorer. Born at Ludingworth
in Holstein, he joined an expedition sent by
Frederic V of Denmark in 1761 to explore
Arabia. He traveled in Egypt, Syria, Palestine
and Egypt before sailing for Bombay. The sole
survivor of the expedition, he stayed at
Bombay for a year before traveling to
Mesopotamia and Persia, where he spent three
weeks at Persepolis in March 1765. He made
fine copies of the cuneiform inscriptions, in the
study of which he made great advances.

Nike Greek goddess of victory.

Nirvana Extinction of all desires and passions,
and the attainment of perfect contentment; the
goal of **Buddhism**.

Ottomans Turkish dynasty who began ruling
a minor principality in western Turkey in the
late 13th century. They greatly increased the
territory under their control and were one of
the principal enemies of the Safavid kings,
who sought alliances with European princes
against their common enemy.

Ouseley, Sir William (1767–1842) English Orientalist and scholar. He studied Persian at Paris and Leyden, and accompanied his brother Sir Gore Ouseley on his mission to Persia, 1810–12. His published books include one on his Persian travels.

Pahlavi Language of Iran during the time of the Parthian and Sasanian dynasties.

Palaestra Gymnasium.

Parsees Community of Persians, followers of Zoroaster, who, to escape Islam, fled to India and settled around Bombay. They have maintained their identity and faith through the centuries to the present day.

Parthians Tribe of Iranian nomads who took the name "Parthian" from the country in which they settled, the old Achaemenian satrapy of Parthava, situated to the east of the Caspian Sea. Initially vassals of the **Seleucid** kings, they achieved independence in the mid-3rd century. Their ruling family, called **Arsacids**, gradually expanded Parthian territory and, despite some reverses, had conquered most of the eastern Seleucid empire by the mid-2nd century BC. Thereafter they ruled an empire stretching from Syria to Central Asia. They were a strong and warlike people, superb horsemen and archers. They were famous for firing arrows back over their shoulders, while apparently retreating (the "Parthian shot"), and for being even more formidable when apparently retreating than when attacking. They stopped Roman expansion eastward, and several times threatened Rome's eastern territories.

As a result of coming into contact with the **Han dynasty** of China in Central Asia, the luxury trade in silk was begun. Parthia's strategic position between east and west enabled her to profit from Rome's insatiable demand for silks and other eastern luxuries.

Peristyle Row of columns surrounding a temple or courtyard.

Persian, Middle See **Pahlavi**.

Persian, Old Official language of Iran during the Achaemenian empire and that recorded in cuneiform on sculptures and foundation tablets. The lingua franca of the empire was Aramaic, while much of the day-to-day administration was carried out by Elamite scribes. Old Persian was probably first written during the first 50 years of empire. The script was a semi-alphabetic form of cuneiform, the system of writing devised by the Sumerians more than two millennia earlier.

Persians Iranian tribe, first heard of in the Assyrian Annals of the 9th century BC, by which time they were already living in the Zagros mountains. By the 7th/6th century

their homeland approximated to the modern province of Fars or Pars. Led by Cyrus II (559–530 BC), they formed, together with the **Medes**, the first world empire, the **Achaemenian** empire.

Persians continued to live in Pars or Persis after the defeat of the Achaemenian empire in 330 by **Alexander the Great**. Thereafter a series of Persian vassal kings ruled, known as the Fratadara. By the 2nd century AD the Persian Sasan was king of Persis, with his capital at Istakhr, the city site near ancient Persepolis. The Persians expanded their territories in the late 2nd century and Ardashir I challenged and defeated the last Parthian king, Artabanus, in 224 AD. He formed the **Sasanian** empire, which ruled for 400 years: this was the second Persian empire.

Philhellene Lover or supporter of the Hellenes or Greeks, followers of Greek culture.

Phyllite Rock used by Gandharan sculptors: it is between a clay-state and a mica-schist.

Plutarch (46–120 AD) Roman traveler, writer and historian. He opened a school in Rome under the protection of Trajan; then retired to Chaeronea, where he wrote most of his books including his famous *Lives*.

Pompey, Gnaeus (106–48 BC) Brilliant Roman general. In 67 BC he cleared the Mediterranean of pirates in four months. He conquered Sicily and all the Roman territories of Africa. Recalled to Rome, he was given the name Magnus ("the Great"). Made consul c. 73 BC, he continued his military campaigns, conquering Judaea and parts of Arabia, and settled Rome's eastern territories. He returned to Rome in 62 BC with overwhelming power, but was a poor politician. Eventually he joined **Caesar** and Crassus in the first triumvirate, but was defeated by Caesar in the civil war.

Quatrefoil column.

Pope, Arthur Upham (died 1969) American art-historian of Islamic architecture. He edited the monumental *Survey of Persian Art* (1938–39). He returned to Iran in the 1960s at

the invitation of the shah to found the Asia Institute in Shiraz. In 1965 he published *Persian Architecture*.

Porter, Sir Robert Ker (1777–1842) English artist and traveler. Academy student at Somerset House, 1790; scene painter at Lyceum Theatre, London, 1800; historical painter to the czar of Russia, 1804–06. He accompanied Sir John Moore throughout his Corunna campaigns; then he returned to Russia and married a princess in 1812. He traveled in Georgia, Persia, Armenia and Mesopotamia, 1817–20, with the express purpose of recording ancient sites – his two-volume work was published in 1821. His diaries and numerous unpublished drawings and watercolors are in the Manuscript Room of the British Library.

Procopius (born c. 500 AD) Greek historian of Caesarea in Palestine, secretary to Belisarius. He wrote a history of the reign of **Justinian**, which is useful but full of scandal and malicious gossip.

Pronaos Vestibule of a temple, the room between the porch (*propylon*) and sanctuary (*cella*).

Propylon Entrance vestibule, porch or gateway.

Ptolemy or **Ptolemaeus I** (died c. 284 BC) First of the Macedonian kings of Egypt. The illegitimate son of Philip of Macedon, he was educated at the Macedonian court. He accompanied **Alexander the Great** throughout his Asian campaigns, behaving with great courage. On the division of the Macedonian empire after Alexander's death Ptolemy obtained Egypt, which he ruled wisely and well. He conquered much of Palestine and the Syrian coast; he brought many prisoners back to Egypt whom he settled in his new capital, Alexandria. His successors were also known as Ptolemy.

Qajars Dynasty founded by Agha Muhammad Shah in 1794 which ruled Iran until Reza Shah Pahlavi ascended the throne in 1926.

Quatrefoil column Column which in plan appears to have four petals.

Rawlinson, Sir Henry Creswicke (1810–95) English Orientalist and scholar who succeeded in translating cuneiform. He entered the service of the East India Company and arrived in India in 1827. He learned Persian, Arabic and Hindustani. Sent as military adviser to the shah's brother in 1833 to Kermanshah, he began his study of the inscriptions at Bisitun. A splendid horseman (he once rode 750 miles in 150 consecutive hours), he traveled widely in Persia, recording ancient monuments. Among numerous other sites he visited Takht-i Sulaiman and Qaleh-i Zohak. He took up his post as Political Agent in Turkish Arabia in Baghdad in 1843, and succeeded in completely copying the Bisitun inscription. He returned to England in 1855 and became a Member of Parliament and President of the Royal Asiatic Society and of the Royal Geographical Society.

Reliquary Small box or casket in which relics are kept.

Reuther, Oscar German archaeologist and architect who first worked with **Andrae** at Assur, and later directed the German excavation at Ctesiphon in 1928–29. His contributions to the *Survey of Persian Art* on Parthian and Sasanian architecture are brilliant accounts of the extant buildings and construction techniques.

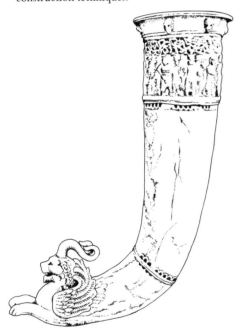

Ivory rhyton from Nysa.

Rhyton Drinking vessel in the form of a horn, usually ending in an animal's head.

Roundel Circular frame.

Rubble masonry Method of building, widely used on the Iranian plateau in the Sasanian period and also, as discoveries at Yazdigird have proved, in the late Parthian period. A mixture of loose stones and gypsum mortar was poured into a frame of wooden planks or shuttering. The mortar set quickly and held the stones in position. This somewhat clumsy technique is extremely long lasting

Russian and Muscovy Company Group of English merchants, formed in 1555, to trade with Russia.

Sacy, Silvestre de French Orientalist, who worked on Pahlavi inscriptions at the end of the 18th century and succeeded in translating them. He also published antiquities in his *Mémoires sur les antiquités de la Perse.*

Safavids Dynasty which ruled Iran from 1491 to 1722. Shah Abbas I (1587–1628) moved his capital to Isfahan, where he built up a brilliant court and constructed numerous colorful mosques and palaces. He enjoyed frequent contact with European kings.

Saka or **Scythians** Large group of Iranian nomads, based in Central Asia, first heard of in the 7th century BC, when they invaded the Zagros Mountain area. Initially allied with the **Assyrians**, they later joined the **Medes** and Babylonians in destroying the Assyrian empire. Various groups of Scythians, including the Saka Tigrakhauda or Pointed-Hat Scythians, were vassals of the Achaemenian empire. There were important Scythian settlements along the northern Black Sea coast: the excavation of barrows there has produced superb works of art in a vigorous style, as well as many beautiful objects made by Greek artists. In about 130 BC fresh Saka movements caused the collapse of the Greco-Bactrian dynasty and nearly overwhelmed the newly formed Parthian empire. Conquered by Mithradates II, one group settled in Seistan (Sakastan) and was ruled by an Indo-Parthian dynasty, the greatest king of which was Gondophares. An extensive Indo-Parthian city has been excavated at Taxila in NW India. Legend claims that St Thomas worked as a carpenter at Gondophares' court.

Sarre, Friedrich (1865–1945) German archaeologist. He traveled with **Herzfeld** in the early years of the 20th century, with whom he collaborated in a number of important publications, including *Iranische Felsreliefs* (1910), which was illustrated with his own excellent photographs, and the first volumes on Ctesiphon. Founder and first Director of the Islamic Department of the Berlin Museum, he began the serious study of Islamic art history in Germany.

Sasanians Persian dynasty, 224–637 AD. Named after Sasan, king of Persis, the Sasanians claimed to be heirs of the **Achaemenian** Persians (550–330 BC). They ruled an empire stretching from Syria to Central Asia which was the principal eastern enemy of Rome and of Byzantium. They were finally overcome by the Arabs fighting under the banner of Islam. The state religion was **Zoroastrianism** and religious minorities were, from time to time, persecuted.

Satrap Provincial governor.

Schist Metamorphic rock used for Gandharan sculptures.

Schmidt, Erich 20th-century American archaeologist, who excavated at Tepe Hissar, Persepolis, Naqsh-i Rustam, Istakhr, Rayy and Rumishqan. He pioneered the use of aerial reconnaissance as an archaeological aid in Iran.

Scrim Loose-weave material used by plasterers to help the plaster adhere to the surface of rock.

Seleucids Dynasty formed by Seleucus, formerly Macedonian chief of cavalry in Alexander's army. They ruled much of the Near East from 311 BC until defeated by the Parthians in the middle of the 2nd century BC. Their last kingdom (in Syria) was defeated by Rome.

Senmurv Mythical creature, half-bird, half-beast, frequently illustrated on Sasanian stucco, silver and seals. It was believed to bring good luck.

Senmurv.

Severus, Lucius Septimius (145–211 AD) Roman emperor. Born at Leptis in North Africa of a noble family, he occupied all the major offices of state. He assumed the imperial purple, but had to fight another contender, Pescennius Niger, who was supported by among others the Parthians. Severus defeated and killed Niger, and then defeated another rival Albinus. With his sons, Caracalla and Geta, Severus then marched east and began a successful campaign against Parthia, capturing Seleucia, Ctesiphon and Babylon. After visiting Egypt, he marched to Britain, which was in revolt. Having concluded peace, he died at York on 4 February.

Shah Persian for king – *shah-an-shah*, king of kings.

Shah-Nameh *Book of Kings.* The national epic of Persia, composed principally by the poet **Firdausi** in the 11th century. It consists of a collection of Persian legends covering the creation of the world and the exploits of great heroes like Rustam, a version of the Alexander Romance, and a partially historical account of the Sasanian dynasty.

Shirley, Sir Anthony (1565–1635?) English soldier and adventurer. He fought in the Netherlands in 1586 and under Essex in Normandy in 1591. Knighted by Henry of Navarre, he commanded an expedition against the Portuguese in South America in 1596. In 1599 he was instructed by Essex to travel to the court of Shah Abbas, by whom he was employed as an envoy to Europe. Disclaimed by the English government, he was imprisoned in Venice (1603). He undertook an unsuccessful mission for Spain to the Levant in 1609 and thereafter lived in poverty in Madrid.

Shirley, Sir Robert (c. 1581–1628) English adventurer and envoy. He traveled with his brother Anthony to the court of Shah Abbas in 1599, by whom he was employed as an adviser on military matters. He married a Circassian lady. In 1608 he returned to Europe as Abbas' ambassador, trying to negotiate anti-Turk alliances. He reported on his mission in 1615 and was dispatched again almost immediately. He came back to Iran with Sir Dodmore **Cotton** in 1627 and died a year later, discredited and penniless in Qazvin.

Slavs People who originated in the Carpathian mountains and settled in about the 7th century AD in the middle and upper reaches of the River Dnieper.

Socle Architectural term for a base or pedestal.

Sondage Trial excavation, limited in extent.

Spahbad General of one of the four great military zones into which Iran was divided by Khusrau I.

Spandrel Architectural term for the triangular space at each side of an arch.

Stein, Sir Mark Aurel (1862–1943) Scholar, explorer, archaeologist and geographer. Born a Hungarian, he worked for many years for the government of India and adopted British nationality in 1904. He undertook four Central Asian expeditions between 1900 and 1930, during which he made valuable discoveries and collections, and as a result of which he published numerous volumes including *Innermost Asia* (4 volumes). Between 1927 and 1936 he surveyed extensively in southwest and southeast Iran, the results of which he also promptly published: *Archaeological Reconnaissances in N.W. India and S.E. Iran* (1937) and *Old Routes of Western Iran* (1940). He died in Kabul, still exploring. His papers are currently in the India Office Library in London.

Stucco Plaster used for coating walls. By means of molds large areas could be quickly and economically covered. This form of

Stucco bust of Shapur II.

architectural decoration came into favor in the Hellenistic period and was fully exploited in the succeeding Parthian period, when it was used to cover the entire facade of a monumental courtyard at Assur. As has been found at Qaleh-i Yazdigird (see pages 67–72), the stucco panels were brightly painted. In the early Sasanian period stucco decoration was restrained in appearance, but by mid and late Sasanian times a rich repertoire of motifs, both figural and geometric, was employed.

Stupa Buddhist monument built around a reliquary.

Model stupa from Taxila.

Tavernier, Jean Baptiste (1605–89) French jeweler who, like **Chardin**, worked at the courts of the Great Sophy and Great Mogul. He made six visits to Persia, once accompanied by André Daulier des Landes, a young French artist, another time by the Dutch painter **Angel**. His book *Les Six Voyages* was published posthumously in Utrecht in 1712.

Terracotta Unglazed pottery of a brownish red shade.

Tetradrachm Greek silver coin worth 4 drachms, also minted by the Parthians and the Sasanians. The leading denomination was the drachm, usually coined in silver. Both the Parthian and the Sasanian drachm had the same weight from beginning to end – about 4 grams on average.

Theriac Antidote to poison, especially from snake venom.

Toga Flowing Roman outer garment consisting of a single piece of cloth.

Parthian coin showing a torque.

Torque Collar, necklace, armlet or bracelet, usually made of a twisted band or strip of precious metal, and often ending in an animal's head.

Torus Architectural term for a large convex molding, of semicircular profile, usually at the base of a column.

Trajan (53–117 AD) Roman emperor. Trajan became emperor at the age of 45 after a successful military career, and he was the first emperor to receive the title of "Optimus," the best. He followed a policy of conquest and expansion in the east. Having annexed Armenia, he swept through Mesopotamia and reached the shores of the Persian Gulf. These gains did not survive his death.

Turkoman Turkish nomads.

Valle, Pietro Della (1586–1652). Italian traveler. He spent five years traveling in Assyria, Babylonia and Persia, during which period he married a Nestorian Christian. He was the first to identify the ruins of Babylon. His letters to his friend Mario Schiparo were published from 1658 to 1663 as *Viaggi di Pietro della Valle, il pellegrino, descritti da lui medesimo in lettere familiari.*

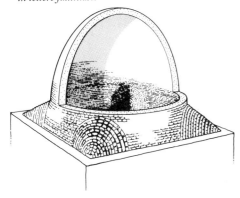

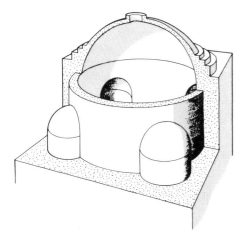

Above: *Iranian dome on squinches*; below: *Roman domed rotunda. See pp. 83–4.*

Vaulting Method of roofing. Although it had been known since at least the third millennium BC, it was only in the later Parthian period that vaulting was employed in monumental buildings to roof the great span of *iwans* and other large halls. This technological breakthrough was made possible by the use of a new mortar, gypsum mortar, which set quickly: it held the bricks in position almost as soon as they were laid, and thus expensive scaffolding was no longer required.

Verethragna Old Iranian deity, the god of victory, often portrayed as a boar.

Vertical brick lay Unusual brick lay, typically Parthian, though used in later periods as well. The bricks were laid vertically rather than horizontally. This same lay was also used to form round brick columns.

Vihara Buddhist monastery.

Volute Spiral scroll or twist.

White Sheep Dynasty Confederation of Turkoman tribes ruling in northwest Iran c. 1350–1500. Its most famous ruler was Uzun Hasan (1466–78).

Yakshi Indian fertility spirit.

Yüeh-chih See **Kushans**.

Zand Dynasty controlling Shiraz area in the later 18th century. Its best-known ruler was Karim Khan Zand.

Zeus Great god of the Greeks and king of Olympus. Identified by the Iranians with **Ahuramazda**, and by the Romans with Jupiter.

Zoroastrianism National faith of Iran from the Achaemenian period until the advent of Islam, still practiced by some communities in Iran, principally in the Yazd area, and by the Parsees of Bombay. Its prophet, Zoroaster, who probably lived in eastern Iran in about

Zoroastrian fire altar.

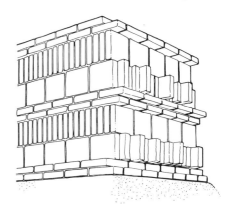

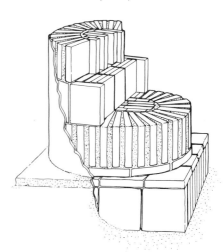

Vertical brick lay for a wall (above) and a column (below).

the 7th century BC (the date is disputed), tried to reform Iranian religion, which consisted of the worship of numerous different *ahuras* and *daevas*. He promoted an essentially monotheistic vision, proclaiming **Ahuramazda** as the single supreme god, and he stressed man's free choice between good and evil, truth and falsehood. Despite his prohibition, worship of other Iranian deities, such as **Mithra** and **Anahita**, continued alongside that of Ahuramazda.

Fire worship probably preceded Zoroaster and continued to form an essential part of the Zoroastrian faith. The foundation of new fires was regularly undertaken by each new monarch. The tribe of the **Magi** acted as priests, and the exposure of the dead was probably an old Iranian custom continued by them.

Index